Fertility, Education, Growth, and Sustainability

Fertility choices depend not only on the surrounding culture but also on economic incentives, which have important consequences for inequality, education, and sustainability. This book outlines parallels between demographic development and economic outcomes, explaining how fertility, growth, and inequality are related. It provides a set of general equilibrium models in which households choose their number of children, analyzed in four domains. First, inequality is particularly damaging for growth as human capital is kept low by the mass of grown-up children stemming from poor families. Second, the cost of education can be an important determining factor on fertility. Third, fertility is sometimes viewed as a strategic variable in the power struggle between different cultural, ethnic, and religious groups. Finally, fertility might be affected by policies targeted at other objectives. Incorporating new findings with the discussion of education policy and sustainability, this book is a significant addition to the literature on growth.

DAVID DE LA CROIX is Professor of Economics and a member of both IRES and CORE at UCLouvain, Belgium. He is associate editor for the *Journal of Economic Dynamics and Control*, the *Journal of Development Economics*, and, the *Journal of Public Economic Theory*. His research interests cover growth theory, human capital, demographics, and overlapping generations.

The CICSE Lectures in Growth and Development

Series editor
Neri Salvadori, University of Pisa

The CICSE lecture series is a biannual lecture series in which leading economists present new findings in the theory and empirics of economic growth and development. The series is sponsored by the Centro Interuniversitario per lo studio sulla Crescita e lo Sviluppo Economico (CICSE), a centre devoted to the analysis of economic growth and development supported by seven Italian universities. For more details about CICSE see their website at http://cicse.ec.unipi.it/.

Fertility, Education, Growth, and Sustainability

DAVID DE LA CROIX

CAMBRIDGE
UNIVERSITY PRESS

CAMBRIDGE
UNIVERSITY PRESS

32 Avenue of the Americas, New York NY 10013-2473, USA

Cambridge University Press is part of the University of Cambridge.

It furthers the University's mission by disseminating knowledge in the pursuit of education, learning and research at the highest international levels of excellence.

www.cambridge.org
Information on this title: www.cambridge.org/9781107029590

© CICSE 2013

This publication is in copyright. Subject to statutory exception and to the provisions of relevant collective licensing agreements, no reproduction of any part may take place without the written permission of Cambridge University Press.

First published 2013

A catalogue record for this publication is available from the British Library

Library of Congress Cataloguing in Publication data
La Croix, David de.
Fertility, education, growth, and sustainability / David de la Croix.
p.   cm.
Includes bibliographical references and index.
ISBN 978-1-107-02959-0 (hardback)
1. Fertility, Human–Economic aspects.   2. Population.   I. Title.
HB901.L32 2012
304.6′32–dc23   2012019854

ISBN 978-1-107-02959-0 Hardback

Cambridge University Press has no responsibility for the persistence or accuracy of URLs for external or third-party internet websites referred to in this publication, and does not guarantee that any content on such websites is, or will remain, accurate or appropriate.

Contents

List of figures		*page* ix
List of tables		xi
List of symbols		xiii
List of definitions		xv
List of propositions		xvi
Introduction		**1**
PART ONE DIFFERENTIAL FERTILITY		**7**
1	**Benchmark model**	**9**
	1.1 The model	9
	1.2 Introducing a lump sum transfer	16
	1.3 Numerical illustration	17
2	**Implications for the growth–inequality relationship**	**20**
	2.1 The model economy	22
	2.2 Theoretical results	25
	2.2.1 The tradeoff between the quality and quantity of children	25
	2.2.2 The balanced growth path	28
	2.2.3 The dynamics of individual human capital	31
	2.2.4 Extension with endogenous child rearing time	33
	2.3 Computational experiments	35
	2.3.1 Calibration	35
	2.3.2 Initial inequality, fertility, and growth	39
	2.3.3 The dynamics of inequality, fertility, and growth	41
	2.4 Conclusion	46

3   Understanding the forerunners in fertility decline   48
  3.1   Rouen and Geneva data   49
  3.2   A simple model of fertility   52
  3.3   Numerical experiments – calibration   58
  3.4   Numerical experiments – comparative statics   60
  3.5   Additional data   63
  3.6   Conclusion   65

        PART TWO EDUCATION POLICY   67

4   Education policy: private versus public schools   69
  4.1   The model   72
         4.1.1   The set-up with private education   72
         4.1.2   Fertility and education choices under
                 private education   74
         4.1.3   The set-up with public education   75
         4.1.4   Fertility and policy choices under public education 76
  4.2   Comparing private and public education   77
         4.2.1   Long-run dynamics   77
         4.2.2   Implications for growth   81
  4.3   Growth and inequality over time   84
         4.3.1   Calibration   85
         4.3.2   Initial conditions and growth   85
         4.3.3   Human capital accumulation and inequality
                 dynamics   87
  4.4   Conclusion   89

5   Education politics and democracy   91
  5.1   The model economy   93
         5.1.1   Preferences and technology   93
         5.1.2   Timing of events and private choices   94
         5.1.3   The political mechanism   97
         5.1.4   The equilibrium   100
  5.2   Comparing the education regimes   102
  5.3   Political power and multiple equilibria   106
  5.4   Alternative timing assumptions   112
         5.4.1   Outcomes with full government commitment   112
         5.4.2   Outcomes with partial government commitment   114
  5.5   A dynamic extension   116
         5.5.1   The model economy   116
         5.5.2   Private choices   117

	5.5.3 The political mechanism	117
	5.5.4 The equilibrium	118
	5.5.5 Comparing the education regimes	119
	5.5.6 The dynamics of education regimes	123
5.6	Extensions to an ethnic dimension	128
5.7	Conclusion	129
6	**Empirical evidence**	**130**
6.1	Inequality, fertility, and schooling across US states	130
6.2	Determinants of fertility and public versus private schooling at the household level	134
6.3	Schooling over time	138
6.4	Inequality, fertility, and schooling across countries	141
6.5	Public education spending and democracy	147
6.6	Conclusion	149
	PART THREE SUSTAINABILITY	151
7	**Environmental collapse and population dynamics**	**153**
7.1	Historical evidence	155
7.2	The model	158
	7.2.1 Preferences and technology	159
	7.2.2 The bargaining problem	161
	7.2.3 The fertility choice	164
	7.2.4 Dynamics	171
7.3	Numerical simulations and robustness analysis	173
	7.3.1 The Nash Equilibrium	173
	7.3.2 Resources and population dynamics	175
	7.3.3 Simulation of transition paths	177
7.4	Extension to the sustainability of diverse societies	178
7.5	Conclusion	180
7.6	Additional material – concave utility	181
8	**Production, reproduction, and pollution caps**	**184**
8.1	The model	186
	8.1.1 Production and pollution	186
	8.1.2 Households	187
	8.1.3 Aggregate dynamics	189
8.2	Pollution cap and tradable rights	191
	8.2.1 Households	191

	8.2.2	Equilibrium	193
	8.2.3	Dynamics	194
8.3	Numerical experiment		198
	8.3.1	Calibration	198
	8.3.2	Simulation	200
8.4	Conclusion		203

9   Population policy — **205**
9.1   Procreation entitlements — 207
9.2   Implementing tradable procreation rights — 208
9.3   Effects on inequality — 218
9.4   Effects on education — 226
9.5   Moving from national to global level — 228
9.6   Conclusion — 232

10   Conclusion: endogenous fertility matters — **233**

Bibliography — 235
Author index — 245

Figures

1.1   Fertility as a function of parents' human capital   *page* 13
1.2   Construction of the Gini coefficient with two groups   14
1.3   Calibrated fertility and education relationships   18
2.1   Completed Fertility of Married Mothers, USA 1990   21
2.2   Steady state human capital as a function of τ 32
2.3   The relationship of inequality and growth with endogenous fertility (solid), exogenous fertility (dashed), and in Barro's regression (dotted)   40
2.4   Growth, fertility, inequality, and differential fertility for $\tau = 0.05$ (solid) and $\tau = 0.2$ (dashed)   42
2.5   Density functions after eighteen periods   44
2.6   Exogenous versus endogenous growth: $\kappa = 1 - \tau$ (solid), $\kappa = 0.1$ (dashed), data (dots)   45
3.1   Fertility as a function of human capital when $\theta > \epsilon > 0$ 58
3.2   Fertility rates: calibration and simulation   60
3.3   Literacy rates: calibration and simulation   61
3.4   Fertility of aristocrats versus whole population   64
4.1   Private education and rural inequality circa 2000 across Indian states   70
4.2   Private education and growth circa 2000 across Indian states   70
4.3   Initial conditions for which growth is higher with public education   86
4.4   Dynamics with public (solid) and private (dashed) education over time $- \tau = 0.22$ 87
4.5   Public (solid) and private (dashed) education over time $- \tau = 0.5$ 88
5.1   Probabilistic voting versus median voter   98
5.2   The fixed point with $\sigma = 0.5$ (left) and $\sigma = 0.8$ (right)   102

5.3	The fixed point with multiple equilibria ($\sigma = 0.5$, $\bar{x} = 0.7$)	110
5.4	The education regimes	123
5.5	Example of a period-2 cycle	126
6.1	Education spending per capita versus share of private education across states	133
6.2	Education spending per student versus share of private education across states	134
6.3	Share of public education over time – declining cases	139
6.4	Share of public education over time – high and constant cases	139
6.5	Share of public education over time – increasing cases	140
6.6	Inequality and education systems across countries	141
6.7	Density of public education spending (percent of GDP)	148
7.1	Population of Easter Island and Tikopia	156
7.2	Forest coverage on Easter Island	157
7.3	Easter Island and Tikopia	158
7.4	Fertility reaction functions (r_1, r_2) and comparative statics	167
7.5	Fertility reaction functions: case I (solid); case II (dashed)	174
7.6	Collapse zones as a function of parameters	176
7.7	Simulation for environmental collapse and no collapse	178
8.1	Steady state population with pollution cap	195
8.2	Income and population dynamics in the examples	202
9.1	Solution to the individuals problem: regimes R1 to R4	215
9.2	Fertility as a function of income and procreation price	216
9.3	Redistributive nature of tradability	223
9.4	Fertility as a function of income and procreation price in the example. Unskilled (solid line) and skilled (dashed)	227
9.5	The procreation price in the example. Anti-natalist (dots), neutral (short dashes), pro-natalist (long dashes)	227
9.6	The ratio of unskilled to skilled. Anti-natalist (dots), neutral (short dashes), pro-natalist (long dashes)	228

Tables

1	Total fertility rates by education	*page* 2
1.1	Estimation results on global data	19
2.1	Calibration: a summary	36
2.2	Initial growth with endogenous and exogenous fertility	39
3.1	Data for Rouen	50
3.2	Data for Geneva	51
3.3	Global trends in forerunners' fertility	52
3.4	Forerunners' fertility and differential fertility	52
3.5	Forerunners' reproduction rates and differentials	52
3.6	Results of the calibration procedure	59
4.1	Calibration: a summary	85
5.1	Share of private resources in total education funding, 2003	92
5.2	Typology of education regimes	103
5.3	Education regimes with two types of households	119
6.1	Public schooling across US states: correlations	132
6.2	Estimation results: households' fertility behavior	136
6.3	Estimation results: households' education behavior	137
6.4	PISA data: education, fertility, and social status (1)	143
6.5	Statistics for countries with different education regimes	146
6.6	Public education spending and the democracy index	148
6.7	Public education spending in democracies and non-democracies	148
7.1	Benchmark parameterization of the population race model	173
7.2	Outcome for generation born at t, cases I and II	174
7.3	Risk aversion (ξ), fertility rates and bargained shares	182
8.1	Calibration: a summary	198
8.2	Benchmark simulation – world economy 1983–2208	200

8.3   Simulation with a constant pollution cap – 1983–2208   201
8.4   Simulation with an increasing pollution cap – 1983–2208   203
9.1   Implementation sequence of procreation entitlements
      for a country   209

Symbols

Notation of parameters is harmonized across chapters.

Parameter	Description	Chapters
α	1−share of labor in output	2,7
β	psychological discount factor	2,3,7
γ	weight of children in utility	1,2,3,4,5,8,9
δ	intrinsic growth rate of natural resource	7
ϵ	goods cost of surviving children	3
ζ	sensitivity of the probability of winning a war to the size of the clan	7
η	rate of return of education spending	1,2,3,4,5,8,9
$\hat{\eta}$	$(1 - \eta)^{1/\eta}$	5
θ	education level reached in the absence of education spending	1,2,3,4,9
ι	importance of space in the cost of rearing children	8
κ	human capital externality at the social level	2
λ	marginal disutility of child rearing	7
μ	efficiency parameter of education technology	1,2,4,5,8
ν	fertility objective of the government	9
ξ	degree of relative risk aversion	7
π	probability of becoming skilled	1,5
π^A	adult survival probability	3
π^C	child survival probability	3
π^ω	probability of winning a war	7
ϖ	political power	5
ρ	growth rate of productivity	2

Parameter	Description	Chapters
ϱ	elasticity of the children's human capital with respect to parental time	2
σ	standard error of the distribution of human capital	2,5
τ	intergenerational transmission of human capital within the family	2,4
υ	average productivity of labor	1,9
ϕ	time cost of rearing children	1,2,3,4,5,8,9
φ	weight of leisure in utility	8
χ	old-age support	7
ψ	additional time cost of rearing children in case of survival	3
ω	cost of war (as % of output)	7

Definitions

1.1	Benchmark inter-temporal equilibrium	*page* 11
2.1	Intertemporal equilibrium with heterogeneity	25
4.1	Private education inter-temporal equilibrium	74
4.2	Public education inter-temporal equilibrium	76
5.1	Political economy equilibrium with perfect foresight	100
5.2	Political equilibrium with two types of agents	118
5.3	Political economy inter-temporal equilibrium	124
7.1	Sustainability	153
7.2	Diverse society	179
7.3	Sustainability of a diverse society	179
9.1	Inter-temporal equilibrium with procreation rights	210

Propositions

1.1	Dynamics of the composition of population	*page* 15
2.1	Existence and uniqueness of the equilibrium	29
2.2	Balanced growth path and limiting distribution	30
2.3	Dynamics around the transcritical bifurcation	33
4.1	Balanced growth path with private education	78
4.2	Balanced growth path with public education	80
4.3	Public and private education in the long run	82
4.4	Comparison of public and private regime	83
5.1	Existence and uniqueness of equilibrium	101
5.2	Occurrence of education regimes	103
5.3	Inequality and segregation	105
5.4	Multiplicity of equilibria for $\bar{x} > 1 - \sigma$	108
5.5	Coverage of public education as a function of $\bar{x}$	111
5.6	Equilibrium with commitment	114
5.7	Occurrence of education regimes	120
5.8	Existence and uniqueness of inter-temporal equilibria	125
5.9	Global dynamics	125
5.10	Dynamics with public education	127
7.1	Bargaining outcome as a function of population	163
7.2	Population race as a Nash Equilibrium	165
7.3	Sustainable initial populations	172
8.1	Equilibrium with binding and non-binding cap	193
8.2	Population and the pollution cap	197
9.1	Solution to the individual problem	212
9.2	Fertility, education and income	214

9.3   Fertility and procreation price   215
9.4   Existence and uniqueness of equilibrium   217
9.5   Redistributive nature of tradability   222
9.6   Education and procreation price   226

Introduction

Population economics studies how demographic variables such as fertility and mortality respond to economic incentives and affect the economic development of societies. The population of a country changes very slowly over time: most of the people who will populate a given territory next year are already alive this year. However, despite slow dynamics and high predictability in the short–medium run, the effect of population on the economic outcomes are far from negligible. On the contrary, as time passes, changes in the population size and composition have dramatic effects. In some sense, as formulated by Pearce (2010):

> Demography is destiny.

Population change depends on fertility, mortality, and migration. We focus on fertility, and, more precisely, on the relationship between fertility and resources (or income in a broad sense). Starting from the data, this relationship is characterized by four stylized facts:

Fact 1: In all species, when available resources are more abundant, reproduction increases. This is true for plants, animals, and humans before the Industrial Revolution.

Fact 2: Before the Industrial Revolution, the rich had more surviving children than the poor.

Fact 3: The transition from income stagnation to economic growth is accompanied by a demographic transition from high to low fertility.

Fact 4: Now, both within and across countries, the rich and educated households have fewer children than poor and unskilled households.

The first fact is well known from the biology literature. For humans, it was stressed by Malthus in his *Essay on the Principle of Population* (1798).

1

Table 1. *Total fertility rates by education*

Survey	Countries	Total fertility rate		
		<Elementary	Elementary	Secondary+
WFS, 1975–1979	13 rich	2.40	2.17	1.79
WFS, 1974–1982	30 poor	6.5	5.5	4.0
DHS, 1985–1989	26 poor	5.7	4.9	3.6
DHS, 1990–1994	27 poor	5.29	4.72	3.29

Source: Kremer and Chen (2002).
WFS: World Fertility Survey. DHS: Demographic and Health Survey. "Secondary+" is the average of low secondary, high secondary, and post-secondary, where appropriate.

The second fact is the cross-section implication of the first. It is less documented, but the available evidence in Clark's (2007) seems indeed to suggest that the rich had more reproductive success than the poor, and most authors seem to accept this evidence.

The third fact is one of the most important phenomena of the last two centuries. As countries shifted one after another into a regime of sustained growth in per capita income, their mortality rate first declined, followed by a decline in fertility. This happened in almost every country of the world. Economic modeling of this process has been developed in the last ten years by Galor and various co-authors (see his magnum opus entitled *Unified Growth Theory*, Galor (2011)).

Fact 4 is stressed by Jones and Tertilt (2008) for the US. In a broader perspective, Skirbekk (2008) carries out a meta-analysis of the large empirical literature in demography on the correlation between education and fertility. The results show a strong and stable pattern of differential fertility, with lower fertility of households with higher educational background. Table 1 shows that fertility falls with the mother's education both in developed countries (first row) and in developing countries (last three rows). The fertility differential between women with high and low education is especially large in developing countries.

There is a fifth fact, not as firmly established as the ones above:

Fact 5: Most of the literature finds that the income of the father positively affects fertility, while the income of the mother negatively affects fertility.

Three references are Baudin (2009), Hotz and Miller (1988), and Merrigan and Saint-Pierre (1998). If Fact 5 is true, it would support the economic approach to fertility, according to which a higher wage of the mother implies a higher opportunity cost of having children, while a higher wage of the father entails a simple income effect.

It is fair to acknowledge that demographers and economists largely disagree on the forces underlying these observations. Demographers stress the knowledge of and access to contraception technology as important factors underlying the demographic transition. They also stress the importance of norms and culture (the Princeton European Fertility Project found that drops in fertility across Europe often followed linguistic and religious contours).

Economists, on the contrary, do not believe that a significant part of observed fertility is involuntary and would not have materialized if contraception was available. They insist on the influence of incentives faced by parents to have many or fewer children. For example, according to Pritchett (1994), 90 percent of the differences across countries in total fertility rates are accounted for solely by differences in women's reported desired fertility.

Economists have accordingly developed different models where the number of children flows as a result of households optimization problem. Most of the literature uses the notion of the quantity–quality tradeoff introduced by Becker (1960) and Becker and Lewis (1973): parents face a tradeoff between having many children and spending large resources on the health and education of each of them. This tradeoff results from the budget constraint of the family:

Income = number of children × spending per child + other spending

Having more children impedes parents' ability to spend much on the quality education, health, etc. of each of them.

What is the motive for having many children, and why has this motive been weakened during the demographic transition? One school of thought models children as a way to save resources for the future and to obtain some support when old (see Ehrlich and Lui (1991)). The introduction of a state pension system thus weakened the need for children. This is the old-age support hypothesis. A second school of thought studies the interplay between fertility and child mortality, stressing that lower mortality reduces the need for high fertility in order to obtain the same number of children reaching adulthood (see Bar and Leukhina (2010b) and Doepke (2005)). This is the child replacement hypothesis. A third idea explains fertility decline during the demographic transition as a consequence of the rise in the income and education of mothers. Since for educated women the opportunity cost of child-rearing time is high, they will prefer to invest in the education or "quality" of a small number of children. For less educated women, by contrast, the opportunity cost of raising children is low, while providing education is expensive relative to their income. As women's education and income improved during the nineteenth century, those with better education and a higher income preferred to have fewer children but invest more in the education of each child. A fourth strand of the literature stresses that, if the skill premium increases, because of, for example, the demand by industrial firms for more educated workers, the rate of return of quality rises relative to the implicit return of quantity. Again this may trigger the demographic transition as parents cannot invest more in quality without reducing the quantity (Galor and Weil (2000)).

While the quantity–quality model can account for the behavior of fertility over time in the demographic transition, it was originally developed to account for fertility rates in the cross-section of a given country. In almost every country, fertility in the population at a given moment of time is a negative function of income. The quantity–quality model explains this observation in the same way it accounts for the demographic transition. Mothers with little education and low income have many children but invest little in the education of each child. From recent research on developing economies we know that fertility differentials between highly and poorly-educated mothers can be quite large (Kremer and Chen (2002)).

The purpose of this book is to develop a model where heterogeneous households decide about fertility and education in the spirit of quantity–quality tradeoff models. Heterogeneity will imply that different types of households will have different numbers of children. Our objective is to look at the consequences of this differential fertility for future inequality, growth, education, and sustainability. When we started to work on the subject in 2000, Althaus (1980) was the only existing model to analyze the effects of differential fertility on growth. However, in Althaus' model fertility differentials are exogenously given, and the role of human capital is not considered.

Our analysis provides a new perspective on the link between economic growth and population growth. Existing studies have found little correlation between the growth rates of population and output per capita (see Kelley and Schmidt (1999)), which has led some researchers to conclude that population does not matter for growth. The results in this book suggest that it is not overall population growth but the changes in the composition of the population and the distribution of fertility within the population which are important. In other words, who is having the children and whether children are socially mobile matters more than how many children there are overall.

Outline of the book

The benchmark model of Chapter 1 has endogenous inequality (measured below by the Gini coefficient) and income per capita. In Chapter 2 we will explore in more detail the link between inequality and growth in income. In particular, we will analyze the contribution of endogenous fertility to the relationship between inequality and growth. To this end, the benchmark model will be extended in several directions: introduction of a third period of life (retirement) to give a motive for individual savings and capital formation, and introduction of technical progress and human capital externalities to discuss the basic ingredients of growth models. Finally, rather than relying on two classes of workers, we will introduce a continuous distribution of human capital to get closer to the data.

In Chapter 3 we wonder whether the model developed in Chapters 1 and 2 can be useful to understand the fertility decline during the demographic transition. To this aim we focus on forerunners: groups within Europe that experienced substantial fertility decline decades or even centuries before the mass of the population. To allow for alternative explanations for fertility decline in addition to the channels at the heart of the quantity–quality literature, we extend the model to take account of the role of mortality, on both the child and the adult level.

If fertility and education are joint decisions, government policies regarding education will also have an effect on fertility behavior. In Chapter 4 we analyze the properties of different education systems in a framework that accounts for the joint decision problem of parents regarding fertility and education. We consider separately public and private education regimes.

In most countries, public and private education coexist. In Chapter 5 we therefore extend the set-up developed in Chapter 4 to allow for this coexistence. Households still decide about fertility and education, but also vote for the quality of public schools and the corresponding tax rate. Households are allowed to opt out of the public education regime if the decided quality is not high enough for them. This model focuses on the determinant of the mix of public and private funding at a given period (the dynamic implications are not considered here).

Chapter 6 compares some predictions of Chapters 4 and 5 to various data. We look at US states, data on education funding, at household data on fertility, education, and income from the US Census, at World Bank cross-country data on public and private education spending, and, finally, at data from the OECD Program for International Student Assessment (PISA).

In the following chapters we move to implications of the theory for policy and sustainability. There are many definitions of sustainability in the literature. Here, we consider that a given policy or institution is sustainable if the corresponding competitive equilibrium exists. In Chapter 7 we abandon temporarily the set-up with endogenous education to focus on a new motive to have children: the gain of political power. When distinct population groups compete for political power, and if group size is an important factor, there can be a population race between groups, leading to a higher level of population than that resulting from a cooperative outcome. Moreover, in the context of a fragile ecosystem, such a population race can lead to unsustainable outcomes. The model of Chapter 7 accordingly describes the joint dynamics of population, relative size of groups, and environment. It is applied to the historical case of Easter Island, which has become a classical allegory for environmental collapses.

In Chapter 8 we go back to our benchmark model and consider the effect of an environmental tax. As a tax on output would affect the wages and hence the opportunity cost of children, households would reallocate their time towards non-market activities, such as leisure and reproduction. As reproduction today generates pollution tomorrow, the problem will be even worse in the future. Population will tend to increase and production per capita to decrease as generations pass. The conclusion of the endogenous fertility model would therefore be that capping emissions will gradually lead to larger and poorer successive generations.

Chapter 9 proposes a solution to the issue highlighted in Chapter 8. It looks at a population policy from a specific angle: Boulding's proposal of tradable procreation rights. We generalize those entitlements, aimed at combating over population, to both cases of pro-natalist and anti-natalist policy. Procreation rights can be seen as a generalization of current policies such as child allowances in France or the one-child policy in China, in which the intensity of the policy depends on the state of the population. We consider the effect of these policies on fertility, education, and, most importantly, inequality.

PART ONE

Differential fertility

1

Benchmark model

In this chapter, we present the simplest possible dynamic set-up in which skilled and unskilled households have different numbers of children. We then calibrate the model on world data.

1.1 The model

The model economy is populated by overlapping generations of people who live for two periods: childhood and adulthood. Time is discrete and runs from 0 to ∞. All decisions are made in the adult period of life. We assume a unitary representation of the household, neglecting the possible bargaining between spouses. There are two types of agents, indexed by i, unskilled (group $i = A$) and skilled (group $i = B$), who differ only in their wage w_t^i. The size of each group is denoted P_t^i. Agents represent households within a country, but we can also interpret them as countries within the global economy. Adults care about their own consumption c_t^i, the number of their children n_t^i, and the probability $\pi(e_t^i)$ that their children will become skilled. This probability depends on the education e_t^i they receive. Preferences are represented by the following utility function:[1]

$$\ln[c_t^i] + \gamma \ln[n_t^i \pi(e_t^i)]. \tag{1.1}$$

The parameter $\gamma > 0$ is the weight attached to children in the household's objective. Notice that parents care about both child quantity n_t^i and quality $\pi(e_t^i)$. As we will see below, the tradeoff between quantity and quality of children is

---

[1] The logarithmic utility function is chosen for simplicity; any utility function representing homothetic preferences over the bundle (c, n, e) would lead to the same results.

affected by the human capital endowment of the parents. Notice also that parents do not care about their children's utility, as would be the case with dynastic altruism, but they care about their future human capital. $\gamma \ln[\pi(e_t^i)]$ reflects an ad-hoc altruism factor which is referred to in the literature as "joy-of-giving" (or warm glove), because parents have a taste for giving (see e.g. Andreoni (1989)). In the usual "joy-of-giving" framework, the utility obtained from leaving a bequest or making a gift depends only on the size of the bequest or the gift. Here, it also depends on the efficiency of the gift in bringing quality, through the function $\pi()$. The alternative set-up with dynastic altruism is proposed by Barro and Becker (1989). Recent results using this set-up can be found in Jones and Schoonbroodt (2007) (quantitative theory) and Baudin (2011) (normative aspects). Finally, notice that the logarithmic formulation prevents households from choosing $n_t^i = 0$ (a utility allowing for voluntary childlessness is proposed by Gobbi (2011)).

To attain human capital, children have to be educated. Parents freely choose the education spending per child e_t^i. Apart from the education expenditure, raising one child also takes a constant fraction $\phi \in (0, 1)$ of an adult's time. This fraction of time cannot be cut down. Therefore it limits to $1/\phi$ the number of children one family can possibly raise.

Parents provide education to their children because it raises the probability that their children will be skilled. Specifically, given education e, the probability $\pi^i(e)$ of becoming skilled is given by:

$$\pi^i(e) = \mu^i \, (\theta + e)^\eta, \quad \eta \in (0, 1).$$

The parameter $\theta \geqslant 0$ measures the education level reached by a child in the absence of any education spending by the parents. This education level is obtained for free and is a perfect substitute to the education provided by the parents. η measures the elasticity of success to total educational input $\theta + e$. The parameter μ^i depends on the type i, and we assume the children of skilled parents have, ceteris paribus, a greater chance of becoming skilled themselves, i.e. $\mu^B > \mu^A$. Note that, in what follows, e is always bounded from above; hence we can always define the constant term μ^i as a function of the other parameters of the model such that the function $\pi^i()$ returns values in the interval [0, 1].

The budget constraint for an adult with wage w_t^i is given by:

$$c_t^i = \left[w_t^i(1 - \phi n_t^i) - n_t^i e_t^i \right]. \tag{1.2}$$

The only friction in the model is that children cannot borrow to finance their own education. Instead, education has to be paid for by the parents. This assumption is made in most studies of the joint determination of fertility and education. In the real world, children generally do not finance their own education (at least up to the secondary level).

The aggregate production function for the consumption good is linear in both types of labor input. We have:

$$Y_t = v^A L_t^A + v^B L_t^B.$$

The marginal product of each type of worker is constant and equal to v^A and $v^B > v^A$ respectively. The total input of the groups is given by L_t^A and L_t^B. The equilibrium condition on both labor markets

$$P_t^i(1 - \phi n_t^i) = L_t^i$$

will imply that wages are equal to marginal productivity:

$$w_t^i = v^i.$$

Denoting the equilibrium outcome in the benchmark case with hatted variables, we end up with Definition 1.1.

Definition 1.1 Benchmark inter-temporal equilibrium
Given initial population sizes P_0^A and P_0^B, an equilibrium is a sequence of individual quantities $(\hat{c}_t^i, \hat{e}_t^i, \hat{n}_t^i)_{i=A,B,t\geqslant 0}$ and group sizes $(\hat{P}_t^i)_{i=A,B,t\geqslant 0}$ such that

- *consumption, education and fertility maximize households' utility (1.1) subject to the budget constraint (1.2);*
- *group sizes evolve according to:*

$$\begin{bmatrix} \hat{P}_{t+1}^A \\ \hat{P}_{t+1}^B \end{bmatrix} = \begin{bmatrix} \hat{n}_t^A(1 - \pi^A(\hat{e}_t^A)) & \hat{n}_t^B(1 - \pi^B(\hat{e}_t^B)) \\ \hat{n}_t^A \pi^A(\hat{e}_t^A) & \hat{n}_t^B \pi^B(\hat{e}_t^B) \end{bmatrix} \begin{bmatrix} \hat{P}_t^A \\ \hat{P}_t^B \end{bmatrix} \quad (1.3)$$

- *labor market clears, i.e.*

$$\hat{P}_t^i(1 - \phi \hat{n}_t^i) = L_t^i \qquad \forall i. \qquad (1.4)$$

Let us now analyze the solution to the individual maximization problem. Parents face a tradeoff between the number of children they have and the amount of goods they spend on the education of each child. For, since productivity is fixed, having more children necessarily entails less spending per child. For educated parents, as the opportunity cost of child-rearing time is higher, they will prefer to invest in the education or "quality" of a small number of children. For less educated parents, by contrast, the opportunity cost of raising children is lower, while providing education is expensive relative to their income. Parents with low income would therefore choose to have many children but invest less in the education of each child. This notion of a quantity–quality tradeoff in the decisions on children was first introduced by Becker (1960) and is supported by empirical evidence on the cross-sectional distribution of fertility and education. Maximizing utility (1.1) subject to the constraint (1.2) leads to the following conditions. If $w_t^i > \theta/(\eta\phi)$ [interior regime],

$$\hat{e}_t^i = \frac{\eta\phi w_t^i - \theta}{1 - \eta}, \qquad \text{and:} \tag{1.5}$$

$$\hat{n}_t^i = \frac{(1 - \eta)\gamma w_t^i}{(\phi w_t^i - \theta)(1 + \gamma)} \tag{1.6}$$

otherwise,

$$\hat{e}_t^i = 0, \qquad \text{and:} \tag{1.7}$$

$$\hat{n}_t^i = \frac{\gamma}{\phi(1 + \gamma)} \tag{1.8}$$

This simple model displays the two important properties of quantity–quality tradeoff models: $\partial\hat{e}/\partial w \geq 0$, i.e. parental education spending increases with income, and $\partial\hat{n}/\partial w \leq 0$, i.e. fertility decreases with income. Since income in this model reflects human capital, fertility is a decreasing function of the human capital of the parents. Notice also the role of parameter θ, which captures the education children receive for free (by nature or society). A higher θ pushes parents to substitute education with number of children.

The lowest possible fertility rate is given by:

$$\lim_{x_t \to \infty} n_t = \frac{\gamma(1 - \eta)}{\phi(1 + \gamma)}.$$

Fertility as a function of human capital is plotted in Figure 1.1. The horizontal part of the relationship corresponds to the range of human capital which leads to a choice of zero for education e_t. Fertility depends negatively on human capital

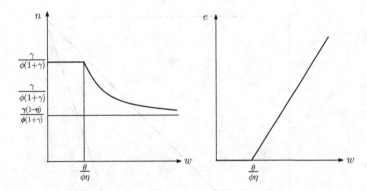

Figure 1.1 Fertility as a function of parents' human capital

and moves within a finite interval. The upper bound on the fertility differential is given by:

$$\frac{\lim_{x_t \to 0} n_t}{\lim_{x_t \to \infty} n_t} = \frac{1}{1 - \eta}. \tag{1.9}$$

This relationship will turn out to be helpful in interpreting the role of the parameter η and calibrating its value.

Denote individual income by $y^i = v^i(1 - \phi \hat{n}^i)$. The Gini coefficient can be computed using Figure 1.2. The surface between the 45-degree line and the Lorenz curve is equal to $1/2$ minus the surface of the light grey triangle ($= (1/2)P^B/(P^A + P^B)$) minus the surface of the darker triangle (which is equal to $(1/2)P^A y^A/(P^A y^A + P^B y^B)$). It is thus equal to:

$$\text{Gini} = \frac{P^B}{P^A y^A/y^B + P^B} - \frac{P^B}{P^A + P^B}.$$

In Chapter 7 we will use a simpler measure to assess the effect of procreation rights on income differences. Observed income inequality Δ^B (B for benchmark) can be measured by the difference between high-skilled and low-skilled income:

$$\Delta^B = y^B - y^A. \tag{1.10}$$

Notice that Δ^B can be interpreted as a first-order approximation of the Gini coefficient at given group sizes.

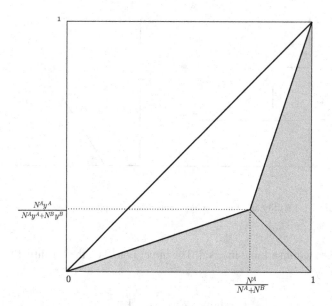

Figure 1.2 Construction of the Gini coefficient with two groups

The dynamic properties of the model can be analyzed by defining the following population ratio:

$$z_t = \frac{P_t^A}{P_t^B}.$$

Notice that, since in our dynastic framework a period corresponds to one generation, the dynamics of the model are to be interpreted as changes which occur over a horizon of a century or more. The dynamic system (1.3) can be reduced to a first-order difference equation $z_{t+1} = f(z_t)$:

$$z_{t+1} = \frac{n^A(1 - \pi^A)z_t + n^B(1 - \pi^B)}{n^A\pi^A z_t + n^B\pi^B} \equiv f(z_t).$$

The function f has the following properties:

$$f(0) = \frac{1 - \pi^B}{\pi^B} > 0$$

$$f'(z) = \frac{n^A n^B (\mu^B - \mu^A)}{(n^A \pi^A z + n^B \pi^B)^2} > 0$$

$$f''(z) = \frac{2(n^A)^2 \pi^A n^B (\mu^A - \mu^B)}{(n^A \pi^A z + n^B \pi^B)^3} < 0$$

The last two results are guaranteed by the fact that $\mu^B > \mu^A$.

Proposition 1.1 Dynamics of the composition of population
The dynamics of z_t given by $z_{t+1} = f(z_t)$ admit a single positive steady state:

$$\bar{z} = \frac{n^A(1 - \pi^A) - n^B \pi^B \sqrt{(n^B \pi^B - n^A(1 - \pi^A))^2 + 4n^A \pi^A n^B (1 - \pi^B)}}{2n^A \pi^A},$$

which is globally stable.

Proof: As $f(z)$ is continuous and non-decreasing on $\mathbb{R}_+$, the time-path satisfying $z_{t+1} = f(z_t)$ given z_0 is a monotonic sequence.

It never goes from one side of a steady state to the other. Indeed, consider any steady state $\bar{z} \in \mathbb{R}_+$ and assume for example $z_0 \leqslant \bar{z}$. Then $z_1 = f(z_0) \leqslant f(\bar{z}) = \bar{z}$, and by induction for all t, $z_t \leqslant \bar{z}$. Similarly, if $z_0 \geqslant \bar{z}$ then $z_t \geqslant \bar{z}$ for all t.

This sequence thus either converges to a steady state $\bar{z} \in \mathbb{R}_+$ or it goes to a boundary of the set $\mathbb{R}_+$.

For all $z_t \in [0, \bar{z}[$, we have $z_{t+1} = f(z_t) > z_t$. The sequence z_t is increasing away from 0, converging asymptotically to $\bar{z}$.

For all $z_t \in]\bar{z}, +\infty[$, we have $z_{t+1} = f(z_t) < z_t$. The sequence z_t is decreasing, converging asymptotically to $\bar{z}$. ∎

Average income per capita is given by:

$$\frac{Y_t}{P_t^A + P_t^B} = \frac{\upsilon^A P_t^A (1 - \phi n^A) + \upsilon^B P_t^B (1 - \phi n^B)}{P_t^A + P_t^B}$$

$$= \frac{\upsilon^A z_t (1 - \phi n^A) + \upsilon^B (1 - \phi n^B)}{z_t + 1},$$

and is a negative function of z_t. Income inequality as measured by the Gini coefficient is:

$$\text{Gini}_t = \frac{P_t^B y^A}{P_t^A y^A + P_t^B y^B} - \frac{P_t^B}{P_t^A + P_t^B}$$

$$= \frac{\upsilon^B (1 - \phi n^B)}{z_t \upsilon^A (1 - \phi n^A) + \upsilon^B (1 - \phi n^B)} - \frac{1}{z_t + 1}$$

It is equal to 0 when $z_t = 0$ or when $z_t \to \infty$. Computing the first-order derivative with respect to z_t and equalizing it to zero yields a unique value:

$$\hat{z} = \sqrt{\frac{\upsilon^B(1 - \phi n^B)}{\upsilon^A(1 - \phi n^A)}}$$

for which the Gini coefficient is at its maximum.

Considering now a dynamic path starting with a large z_0 (many unskilled relative to skilled), z_t is going to decrease monotonically, income per capita will also rise monotonically, while the Gini coefficient will first rise and then decline, provided that the steady state $\bar{z} < \hat{z}$.

1.2 Introducing a lump sum transfer

Let us now consider a lump sum transfer T_t added to the income of the family:

$$c_t^i = \left[w_t^i(1 - \phi n_t^i) - n_t^i e_t^i + T_t \right]. \tag{1.11}$$

This transfer can be understood either as a policy (e.g. foreign aid), or as the income of the father. In the latter case, the father is expected not to spend time rearing children: only the wage of the mother is multiplied by the factor $(1 - \phi n_t^i)$.

Maximizing utility (1.1) subject to the new constraint (1.11) leads to the following conditions. If $w_t^i > \theta/(\eta\phi)$ [interior regime],

$$\hat{e}_t^i = \frac{\eta\phi w_t^i - \theta}{1 - \eta}, \qquad \text{and:} \tag{1.12}$$

$$\hat{n}_t^i = \frac{(1 - \eta)\gamma(w_t^i + T_t)}{(\phi w_t^i - \theta)(1 + \gamma)} \tag{1.13}$$

otherwise,

$$\hat{e}_t^i = 0, \qquad \text{and:} \tag{1.14}$$

$$\hat{n}_t^i = \frac{\gamma(\theta + \eta\phi T_t)}{\phi\theta(1 + \gamma)}. \tag{1.15}$$

We observe that the transfer has a positive effect on fertility in both regimes, and no effect on education. If we interpret the transfer as the wage of the father, we obtain a stark prediction for fertility behavior. Fertility should be increasing with the wage of the father and decreasing in the wage of the mother. This is what obtains in Deb and Rosati (2004) for India (approximating wages by education) and Baudin (2009) for France.

This result also has implications for redistribution policies. Taxing the skilled and subsidizing the unskilled tends to increase fertility differentials (see Knowles (1999a)), increasing the proportion of unskilled in the future and reducing total income. Here the policy implications of our model are in stark contrast to other theories linking inequality and growth (for example, Galor and Zeira (1993) argue that equality in sufficiently wealthy economies stimulates investment in human capital and enhances economic growth when there are capital market imperfections).

1.3 Numerical illustration

Understanding agents in our model as countries or sets of countries, all the results developed above for a given period in time can be applied at the global level (analyzing the dynamics would require reinterpreting the function $\pi()$ as in Chapter 2 or 4). In order to associate numerical values to our parameters η, ϕ, θ, and γ, we calibrate the model on a cross-section of countries.

One period in the model lasts twenty-five years. The variables are measured with data from the World Development Indicators, averaging those available for the years 1998–2002. Variable n is computed as the net reproduction rate, i.e. "Fertility rate, total (births per woman)" divided by two in order to obtain a fertility rate per person and multiplied by (1− "Mortality rate, infant (per 1,000 live births)"/1000) to measure net fertility per capita. Total education $\theta + e$ corresponds to the product of "Adjusted savings: education expenditure (% of GNI)" and "GNI per capita, PPP (current international $)" loading to a measure of education spending per capita in PPP dollars. Population size N for each country is proportional to the population aged 15–64. Productivity per person υ is unobservable but can be obtained from gross national income y as follows:

$$y = \upsilon(1 - \phi n). \qquad (1.16)$$

We then calibrate the parameters ϕ, θ, η, and γ of the system (1.5)–(1.6)–(1.16) using the criterion provided by the estimation method of Full Information

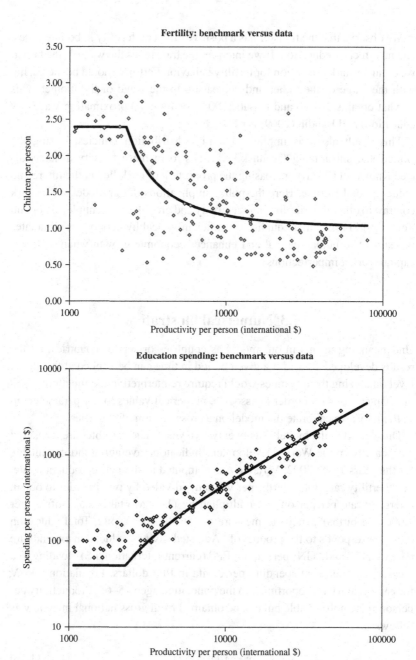

Figure 1.3 Calibrated fertility and education relationships

Table 1.1. *Estimation results on global data*

Number of observations = 158				
Parameter	Estimate	Standard Error	t-statistic	P-value
η	0.572	0.0350	16.34	[.000]
ϕ	0.039	0.0054	7.227	[.000]
θ	51.61	5.3138	9.711	[.000]
γ	0.103	0.0124	8.260	[.000]
Equation	education	fertility		
R-squared	0.88	0.50		

Maximum Likelihood:

$$e_i = \begin{cases} 0 & \text{if } v_i \leqslant \dfrac{\theta}{\eta\phi} \\ \dfrac{\eta\phi v_i - \theta}{1 - \eta} & \text{if } v_i > \dfrac{\theta}{\eta\phi} \end{cases} + \varepsilon_i^e \qquad (1.17)$$

$$n_i = \begin{cases} \dfrac{\gamma}{\phi(1 + \gamma)} & \text{if } v_i \leqslant \dfrac{\theta}{\eta\phi} \\ \dfrac{(1 - \eta)\gamma v_i}{(\phi v_i - \theta)(1 + \gamma)} & \text{if } v_i > \dfrac{\theta}{\eta\phi} \end{cases} + \varepsilon_i^n \qquad (1.18)$$

$$y_i = v_i(1 - \phi n_i)$$

The calibration results are presented in Table 1.1. The point estimate for the parameter η, which measures the elasticity of income to schooling, is located well within the range of estimates of the elasticity of earnings with respect to schooling (see the discussion in Chapter 2). The calibrated value for ϕ implies that one child takes 4 percent of available time during twenty-five years.

Relationships (1.17)–(1.18) are presented in Figure 1.3. The curves stand for two theoretical relationships: the productivity–fertility one (top figure) and the productivity–education one (bottom figure). Points correspond to countries. Notice that we provide an estimation of the productivity level below which no education takes place $e = 0$. It is equal to $\theta/(\phi\eta) = \$2313$ per person and per year. The curves fit with R-squared of 0.88 and 0.50 respectively.

2

Implications for the growth–inequality relationship

The quantity–quality model was originally developed to account for fertility rates in the cross-section of a given country. In almost every country, fertility in the population at a given moment in time is a negative function of income. The quantity–quality model explains this observation in the same way that it accounts for the demographic transition. Since for educated women the opportunity cost of child-rearing time is high, they will prefer to invest in the education or "quality" of a small number of children. For less educated women, by contrast, the opportunity cost of raising children is low, while providing education is expensive relative to their income. Mothers with little education and low income would therefore prefer to have many children but invest little in the education of each child. Figure 2.1 illustrates this fact with detailed and robust data using twelve education categories for married mothers aged 45–70 in the US Census 1990.[1] It shows that completed fertility drops monotonically with the education of the mother. Such a pattern for the USA was contested recently by Hazan and Zoabi (2011), who find a U-shaped relationship between period fertility and mother's education. However, even in their study, the fertility at the low end of the education distribution remains higher than the fertility of mothers with high education.

From recent research on developing economies we know that fertility differentials between high- and low-educated mothers can be quite large (Kremer and Chen (2002)). We extend the model of Chapter 1 to capture the channel from inequality to growth going through fertility. One difference with the model of Chapter 1 is that the distribution of human capital is a continuous distribution instead of a two-point distribution. This allows us to represent the real world more accurately, which is important if we want to capture the link between

This chapter uses some material published in de la Croix and Doepke (2003).

[1] For a more detailed description of these data, see Baudin et al. (2011).

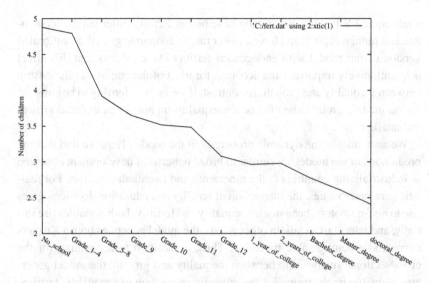

Figure 2.1 Completed Fertility of Married Mothers, USA 1990

inequality and growth quantitatively. The cost to pay when using this distribution will be in terms of theoretical results. We will still be able to characterize the steady state. But it will not be possible to prove that the distribution of human capital converges. We will, however, be able to give some insight into the dynamics by relying on a partial analysis.

The majority of the existing literature on inequality and growth concentrates on channels where inequality affects growth through the accumulation of physical capital (see Bénabou (1996)). Endogenous fertility differentials arise in Dahan and Tsiddon (1998), but since their model does not allow for long-run growth, the analysis concentrates on the transition to the steady state. In Galor and Zang (1997), inequality affects growth through its effect on overall fertility and human capital. Financial market imperfections play a crucial role in their analysis. Morand (1999) has a model of inequality and fertility in which the sole motive for fertility is old-age support. He concentrates on the possibility of poverty traps when the initial level of human capital is too low.

As in Chapter 1, both fertility and education are chosen endogenously. Parents face a quality–quantity tradeoff in their decision on children, and education increases with the income of a family (richer families can afford more education), while fertility decreases with income (the time cost of child rearing is high for rich parents). The aggregate behavior of the model depends on the initial distribution of income. Other things being equal, we find that economies with a less equitable income distribution have higher fertility differentials, accumulate less human capital, and have a lower rate of economic growth. A calibrated version of our model with endogenous fertility choice shows that this effect is quantitatively important and accounts for most of the empirical relationship between inequality and growth. In contrast, if we impose fertility to be constant across income groups, the effects of inequality on human capital and growth are small.

We also analyze the dynamic properties of the model. Here we find that the predictions of the model are similar to broad patterns of development observed in industrializing countries in the nineteenth and twentieth centuries. For realistic parameter values, the interaction of fertility and education decisions gives rise to non-monotone behavior in inequality and fertility: both variables rise initially, and later start to fall. In other words, the model generates both a Kuznets curve and a demographic transition. Thus, in addition to accounting for the cross-sectional relationship between inequality and growth, the model generates plausible implications for the dynamic interaction of inequality, fertility, and growth over long time horizons.

These results have policy implications, in terms of both education policy and population policy. Education policy is the subject of Part II. Population policy will be addressed in Chapter 9.

2.1 The model economy

We extend the benchmark model of the previous chapter to include some key factors of growth: physical capital and technological progress are introduced. We also assume that the distribution of human capital is continuous, to enhance the realism of the set-up.

Consider an economy that is populated by overlapping generations of people who live for three periods: childhood, adulthood, and old age. All decisions are made in the adult period of life. People care about adult consumption c_t, old-age consumption d_{t+1}, their number of children n_t, and the human capital of children h_{t+1}. Parents decide about the education of the children.[2] The utility function is given by:

$$\ln(c_t) + \beta \ln(d_{t+1}) + \gamma \ln(n_t h_{t+1}).$$

---

[2] A similar model, but where households decide about their own education instead of their children's education, is proposed by Chen (2008) to analyze the effect of life expectancy on the incentive to get an education.

The parameter $\beta > 0$ is the psychological discount factor and $\gamma > 0$ is the altruism factor. Compared with Chapter 1, we introduce old-age consumption in order to provide a motive for savings and therefore generate an endogenous supply of capital. Raising one child takes fraction $\phi \in (0, 1)$ of an adult's time. The assumption that the time required to raise a child is fixed is standard in the literature, but offensive. Surely parents can choose how much time to allocate to each child – see Section 2.2.4.

An adult has to choose a consumption profile c_t and d_{t+1}, savings for old age s_t, number of children n_t, and schooling time per child e_t. The budget constraint for an adult with human capital h_t is:

$$c_t + s_t + e_t n_t w_t \bar{h}_t = w_t h_t (1 - \phi n_t),$$ (2.1)

where w_t is the wage per unit of human capital. We assume that the average human capital of teachers equals the average human capital in the population $\bar{h}_t$, so that education cost per child is given by $e_t w_t \bar{h}_t$. The assumption that teachers instead of parents provide education is crucial for generating fertility differentials. It implies that the cost of education is fixed and does not depend on the parent's wage. Education is therefore relatively expensive for poor parents. In contrast, since raising each child takes a fixed amount of the parent's time, having many children is more costly for parents who have high wages.

The budget constraint for the old-age period is:

$$d_{t+1} = R_{t+1} s_t.$$ (2.2)

R_{t+1} is the interest factor. The human capital of the children h_{t+1} depends on human capital of the parents h_t, average human capital $\bar{h}_t$, and education e_t:

$$h_{t+1} = \mu_t (\theta + e_t)^\eta (h_t)^\tau (\bar{h}_t)^\kappa.$$ (2.3)

Here the parameter $\tau \in [0, 1]$ captures the intergenerational transmission of human capital within the family, whereas $\kappa \in [0, 1 - \tau]$ represents an externality at the community or society level. Alternatively, κ can be interpreted as measuring the effect of the quality of schooling, since $\bar{h}$ is the average human capital of teachers. The efficiency parameter μ_t increases deterministically at a constant rate:

$$\mu_t = \mu (1 + \rho)^{(1-\tau-\kappa)t}.$$ (2.4)

The parameters satisfy $\mu, \theta > 0$ and $\eta \in (0, 1)$. The presence of θ guarantees that parents have the option of not educating their children, because even with $e_t = 0$

future human capital remains positive. As in Rangazas (2000), equations (2.3)–(2.4) are compatible with endogenous growth for $\kappa = 1-\tau$, and with exogenous growth otherwise. We will later explore the implications of exogenous versus endogenous growth for the long-run behavior of the economy.

Production of the consumption good is carried out by a single representative firm which operates the technology:

$$Y_t = AK_t^{\alpha} L_t^{1-\alpha},$$

where K_t is aggregate capital, L_t is aggregate labor supply, $A > 0$ and $\alpha \in (0, 1)$. Physical capital completely depreciates in one period. The firm chooses inputs by maximizing profits $Y_t - w_t L_t - R_t K_t$. Compared with Chapter 1, marginal productivity is decreasing and wages will be endogenous.

Human capital is distributed over the adult population according to the distribution function $F_t(h_t)$. Total population P_t evolves over time according to:

$$P_{t+1} = P_t \int_0^{\infty} n_t \ dF_t(h_t), \tag{2.5}$$

and the distribution function of human capital, $F_t(h)$, evolves according to:

$$F_{t+1}(h) = \frac{P_t}{P_{t+1}} \int_0^{\infty} n_t \ I(h_{t+1} \leqslant h) \ dF_t(h_t). \tag{2.6}$$

Here $I(\cdot)$ is an indicator function, and it is understood that the choice variables n_t and h_{t+1} are functions of the individual state h_t. Average human capital $\bar{h}_t$ is given by:

$$\bar{h}_t = \int_0^{\infty} h_t \ dF_t(h_t). \tag{2.7}$$

The market-clearing conditions for capital and labor are:

$$K_{t+1} = P_t \int_0^{\infty} s_t \ dF_t(h_t), \tag{2.8}$$

and:

$$L_t = P_t \left[\int_0^{\infty} h_t(1 - \phi n_t) \ dF_t(h_t) - \int_0^{\infty} e_t n_t \bar{h}_t \ dF_t(h_t) \right]. \tag{2.9}$$

This last condition reflects the fact that the time devoted to teaching is not available for goods production. We are now ready to define an equilibrium for our economy:

Definition 2.1 Intertemporal equilibrium with heterogeneity
Given an initial distribution of human capital $F_0(h_0)$, an initial stock of physical capital K_0, and an initial population size P_0, an equilibrium consists of sequences of prices $\{w_t, R_t\}$, aggregate quantities $\{L_t, K_{t+1}, \bar{h}_t, P_{t+1}\}$, distributions $F_{t+1}(h_{t+1})$, and decision rules $\{c_t, d_{t+1}, s_t, n_t, e_t, h_{t+1}\}$ such that:

(1) *the households' decision rules c_t d_{t+1}, s_t, n_t, e_t, h_{t+1} maximize utility subject to the constraints (2.1), (2.2), and (2.3);*
(2) *the firm's choices L_t and K_t maximize profits;*
(3) *the prices w_t and R_t are such that markets clear, i.e. (2.8) and (2.9) hold;*
(4) *the distribution of human capital evolves according to (2.6);*
(5) *aggregate variables P_t and $\bar{h}_t$ are given by (2.4), (2.5), and (2.7).*

2.2 Theoretical results

We begin the analysis of the model by characterizing the quality–quantity tradeoff faced by individuals. To examine the long-run implications of the model, we characterize the balanced growth path. Finally, we examine the dynamics of individual human capital as a function of the parameters.

2.2.1 The tradeoff between the quality and quantity of children

The key variable for decisions in our economy is the human capital h_t of a family relative to the average human capital $\bar{h}_t$ of the population. We denote the relative human capital of a household as:

$$x_t \equiv \frac{h_t}{\bar{h}_t}.$$

For a household that has enough human capital such that the condition $x_t > \frac{\theta}{\phi\eta}$ holds, there is an interior solution for the optimal education level. Substituting the constraint (2.1) into the objective, the maximization problem can be written as:

$$\max_{s_t, e_t, n_t} \ln(w_t h_t (1 - \phi n_t) - s_t - e_t n_t w_t \bar{h}_t) + \beta \ln(d_{t+1}) + \gamma \ln(n_t h_{t+1})$$

and the first-order conditions imply:

$$s_t = \frac{\beta}{\beth} w_t h_t, \qquad (2.10)$$

$$e_t = \frac{\eta\phi x_t - \theta}{1 - \eta}, \qquad (2.11)$$

$$n_t = \frac{(1 - \eta)\gamma x_t}{(\phi x_t - \theta)\beth} \qquad (2.12)$$

with $\beth = 1 + \beta + \gamma$. It will be noticed that the budget constraint (2.1) is not linear in control variables, because of the term $e_t n_t$. The constraint set is not convex, and, as a consequence, the first-order conditions are necessary but not sufficient for a maximum. This is one important difference with standard consumption theory. Moreover, we cannot use the Alvarez (1999) way of circumventing this problem, which applies only when there is dynastic altruism. Therefore, we need to verify the second-order condition for a maximum. The matrix of second derivatives is:

$$\begin{pmatrix} -\dfrac{\beta}{s_t^2} - \dfrac{1}{\Gamma_t} & -\dfrac{n_t w_t \bar{h}_t}{\Gamma_t} & -\dfrac{w_t(e_t \bar{h}_t + \phi h_t)}{\Gamma_t} \\[2ex] -\dfrac{n_t w_t \bar{h}_t}{\Gamma_t} & -\dfrac{n_t^2 w_t^2 \bar{h}_t^2}{\Gamma_t} - \dfrac{\gamma\eta}{(\theta + e_t)^2} & \dfrac{w_t \bar{h}_t(s_t - w_t h_t)}{\Gamma_t} \\[2ex] -\dfrac{w(e\bar{h}_t + \phi h_t)}{\Gamma_t} & \dfrac{w_t \bar{h}_t(s_t - w_t h_t)}{\Gamma_t} & \dfrac{w_t^2(e_t \bar{h}_t + \phi h_t)^2}{\Gamma_t} - \dfrac{\gamma}{n_t^2} \end{pmatrix}$$

with

$$\Gamma_t = (s_t + w_t(e_t n_t \bar{h}_t - (1 - \phi n_t)h_t))^2$$

Substituting the first-order conditions into this matrix and simplifying leads to:

$$\begin{pmatrix} -\dfrac{(1 + \beta)\beth^2}{\beta w_t^2 h_t^2} & \dfrac{\gamma \bar{h}_t \beth(\eta - 1)}{w_t h_t(\phi h_t - \theta \bar{h}_t)} & \dfrac{\beth^2(\phi h_t - \theta \bar{h}_t)}{w_t h_t^2(\eta - 1)} \\[2ex] \dfrac{\gamma \bar{h}_t \beth(\eta - 1)}{w_t h_t(\phi h_t - \theta \bar{h}_t)} & -\dfrac{\gamma \bar{h}_t^2(\eta - 1)^2(1 + \gamma\eta)}{\eta(\theta \bar{h}_t - \phi h_t)^2} & -\dfrac{\bar{h}_t(1 + \gamma)\beth}{h_t} \\[2ex] \dfrac{\beth^2(\phi h_t - \theta \bar{h}_t)}{h^2 w(\eta - 1)} & -\dfrac{\bar{h}_t(1 + \gamma)\beth}{h_t} & \dfrac{(1 + \gamma)\beth^2(\phi h_t - \theta \bar{h}_t)^2}{\gamma(\eta - 1)^2 h_t^2} \end{pmatrix}$$

The condition for a relative maximum is that the matrix must be negative definite. Let us compute the three principal minors of the matrix:

$$-\frac{(1+\beta)\beth^2}{\beta w_t^2 h_t^2} < 0$$

$$\frac{\gamma(1-\eta)\beth\bar{h}_t \left(2w_t h_t(\phi h_t - \theta\bar{h}_t) + \frac{\bar{h}_t(1+\beta)(1-\eta)\beth(1+\gamma\eta)}{\beta\eta}\right)}{w_t^2 h_t^2(\theta\bar{h}_t - h_t\phi)^2} > 0$$

$$-\frac{\bar{h}_t^2(1-\eta)\beth^5}{\beta\eta w_t^2 h_t^4} < 1$$

As the principal minors alternate in sign, starting with negative values for the first principal minor, the matrix is negative definite and the solution (2.10)–(2.12) is a maximum.

For poorer households endowed with sufficiently little human capital such that $x_t \le \frac{\theta}{\phi\eta}$ holds, the optimal choice for education e_t is zero. The first-order conditions imply equation (2.10) and:

$$e_t = 0, \tag{2.13}$$

$$n_t = \frac{\gamma}{\phi(1+\gamma)}. \tag{2.14}$$

Once a household is at the corner solution and the choice for education is zero, fertility no longer increases as the human capital endowment falls.

Equations (2.11)–(2.12) are qualitatively similar to equations (1.5)–(1.6). They reflect the main effects of inequality on growth that we are interested in. Assuming that all dynasties choose positive levels of education, equation (2.11) shows that education is a linear function of relative human capital. If the dispersion of human capital increases for a given average level of human capital, this linearity implies that the average education choice will still be the same. However, since the production function for human capital is concave in education, future average human capital will be lower if the distribution of human capital is less equal. This would be true even if fertility were constant across families with different human capital levels. The fact that fertility is actually higher for people with low human capital greatly amplifies the negative effect of inequality on human capital accumulation.

Exercise: Introduce a good cost of having children in the household's budget constraint. See how fertility is affected. Derive a condition on the good cost for fertility to be still negatively affected by income.

2.2.2 The balanced growth path

To analyze the dynamic behavior of the economy, it is useful to rewrite the equilibrium conditions in terms of variables that are constant in the balanced growth path. The capital/labor ratio k_t, the growth rate of average human capital g_t, the population growth rate N_t, and the deflated level of average human capital $\hat{h}_t$ are defined by:

$$k_t \equiv \frac{K_t}{L_t}, \qquad g_t \equiv \frac{\bar{h}_{t+1}}{\bar{h}_t}, \qquad N_t \equiv \frac{P_{t+1}}{P_t}, \qquad \hat{h}_t \equiv \frac{\bar{h}_t}{(1+\rho)^t}.$$

We also need to define the distribution of the relative human capital levels:

$$G_t(x_t) \equiv F_t(x_t \bar{h}_t).$$

Rewriting equations (2.4), (2.5), (2.6), and (2.7) in terms of the stationary variables leads to:

$$\hat{h}_{t+1} = \frac{g_t}{1+\rho} \hat{h}_t, \tag{2.15}$$

$$N_t = \int_0^\infty n_t \, dG_t(x_t), \tag{2.16}$$

$$G_{t+1}(x) = \frac{1}{N_t} \int_0^\infty n_t \, I(x_{t+1} \leqslant x) \, dG_t(x_t), \tag{2.17}$$

$$1 = \int_0^\infty x_t \, dG_t(x_t). \tag{2.18}$$

Prices follow from the competitive behavior of firms, which leads to equalization of marginal cost and productivity:

$$w_t = A(1-\alpha)k_t^\alpha, \tag{2.19}$$

$$R_t = A\alpha k_t^{\alpha-1}. $$

Schooling and fertility decisions are given by (2.13) and (2.14) for $x_t < \theta/(\eta\phi)$ and by (2.11) and (2.12) otherwise. The number of children for an adult with relative human capital x_t is thus given by:

$$n_t = \min\left[\frac{(1-\eta)\gamma x_t}{(\phi x_t - \theta)\mathfrak{I}}, \frac{\gamma}{\phi\mathfrak{I}}\right]. \tag{2.20}$$

From equation (2.3), the children's human capital is given by:

$$x_{t+1} = \frac{\mu x_t^\tau}{g_t} \left(\theta + \max\left[0, \frac{\eta\phi x_t - \theta}{1 - \eta}\right]\right)^\eta (\hat{h}_t)^{\tau+\kappa-1}. \qquad (2.21)$$

From equation (2.9), labor input satisfies:

$$\frac{L_t}{P_t \bar{h}_t} = \int_0^{\frac{\theta}{\eta\phi}} \frac{(1+\beta)x_t}{\beth} \, dG_t(x_t)$$

$$+ \int_{\frac{\theta}{\eta\phi}}^{\infty} \left(1 - \gamma \frac{\phi(1-\eta)x_t + (\eta\phi x_t - \theta)}{(\phi x_t - \theta)\beth}\right) x_t \, dG_t(x_t)$$

which leads to:

$$\frac{L_t}{P_t \bar{h}_t} = \frac{1+\beta}{\beth}. \qquad (2.22)$$

Using (2.8), (2.10), (2.19), and (2.22), the capital stock evolves according to the following law of motion:

$$k_{t+1} = \frac{\beta}{1+\beta} \frac{1}{g_t N_t} A(1-\alpha)k_t^\alpha. \qquad (2.23)$$

Given initial conditions k_0, $\hat{h}_0$, and $G_0(x_0)$, an equilibrium can be characterized by sequences $\{\hat{h}_{t+1},\ g_t,\ n_t,\ G_{t+1}(x),\ N_t,\ x_t,\ k_{t+1}\}$ such that (2.15), (2.16), (2.17), (2.18), (2.20), (2.21), and (2.23) hold at all dates.

Proposition 2.1 Existence and uniqueness of the equilibrium
Given any initial conditions, an equilibrium exists and is unique.

Proof: This dynamic system is block recursive. Given the initial conditions, we can first use (2.20) to solve for n_t. Then equations (2.18) and (2.21) determine x_{t+1} and g_t. Leading (2.18) by one period and replacing x_{t+1} by its value from (2.21) yields an expression where g_t can be computed as a function of past variables, x_t and $\hat{h}_t$. The new distribution of relative human capital is given by equation (2.17). The variable $\hat{h}_{t+1}$ is obtained from (2.15), the aggregate population growth rate N_t from (2.16), and the future capital–labor ratio k_{t+1} from (2.23). This procedure can be used to compute an equilibrium for any initial conditions. The future distribution of human capital is always well defined. ∎

Concerning the long-run behavior of the economy, it follows from these equations that there is a balanced growth path in which everyone has the same human capital:

Proposition 2.2 Balanced growth path and limiting distribution
If $\eta\phi > \theta$, there is a balanced growth path characterized by $dG(1) = 1$ (i.e. the limiting distribution is degenerate). The growth factor of output and human capital is:

$$g^\star = \mu\left(\frac{\eta(\phi - \theta)}{1 - \eta}\right)^\eta \quad if \quad \kappa = 1 - \tau \ (endogenous\ growth),$$

$$\qquad\qquad 1 + \rho \qquad otherwise\ (exogenous\ growth),$$

and the growth factor of population is:

$$N^\star = \frac{(1 - \eta)\gamma}{(\phi - \theta)\rrbracket}.$$

Proof: **Case $\kappa = 1 - \tau$:** The constant values $g_t = \mu\,(\eta(\phi - \theta)/(1 - \eta))^\eta$, $N_t = n_t = N^\star$, $x_{t+1} = x_t = 1$, and:

$$k_{t+1} = k_t = \left(\frac{A\beta\rrbracket(1 - \alpha)(\phi - \theta)^{1-\eta}}{\mu\gamma(1 + \beta)\eta^\eta(1 - \eta)^{1-\eta}}\right)^{\frac{1}{1-\alpha}}$$

solve equations (2.16), (2.17), (2.18), (2.20), (2.21), and (2.23).
Case $\kappa \neq 1 - \tau$: The constant values $g_t = 1 + \rho$, $N_t = n_t = N^\star$, $x_{t+1} = x_t = 1$,

$$\hat{h} = \left(\frac{\mu}{1 + \rho}\left(\frac{\eta(\phi - \theta)}{1 - \eta}\right)^\eta\right)^{\frac{1}{1-\kappa-\tau}},$$

and:

$$k_{t+1} = k_t = \left(\frac{\beta(\phi - \theta)\rrbracket A(1 - \alpha)}{(1 + \beta)(1 + \rho)(1 - \eta)\gamma}\right)^{\frac{1}{1-\alpha}}$$

solve equations (2.16), (2.17), (2.18), (2.20), (2.21), and (2.23). ∎

Along this balanced growth path, there is no longer any inequality among households. This holds because we have assumed that households differ only in their initial level of human capital. If we had introduced ability shocks on top of an unequal initial distribution of human capital, inequality would persist along the balanced growth path (this is done in the paper version of this chapter, de la Croix and Doepke (2003)).

We will assume $\eta\phi > \theta$ from here on. We now consider the dynamics of the human capital of an individual dynasty (of mass zero) around an aggregate balanced growth path. This will be useful to understand the role of the parameter τ for the dynamic properties of the model.

2.2.3 The dynamics of individual human capital

To study the dynamics of individual human capital, we assume that the economy is on a balanced growth path, so that the growth rate of average human capital is constant over time: $g_t = g^\star$.

In order to understand the dynamics of the model, we examine the function $x_{t+1} - x_t = \Psi(x_t; \tau)$, i.e., the change in x_t as a function of x_t and τ:

$$\Psi(x; \tau) = \frac{\mu x^\tau}{g^\star}\left(\theta + \max\left[0, \frac{\eta\phi x - \theta}{1 - \eta}\right]\right)^\eta (\hat{h}^\star)^{\kappa + \tau - 1} - x.$$

Here $g^\star$ and $\hat{h}^\star$ are the balanced-growth-path values. In the case $\kappa = 1 - \tau$ we replace $g^\star$ by $\mu(\eta(\phi - \theta)/(1 - \eta))^\eta$. In the case $\kappa \neq 1 - \tau$, we replace $g^\star$ by $1 + \rho$ and $\hat{h}^\star$ by $(\frac{\mu}{1+\rho}(\frac{\eta(\phi-\theta)}{1-\eta})^\eta)^{\frac{1}{1-\kappa-\tau}}$. Both substitutions lead to the same expression:

$$\Psi(x; \tau) = \left(\frac{1 - \eta}{\eta(\phi - \theta)}\right)^\eta x^\tau \left(\theta + \max\left[0, \frac{\eta\phi x - \theta}{1 - \eta}\right]\right)^\eta - x. \qquad (2.24)$$

Note that in the endogenous and exogenous growth cases the function $\Psi(x; \tau)$ turns out to be the same.

First consider the limits of this function. We have: $\Psi(0; \tau) = 0$, $\Psi'_x(0; \tau) = +\infty$, and:

$$\lim_{x \to \infty} \Psi(x; \tau) = x^{\tau+\eta}\left(\frac{\phi}{\phi - \theta}\right)^\eta - x,$$

which implies:

$$\lim_{x \to \infty} \Psi(x; \tau) = -\infty \text{ if } \tau + \eta < 1 \text{ and } \lim_{x \to \infty} \Psi(x; \tau) = +\infty \text{ otherwise.}$$

Hence the function Ψ starts from $x = 0$ with an infinite slope and goes to either $-\infty$ or $+\infty$ depending on parameter values.

By definition of the aggregate balanced growth path, $x = 1$ is a steady state and thus $\Psi(1; \tau) = 0$. This steady state is locally stable if and only if $\Psi'_x(1; \tau) < 0$, i.e.:

$$\tau + \frac{\eta\phi}{\phi - \theta} - 1 < 0.$$

At the point:

$$\hat{\tau} = 1 - \frac{\eta\phi}{\phi - \theta}$$

the dynamics of individual capital described by $x_{t+1} - x_t = \Psi(x_t; \tau)$ undergo a transcritical bifurcation, as proved in Proposition 2.3. There are thus two steady-state equilibria, 1 and $\bar{x}$, near $(1, \hat{\tau})$ for each value of τ smaller or larger than $\hat{\tau}$. The equilibrium 1 (resp. $\bar{x}$) is stable (resp. unstable) for $\tau < \hat{\tau}$ and unstable (resp. stable) for $\tau > \hat{\tau}$.

Another point of interest is $x_t = \frac{\theta}{\eta\phi}$. If, at this point, the function Ψ is negative, it crosses the horizontal axes between 0 and $\frac{\theta}{\eta\phi}$. The existence of this steady state results from the infinite slope of Ψ at 0 and from its continuity; uniqueness results from the concavity of the function in the interval $(0, \frac{\theta}{\eta\phi})$. We evaluate:

$$\Psi\left(\frac{\theta}{\eta\phi}, \tau\right) = \left(\frac{\theta(1-\eta)}{\eta(\phi-\theta)}\right)\eta\left(\frac{\theta}{\eta\phi}\right)^{\tau} - \frac{\theta}{\eta\phi}.$$

This is negative if τ is above a threshold $\bar{\tau}$:

$$\bar{\tau} = \frac{(1-\eta)\ln(\theta/\eta) - \ln\phi - \eta\ln((1-\eta)/(\phi-\theta))}{\ln\theta - \ln(\eta\phi)}.$$

We are now able to fully characterize the dynamics of x as a function of the parameter τ. The bifurcation diagram is presented in Figure 2.2. The steady states x are represented on the vertical axis as a function of τ. For small τ there is only one steady state, $x = 1$, which is globally stable. Once τ reaches a

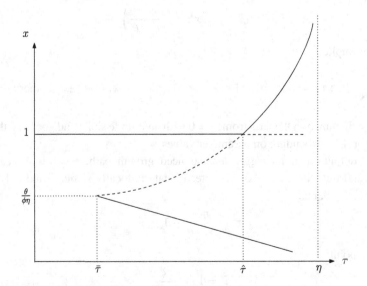

Figure 2.2 Steady state human capital as a function of τ

threshold $\bar{\tau}$, two additional steady states appear. The lower one is stable and the second is unstable. This threshold arises at the point where the cutoff value for an interior solution is a steady state of the individual dynamics.

Proposition 2.3 Dynamics around the transcritical bifurcation
At the point:

$$\hat{\tau} = 1 - \frac{\eta\phi}{\phi - \theta}$$

the dynamics of individual capital described by $x_{t+1} - x_t = \Psi(x_t; \tau)$ *undergo a transcritical bifurcation. There are two steady-state equilibria, 1 and $\bar{x}$, near $(1, \hat{\tau})$ for each value of τ smaller or larger than $\hat{\tau}$. The equilibrium 1 (resp. $\bar{x}$) is stable (resp. unstable) for $\tau < \hat{\tau}$ and unstable (resp. stable) for $\tau > \hat{\tau}$.*

Proof: We check the five conditions that define such a bifurcation in Wiggins (1990), p. 365:

$$\Psi(1, \hat{\tau}) = 0, \quad \Psi_x'(1, \hat{\tau}) = 0, \quad \Psi_\tau'(1, \hat{\tau}) = 0,$$

$$\Psi_{xx}''(1, \hat{\tau}) = -\frac{\eta\theta\phi}{(\phi - \theta)^2} \neq 0, \quad \Psi_{x\tau}''(1, \hat{\tau}) = 1 \neq 0.$$

∎

This bifurcation occurs when an unstable and a stable fixed point collide and exchange stability. That is, the unstable fixed point becomes stable and vice versa. When τ increases beyond $\hat{\tau}$, the high steady state increases and then vanishes once $\tau > \eta$. Thus, for individual dynamics to be stable, it is essential that τ be not too high. In the next section, we calibrate the model parameters to data and find that the stable region for τ is the empirically relevant case. The analysis of the dynamics of x_t at given aggregate conditions is helpful to understand the numerical simulations carried out in the next section. But before that, we look at the robustness of the results if we allow parents to choose how much time to spend with each child.

2.2.4 Extension with endogenous child rearing time

The model is extended to allow parents to choose how much time to spend with each child. For this choice to matter, this parental time input would have to affect the human capital of the child. Specifically, when parents choose the time devoted to child rearing, the parental decision problem is:

$$\max \ln(c_t) + \beta \ln(d_{t+1}) + \gamma \ln(n_t h_{t+1})$$

subject to:

$$c_t + s_t + e_t n_t w_t \bar{h}_t = w_t h_t (1 - \phi n_t - p_t n_t), \qquad (2.25)$$

and:

$$h_{t+1} = \mu_t (\theta + e_t)^\eta (h_t)^\tau (\bar{h}_t)^\kappa p_t^\varrho. \qquad (2.26)$$

Now, p_t is the time spent by parents on raising their children, and ϱ is the elasticity of the children's human capital with respect to p_t. For a household with an interior solution for the education choice ($x_t > \frac{\theta(1-\varrho)}{\phi\eta}$ holds), the first-order conditions imply:

$$s_t = \frac{\beta}{\beth} w_t h_t, \qquad (2.27)$$

$$e_t = \frac{\eta \phi x_t - \theta(1 - \varrho)}{1 - \eta - \varrho}, \qquad (2.28)$$

$$n_t = \frac{(1 - \eta - \varrho)\gamma x_t}{(\phi x_t - \theta)\beth}, \qquad (2.29)$$

$$p_t = \frac{(\phi x_t - \theta)\varrho}{x_t \beth}. \qquad (2.30)$$

For a household endowed with sufficiently little human capital such that $x_t < \frac{\theta(1-\varrho)}{\phi\eta}$ holds, the optimal choice for education e_t is zero. The first-order conditions imply equation (2.10) and:

$$e_t = 0, \qquad (2.31)$$

$$n_t = \frac{\gamma(1 - \varrho)}{\phi \beth}, \qquad (2.32)$$

$$p_t = \frac{\varrho\phi}{1 - \varrho}. \qquad (2.33)$$

Qualitatively, the income–fertility and income–education relationships are the same as in the simpler model ($\varrho = 0$). If we calibrated the more complicated model, estimates for ϱ would be very small, since empirical studies find that parental time has little (if any) direct effects on children's earnings (Hanushek (1992), Leibowitz (1974), Rosenzweig and Wolpin (1994)). In addition, since we calibrate the model such that maximum fertility differentials correspond to data, the values for other parameters would adjust, so that the implications of the two versions of the model for fertility and education would be very similar.

2.3 Computational experiments

The theoretical results in the previous section highlight two channels through which inequality affects growth in this model. First, inequality in human capital leads to inequality in education, and since the production function for human capital is concave, inequality in education lowers future average human capital. Second, people with lower human capital choose not only less education for their children but also a higher number of children. This differential–fertility effect increases the weight in the population on families with little education, which also lowers future human capital. The question arises as to which effect is more important, and how large the effects are quantitatively. To answer this question, we calibrate our model and provide numerical simulations of the evolution of fertility, inequality, human capital, and income. The main findings are that the effects of inequality on human capital accumulation and growth are sizable, and that the differential–fertility effect is crucial for generating this result.

We also use the calibrated model to analyze the dynamic implications of our theory. Here, a key finding is that for reasonable parameterizations, the model generates a "hump-shape" in inequality and population growth, which first increase and then fall during development. This outcome lends additional support to the relationship between inequality, fertility, and growth postulated model.

2.3.1 Calibration

We choose the parameters of the model such that the balanced growth path resembles empirical features of the US economy and population. The production function for human capital is calibrated to match observed fertility differentials, as well as empirical estimates of the effects of education on future earnings. Table 2.1 summarizes the results for the benchmark case and the endogenous growth case (variant).

The model is calibrated under the assumption that one period (or generation) has a length of thirty years. The parameter α is the capital share in the consumption good sector and is set to $1/3$ to match the empirical counterpart. The productivity level A is a scale parameter and is set to $A = 1$. The discount factor β mainly affects the ratio of human capital to physical capital in the balanced

Table 2.1. *Calibration: a summary*

Parameter		Benchmark	Variant
Capital share in production	α	0.333	
Total factor productivity	A	1.000	
Psychological discount factor	β	0.299	
Productivity growth rate	ρ	0.811	
Productivity of education	μ	1.000	0.367
Taste for children	γ	0.271	
Time–cost parameter	ϕ	0.075	
Return to education	η	0.635	
Innate education level	θ	0.012	
Human capital externality at the social level	κ	0.100	0.800
Inter-generational transmission of human capital	τ	0.200	

growth path. Since this ratio depends on the choice of units, it does not provide a convenient basis for calibrating β. Given that β does not influence qualitative features of the model that we are interested in, we choose a value that is standard in the real-business-cycle literature, $\beta = 0.99^{120}$ (i.e. 0.99 per quarter). The implied interest rate per year is 4.7 percent. The productivity growth rate ρ governs output growth in the balanced growth path, and is set to $1.02^{30} - 1$ or 2 percent per year, which approximates the average growth rate in the US. With exogenous growth (i.e. $\kappa < 1 - \tau$) as in our calibration, the overall productivity μ in the production function for human capital is a scale parameter and is set to $\mu = 1$.

The weight γ of children in the utility function governs the growth rate of population in the balanced growth path. In the USA as in other industrialized countries, fertility rates are close to the reproduction level. Accordingly, we choose γ such that the growth rate of population in the balanced growth path is zero. This is achieved by choosing $\gamma = 0.271$.[3] The time–cost parameter ϕ for having a child determines the overall opportunity cost of children. Evidence in Haveman and Wolfe (1995) and Knowles (1999a) suggests that the opportunity cost of a child is equivalent to about 15 percent of the parents' time endowment. This cost accrues only as long as the child is living with the parents. If we assume that children live with parents for fifteen years and that the adult period lasts for thirty years, the overall time cost should be 50 percent of the time cost per year with the child present. Accordingly, we choose $\phi = 0.075$. The parameter ϕ

---

[3] Since convergence to the balanced growth path is slow, the model still allows for substantial population growth for long time periods.

also sets an upper limit on the number of children a person can have. With our choice, a person spending all their time on raising children would have a little above thirteen children. A family of two could have a little under twenty-seven children.

The parameter η influences the elasticity of human capital with respect to education, as well as the maximum fertility differential in the economy. Specifically, the maximum differential written as a ratio is given by $1/(1 - \eta)$. In the Kremer and Chen (2002) data set, the highest fertility ratio between women at the lowest and the highest education levels is 2.74 (Brazil). This differential is achieved by choosing $\eta = 0.635$. Our choice of η guarantees that realized fertility differentials in the model never exceed the maximum differential observed in the data, which ensures that the role of the differential–fertility channel is not inflated. At the same time, for evaluating the differential–fertility channel it is also important that the elasticity of future human capital with respect to education is calibrated realistically. In the model, this elasticity is determined jointly by η and θ. Since θ enters the education choice of parents, it determines aggregate expenditures on education. We choose θ such that in the balanced growth path total education expenditure as a fraction of gross domestic product (GDP) matches the corresponding value in US data, which is 7.3 percent. The implied parameter value is $\theta = 0.0119$. Our combined choices for η and θ imply an elasticity of human capital with respect to education of 0.6 in the balanced growth path.[4]

The remaining parameters κ and τ do not influence individual decisions, but still have an effect on growth rates. The elasticity κ of future human capital with respect to average human capital $\bar{h}$ can be calibrated to evidence on the effects of the quality of schooling. We interpret the education choice e_t as the quantity of schooling (corresponding to years of schooling in the data) while $\bar{h}$ measures the quality of schooling, since it is the average human capital of teachers. Compared with the quantity of schooling, the quality of schooling (such as spending per pupil at a given level of education) has been shown to have smaller effects on earnings with an elasticity of around 0.1 – see Card and Krueger (1996) and Krueger and Lindahl (2001). In line with evidence on

---

[4] This number is within the range of estimates of the elasticity of earnings with respect to schooling. Specifically, estimates of the return to an additional year of schooling range from 7.5 percent in Angrist and Krueger (1991) to 12–16 percent in the study of twins by Ashenfelter and Krueger (1994). The surveys by Krueger and Lindahl (2001) and Psacharopoulos (1994) report estimates of the return to schooling in developed countries of 8–10 percent, with higher estimates for developing countries and low levels of schooling. Assuming that an additional year of schooling raises education expenditure by 20 percent, these returns translate into an earnings elasticity of schooling between 0.4 and 0.8. The elasticity implied by our parameter choices is exactly in the middle of this range.

the effect of the quality of education, we set $\kappa = 0.1$.[5] Our results are robust
with respect to the choice of this elasticity in the sense that κ matters only
for the determination of the growth rate of average human capital. Individual
decisions and the evolution of inequality, fertility, and differential fertility are
independent of κ.

The parameter τ determines the direct effect of parental human capital (or,
equivalently, income) on the children's human capital. Thus, τ captures the
intergenerational transmission of ability, as well as human capital formation
within the family that does not work through formal schooling. Empirical studies detect such effects, but they are relatively small. Rosenzweig and Wolpin
(1994) find that an additional year of the mother's education at the high school
level (roughly a 10 percent increase in education) raises a child's test scores by
2.4 percent. Leibowitz (1974) finds that even after controlling for schooling and
education of the parents, parental income has a significant effect on a child's
earnings. A 10 percent increase in parental income increases a child's future
earnings by up to 0.85 percent. Given that the long-run dynamics of the model
are sensitive to the choice of τ, we choose a moderate degree of intergenerational transmission of human capital ($\tau = 0.2$) as the baseline case, and provide
a sensitivity analysis with respect to alternative choices for τ.

Exercise: Draw the Ψ function for the chosen calibration (using software
such as Matlab, Mathematica, or even Excel). What is the bifurcation value $\hat{\tau}$
from Proposition 2.3? Draw also the Ψ function for $\tau = 0.3$.

In addition to choosing parameters, we need to set the initial conditions for the
simulations. The overall size of the population is a scale parameter which does
not affect the results, and is therefore set to 1. Likewise, the distribution of physical capital does not matter, since capital is owned by old people who have nothing left to decide. We therefore specify only the aggregate value. The initial distribution of human capital follows a log-normal distribution $F(m, \sigma^2)$, where
m and σ^2 are the mean and variance of the underlying normal distribution. The
parameter m is set such that $\hat{h}_t$ is at its balanced-growth level. We provide simulations for different variances of the distribution in order to examine the effects
of inequality. The initial level of physical capital K_0 is chosen such that the ratio
of physical to human capital is equal to its value in the balanced growth path.[6]

---

[5] Alternatively, κ could also be interpreted as a measure of human capital externalities. Existing
evidence (see Acemoglu and Angrist (2000) and Krueger and Lindahl (2001)) suggests that
these externalities are small as well, i.e. the social return to human capital accumulation is only
slightly larger than the private return, confirming our low choice of κ.

[6] The effect of inequality on growth is independent of m and K_0; m and K_0 affect only average
growth rates.

Table 2.2. *Initial growth with endogenous and exogenous fertility*

	Endogenous fertility				Exogenous fertility			
σ^2	g_0	N_0	I_0	D_0	g_0	N_0	I_0	D_0
0.10	2.00	0.00	0.056	0.09	2.00	0	0.056	0
0.75	1.26	0.66	0.404	1.95	1.87	0	0.400	0
1.00	0.80	1.08	0.520	2.76	1.78	0	0.513	0
1.50	0.01	1.71	0.707	2.77	1.53	0	0.700	0

Notes: σ^2: variance of income distribution, g_0: growth rate of human capital per worker, N_0: growth rate of population, I_0: income inequality (Gini coefficient), D_0: fertility differential.

2.3.2 Initial inequality, fertility, and growth

As a first computational experiment, we examine the effect of initial inequality on growth over the first period. Since a period is in fact a generation, the growth rate should be interpreted as a thirty-year average. Table 2.2 presents the initial annualized growth rates of human capital g_0 and population N_0 (in percent), initial inequality I_0, and the initial fertility differential D_0 for different variances of the distribution of human capital. Inequality is measured by the Gini coefficient I_0 computed on the earnings of the working population. Differential fertility is the difference between the average fertility of the top quintile and the bottom quintile; this quantity is then multiplied by two to yield a number per woman. To evaluate the role of differential fertility in our model, we also computed results under the assumption of constant, exogenous fertility.

The results in Table 2.2 show that inequality lowers growth both with and without endogenous fertility, but the effects are much larger when fertility is endogenous. When the variance of the distribution of human capital is low ($\sigma^2 = 0.10$), the difference between endogenous and exogenous fertility is small, and the growth rates are close to their values on the balanced growth path. When we increase the initial variance to $\sigma^2 = 0.75$, substantial fertility differentials within the population begin to arise, and the annual growth rate of human capital drops 0.74 percent below the steady state. With constant exogenous fertility, the drop in the growth rate is six times smaller. Further increases in the initial variance eventually lead to a negative growth rate (for $\sigma^2 > 1.5$) with endogenous fertility, while growth stays positive with exogenous fertility.

The results are robust with respect to the choice of τ. For example, with $\sigma^2 = 0.75$, initial growth with endogenous fertility is 1.22 percent for $\tau = 0.05$, and 1.32 percent for $\tau = 0.3$. With exogenous fertility, it is 1.80 percent for $\tau = 0.05$, and 1.94 percent for $\tau = 0.3$. We carried out the same computations with a uniform instead of a log-normal distribution of initial human capital. We still found that growth declines much faster with inequality when fertility is endogenous. For example, when the Gini index goes from 0 to 0.33, growth drops by 0.7 percent with endogenous fertility and by 0.1 percent with exogenous fertility.

The initial dispersion of human capital also influences the overall growth rate of population. When the variance of human capital rises, fertility of low-skilled households increases, while high-skilled households decide to have fewer children. Because of the shape of the fertility function (see Figure 1.1), the first effect dominates and aggregate fertility rises. This is in line with empirical studies that report a high positive correlation between aggregate fertility rates and Gini coefficients (see Barro (2000)).

Figure 2.3 depicts the growth rate of human capital as a function of the Gini coefficient. The slope is much steeper with endogenous fertility than with exogenous fertility. In the data, income Ginis for a country vary roughly in the range 0.2 to 0.65. In the model, raising the initial Gini from 0.2 to 0.65 lowers the growth rate by only about 0.3 percent with exogenous fertility, but by 1.4 percent with endogenous fertility. In a quantitative sense, fertility differentials within the population are essential for generating the relationship between inequality and growth.

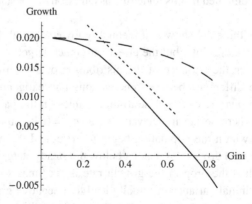

Figure 2.3 The relationship of inequality and growth with endogenous fertility (solid), exogenous fertility (dashed), and in Barro's regression (dotted)

We have also represented the slope of the regression of economic growth on income Ginis run by Barro (2000) when the fertility rate variable is omitted. In this regression, the Gini coefficient captures the intrinsic effect of inequality as well as the one going through fertility. Since actual Gini coefficients lie in the interval [.21, .64], the regression line has been restricted to this interval. Our computational experiment is consistent with the Barro (2000) finding: "A reduction of the Gini coefficient by 0.1 would be estimated to raise the growth rate on impact by 0.4 percent per year."[7]

2.3.3 The dynamics of inequality, fertility, and growth

We now turn to the dynamic implications of our model. So far, we have analyzed only the effects of inequality on growth during the initial period. Since in our dynastic model a period has a length of thirty years, even the initial growth effect extends over a long horizon, and consequently the dynamics of the model are to be interpreted as changes which occur over a horizon of a century or more. We therefore evaluate the dynamic behavior of the model relative to the evolution of income, fertility, and inequality in industrializing countries in the last 200 years. A central feature of the data for this period is that the behavior of population growth and inequality is non-monotone. As a benchmark case, consider England, the first country to industrialize. Fertility rates increased until about 1830 and started to decline rapidly only after 1870 (Chesnais (1992)). Income inequality followed a similar pattern, with increasing inequality until about 1870 and a rapid decline afterwards (Williamson (1985)). The growth rate of income per capita, in contrast, does not display a hump-shape. Growth rates were essentially zero before the Industrial Revolution and then increased slowly throughout the nineteenth century (Maddison (2001)). Similar patterns can be observed for Western Europe as a whole and, starting a little later, in the United States.

To evaluate how our model performs relative to these facts, we simulate the model with the baseline calibration over a horizon of eight periods, correspond-ing to 240 years. Figure 2.4 shows the evolution of the growth rate of human capital, the population growth rate, inequality, and differential fertility for two different values of τ. Growth rates are annualized. The initial distribution of human capital is assumed log-normal with $\sigma^2 = 1$, corresponding to an initial Gini coefficient of 0.5. With a low τ of 0.05, fertility, inequality, and differential fertility converge monotonically to their steady-state values. Initially, inequal-ity reduces growth below its balanced-growth value for the reasons explained

---

[7] Perotti (1996) reports effects of similar magnitude.

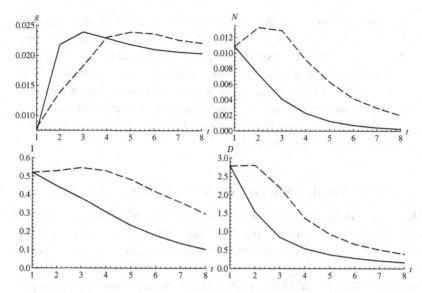

Figure 2.4 Growth, fertility, inequality, and differential fertility for $\tau = 0.05$ (solid) and $\tau = 0.2$ (dashed)

above, but subsequently the growth rate increases. Low initial growth implies that the capital stock increases more slowly than in the balanced growth path. Since productivity growth is exogenous, the effective capital stock falls, and the usual transitional dynamics in exogenous-growth models result in higher subsequent growth. If τ is raised to 0.2, the model generates the hump-shape patterns that characterize the data. Fertility and inequality first rise and then decrease, and the growth rate remains below its balanced-growth value for several periods as long as inequality remains high. A moderate degree of intergenerational persistence in human capital is thus essential for matching the long-run evolution of inequality and fertility to data.

The non-monotone behavior of inequality and fertility is related to the corner solution for education. A fraction of the people in the first period decides not to invest in education. Since this group has the highest fertility rates, their children make up an even larger fraction of the population in the next period. If there is a sufficient degree of intergenerational persistence, these children will be at the corner solution for education as well. This leads to an increase in population growth in the first periods and slow growth of human capital, since investment in education is low. Because of exogenous technological change and human capital externalities, however, after a few periods even the dynasties that initially did not invest in education find it optimal to start educating their children. From this point on, inequality and population growth fall.

This non-monotone behavior occurs only if the initial distribution of human capital is such that some people choose not to invest in education. If everyone is above the threshold initially, convergence to the steady state is monotone even for $\tau = 0.2$. For parameters that lead to an initial rise in fertility and inequality, the time paths for inequality, growth, and fertility look surprisingly similar to the patterns of development in Western Europe between 1800 and 2000 described by Galor and Weil (2000) and others. For example, let us assume that $t = 1$ in figures 2.4 and 2.6 corresponds to the period 1760–1790 in England. Then population growth peaks around 1790–1820, and inequality peaks thirty years later. The timing of the subsequent fall is close to what is observed in the data. For the hump to occur, however, τ cannot be too small, i.e. we need some degree of intergenerational persistence in human capital and earnings.

A unique equilibrium exists even if we increase τ above the bifurcation value of $\hat{\tau} = 0.246$, where we enter the region of the parameter space in which the dynamics of individual human capital are no longer stable. The returns to parental human capital in the education function are not sufficiently decreasing to compensate the centrifugal force of the quality–quantity tradeoff. Computations of the distribution of human capital after a large number of periods indicate that an ever decreasing share of the population accumulates an ever increasing share of human capital. The mass of people with above-average human capital tends to 0, but the fraction of human capital accounted for by them tends to 1.

Figure 2.5 shows the distribution over human capital after eighteen periods for four different values for τ. The graphs for $\tau = 0.05$ and $\tau = 0.2$ confirm that the distribution of human capital converges to a degenerate steady state where everyone has the same human capital. In both cases, most of the mass of the distribution is concentrated around $x = 1$. For the case $\tau = 0.2$, the density has a number of kinks. These kinks correspond to the cutoff points for dynasties that were at the corner solution for education in the first periods. The figure for $\tau = 0.3$ shows a bimodal distribution of human capital. This bimodal distribution reflects the case of two stable steady states for the individual dynamics that we discussed in the bifurcation analysis. However, the fact that the individual dynamics are stable around two steady states does not imply that the limiting distribution is bimodal as well. As long as the dynasties at one of the steady states have higher fertility rates, their fraction of the population will converge to 1, leading to a unimodal limiting distribution. Indeed, our computations indicate that the limiting distribution is degenerate at $x = 1$ even for the case $\tau = 0.3$. In the case $\tau = 0.4$, the distribution of human capital is unimodal

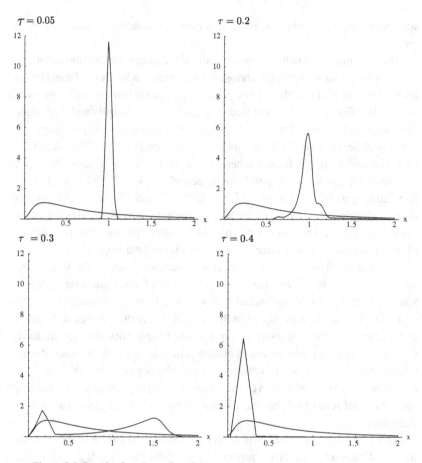

Figure 2.5 Density functions after eighteen periods

around a point x smaller than 1. In this case, there are only few dynasties with
high human capital, but since they invest in a lot of education they account for
a large fraction of total human capital. The mass of people with above-average
human capital tends to zero, but the fraction of human capital accounted for by
them tends to 1.

The main disparity between the model and the data is that in the data
growth rates were slowly increasing throughout the nineteenth century, whereas
the model produces a hump-shape with first rapidly increasing and then
falling growth rates. This behavior of the model is generated by transitional dynamics due to the exogenous-growth assumption. We therefore also
explore how the model performs if we increase the human capital externality

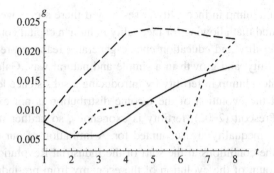

Figure 2.6 Exogenous versus endogenous growth: $\kappa = 1 - \tau$ (solid), $\kappa = 0.1$ (dashed), data (dots)

from $\kappa = 0.1$ to $\kappa = 1 - \tau = 0.8$ to allow for endogenous growth. As stressed above, individual decisions and the evolution of inequality, fertility, and differential fertility are independent of the assumption on κ. However, the dynamic pattern of the growth rate can be affected.[8] Figure 2.6 compares growth rates under the two different regimes with UK data from Maddison (2001). While growth with $\kappa = 0.1$ increases quickly and soon exceeds its balanced-growth value, with $\kappa = 1 - \tau$ growth converges slowly and monotonically to its long-run level. The pattern under the endogenous growth assumption is closer to the observed pattern in England, where the average growth rate of 2 percent was reached only towards the beginning of the twentieth century. Notice, however, that to generate endogenous growth we have to assume a much higher degree of externalities than suggested by empirical estimates in recent data. The result therefore indicates either that externalities played a bigger role in the past, or that another endogenous growth mechanism was at work which generated the slowly increasing growth rates.

Our results complement existing theories of long-run growth. Relative to the literature, the main novelty is that we link the evolution of growth and population to the income distribution. In contrast, the models developed by Boucekkine *et al.* (2002), Galor and Weil (2000), and Hansen and Prescott (2002) abstract from distributional issues. Doepke (2004) has a model of the Industrial Revolution and the demographic transition which does allow for

---

[8] To calibrate the endogenous growth version of the model, we keep τ at 0.2 and set $\kappa = 0.8$. The overall productivity μ in the production function for human capital now governs the growth rate of output per capita. We pick $\mu = 0.367$ which ensures a long-term growth rate of 2 percent per year.

inequality, but a hump in inequality arises only if there are exogenous policy changes. We find that allowing for inequality in human capital combined with endogenous fertility and education choice generates realistic predictions for inequality, fertility, and growth in a simple and natural way. Galor and Weil (2000) generate a hump in fertility by introducing a subsistence level of consumption, but the evolution of the income distribution is not explained. In Hansen and Prescott (2002), fertility is exogenous, so neither the hump in fertility nor in inequality are accounted for. A limitation of our approach is that we take the conditions at the start of the Industrial Revolution as given. For a full account of the evolution of the economy from pre-industrial stagnation to modern growth we would have to add an element to the model that generates the initial stagnation phase. We suspect that this could be done along the lines of unified growth theory (Galor and Weil (2000) or Hansen and Prescott (2002)), but the extension is beyond the scope of the current chapter.

2.4 Conclusion

Most of the theoretical literature on inequality and growth has concentrated on channels where inequality affects growth through the accumulation of physical capital. In this chapter we propose a different mechanism which links inequality and growth through differential fertility and the accumulation of human capital. In our model, families with less human capital decide to have more children and invest less in education. When income inequality is high, large fertility differentials lower the growth rate of average human capital, since poor families who invest little in education make up a large fraction of the population in the next generation. A calibration exercise shows that these effects can be fairly large. In the benchmark case, raising the Gini from 0.2 to 0.65 lowers the initial annual growth rate by 1.4 percent.

We also examine the time-series implications of our model for the joint evolution of inequality, fertility, and growth. Here we find that the model is able to explain key features of the evolution of income, fertility, and inequality in industrializing countries in the last 200 years. Specifically, the model generates an initial increase and ultimate decline in inequality and fertility. The same pattern was observed in many industrializing countries in the nineteenth and early twentieth centuries. In addition, if we specify the model to allow for endogenous growth, the model generates steadily increasing growth rates throughout the transition, which is another stylized feature of the data.

A natural direction for further research concerns the policy implications of our model. Since differential fertility rather than inequality per se is the main source of growth effects, it is not clear that redistribution policies would increase economic growth. Indeed, as we showed in Chapter 1, income redistribution tends to increase fertility differentials, which would lower the growth rate. Compared with income redistribution, policies aimed at equalizing access to education would be more effective. This will be the subject of Part II.

3

Understanding the forerunners in
fertility decline

It is one of the universal facts of development that economic growth is accompanied by a demographic transition from high to low fertility. In recent years a number of authors have used economic theory to analyze the interaction between long-run growth and the demographic transition (see Chapter 2). To explain fertility decline during the demographic transition, the majority of these studies relies on the notion of a quantity–quality tradeoff introduced by Becker (1960).[1] In the quantity–quality model, parents choose both the number and "quality" of children, where quality can be interpreted as investments in children, such as education. As the economy grows and wages rise, having many children becomes more costly, since the value of the parents' time increases and children are costly in terms of time. In contrast, rising income implies that investment in education becomes more affordable. Parents therefore substitute child quality for child quantity, and decide to have smaller families with better education. This explanation for the demographic transition is supported by the observation that in many countries average education levels of children were rising significantly during the phase of rapid fertility decline.

The ability to account for fertility both in the cross-section and over time during the demographic transition is one of the key attractions of the quantity-quality model. The economic literature on the demographic transition, however, is generally silent on the cross-sectional implications of the fertility model employed. To some degree, this is because many studies rely on representative-agent models which do not generate cross-sectional predictions. Another, maybe

This chapter uses some unpublished material worked out with Matthias Doepke.

[1] Work on the quantity–quality tradeoff includes Becker *et al.* (1990) and Tamura (1994). These papers were the first to demonstrate how different development regimes can arise from endogenous fertility decisions.

more important, reason is that little historical data are available on fertility across income groups. Information on the evolution of fertility differentials during the demographic transition would allow us to evaluate more thoroughly the predictions of the quantity–quality model. Moreover, understanding the evolution of fertility by education group or social class can shed light on the mechanisms and underlying changes that led to declining total fertility rates. In this chapter, we provide data on changes in differential fertility in Europe from 1550 to 1900. We use this information to assess whether a basic quantity–quality fertility model can account for both the overall decline in fertility and the changes in differential fertility during the demographic transition.

3.1 Rouen and Geneva data

Two data sets can give hints about fertility by social class before the Industrial Revolution. They cover the population of two cities in continental Europe – Rouen by Bardet (1983) and Geneva by Perrenoud (1975). We already used these data focusing on mortality in de la Croix and Sommacal (2009). Tables 3.1 and 3.2 present the raw data.

Aggregate trends
In both cities, there is a steady reduction in fertility in all social classes over the period 1670–1790. Table 3.3 shows that the drop in fertility over this period varies between −1.5 and −3.9 children per mother.

This reduction in total fertility is stronger than the decline in mortality, if any, so that net reproduction rates fall on average by 0.5 child per person. By the end of the eighteenth century, they end below one for all classes in both cities.

In both cities, literacy, as measured by the ability to sign an official act, expanded steadily for all classes (last column of Table 3.3).

Differences by social classes
In both cities, there are substantial differences in child mortality between social classes, while differences in adult mortality are smaller.

Total fertility in upper classes is below that in the lower classes by the end of the period considered. We observe from Table 3.4 that, in Rouen, this was always the case, but the difference widened slightly over the period. In Geneva,

Table 3.1. *Data for Rouen*

Classes	I Notables	II Merchants	III Craftsmen	IV Workmen
Income				
Rental value – 1773	488.00	266.00	202.00	77.00
Poll tax – 1728	26.80	12.10	9.40	1.22
Indexes	100.00	54.51	41.39	15.78
Notables = 100				
	100.00	45.15	35.07	4.55
Literacy rate				
1670–99	91.99	76.00	60.50	29.50
1700–29	97.42	79.00	71.50	34.00
1730–59	96.11	83.50	77.00	42.50
1760–92	95.70	90.50	82.50	47.50
Fertility per woman	I	II	III	IV
1670–99	6.23	6.53	7.19	7.21
1700–29	4.87	5.51	6.29	6.06
1730–59	4.84	4.81	5.48	5.67
1760–92	3.77	3.28	4.84	4.84
Net reproduction rate				
1670–99	1.37	1.51	1.36	1.20
1700–29	1.30	1.27	1.19	1.00
1730–59	0.88	0.95	0.96	0.80
1760–92	0.73	0.58	0.82	0.68
Change 1670–1792	−0.65	−0.93	−0.54	−0.52
Survival probability 15 → 30				
	0.865	0.875	0.875	0.857
Survival probability 0 → 15				
	0.521	0.474	0.474	0.408

notables had initially more children than workmen, but ended with far fewer children per woman at the end of the period.

Table 3.5 shows differentials in reproduction rates. Net reproduction rates are always higher in upper classes. The decline in net reproduction rates is more

Table 3.2. *Data for Geneva*

Classes	I Notables	III Craftsmen	IV Workmen
Income			
Dowry 1700–4	20160.00	3189.00	1251.00
Dowry 1741–5	25092.00	5057.00	2173.00
Dowry 1770–4	33730.00	2489.00	2311.00
Indexes Notables = 100	100.00	15.82	6.21
	100.00	20.15	8.66
	100.00	7.38	6.85
Literacy rate			
1700–4	86.00	54.50	12.50
1741–5	96.50	83.50	33.50
1770–4	98.50	87.50	58.00
Fertility per woman			
1675–96	6.70	7.10	6.20
1700–4	6.70	7.30	5.50
1741–5	4.70	5.70	4.20
1770–4	2.80	5.20	4.70
Net reproduction rate			
1650–84	1.18	1.07	0.60
1687–04	1.23	0.96	0.66
1725–72	0.84	0.83	0.68
1800–10	0.73	0.59	0.66
Change 1650–1810	−0.45	−0.48	0.06
Survival probability 15 → 30			
	0.89	0.84	0.80
Survival probability 0 → 15			
	0.61	0.452	0.338

pronounced in the upper classes. Consequently, the net reproduction rates tend to converge across classes.

In sum, both cities are forerunners in the fertility decline. In Geneva, the notables clearly precede the poor classes, and differential fertility widens. In Rouen, this trend is less marked, and fertility differentials widen only marginally.

Table 3.3. *Global trends in forerunners' fertility*

		Change in fertility 1670–1790	Change in reprod. rate 1670–1790	Reprod. rate 1790	Change in literacy 1670–1790
Rouen	Notables	−2.46	−0.65	0.73	+3.71
	Merchants	−3.25	−0.93	0.58	+14.50
	Craftsmen	−2.35	−0.54	0.82	+22.00
	Workmen	−2.37	−0.52	0.68	+18.00
Geneva	Notables	−3.90	−0.45	0.73	+12.50
	Craftsmen	−1.90	−0.48	0.59	+33.00
	Workmen	−1.50	0.06	0.66	+45.50

Table 3.4. *Forerunners' fertility and differential fertility*

		Rouen			Geneva	
	Notables	Workmen	Diff.	Notables	Workmen	Diff.
1670	6.23	7.21	−0.98	6.7	6.2	0.5
1770	3.77	4.84	−1.07	2.8	4.7	−1.9

Table 3.5. *Forerunners' reproduction rates and differentials*

		Rouen			Geneva	
	Notables	Workmen	Diff.	Notables	Workmen	Diff.
1670	1.37	1.20	0.17	1.18	0.60	0.58
1770	0.73	0.68	0.05	0.73	0.66	0.07

3.2 A simple model of fertility

In this section we describe the general model that we use to interpret historical observations on fertility decline. Emphasizing a quantity–quality tradeoff in decisions on children, we also want the model to be sufficiently flexible to admit alternative explanations for fertility decline in addition to the channels at the heart of the quantity–quality literature. For this reason, the model explicitly accounts for the role of mortality, at both the child and the adult level, and we allow for multiple periods of child bearing.

In the model, adults live for up to two periods, and they can have children in either period. The expected lifetime utility of an adult maturing in period t is given by:

$$u_t^t + \beta \pi_t^A u_{t+1}^t, \tag{3.1}$$

where β is the discount factor, π_t^A is the probability of surviving into the second period of adulthood, and u_t^t and u_{t+1}^t are the instantaneous utilities in the two periods of life. Adults care about consumption, their number of children, and the education of their children. The instantaneous utility in period i is given by:

$$u_{t+i}^t = \log c_{t+i}^t + \gamma \log \left(\pi_{t+i}^C n_{t+i}^t q_{t+i}^t \right). \quad i = 0, 1$$

Here c_{t+i}^t denotes goods consumption, n_{t+i}^t is the number of newborn children, q_{t+i}^t is the quality achieved by children born in period $t+i$, and π_{t+i}^C is the probability that a child will survive until the first period of adulthood. The quality of a given child is determined by the education it receives, through the function:

$$q_{t+i}^t = (\theta + e_{t+i}^t)^\eta$$

The variable e_{t+i}^t denotes education spending, while the parameter $\theta > 0$ gives the level of education reached without any education spending. η is a parameter measuring the return on education; more precisely, it is the elasticity of children quality to education. Replacing q_{t+i}^t by its value,

$$u_{t+i}^t = \log c_{t+i}^t + \gamma \log \left(\pi_{t+i}^C n_{t+i}^t \right) + \gamma \eta \log(\theta + e_{t+i}^t). \quad i = 0, 1 \tag{3.2}$$

Adults maximize utility subject to the following period budget constraints:

$$c_t^t + s_t + e_t^t n_t^t \pi_t^C + \epsilon n_t^t \pi_t^C = w(1 - \phi n_t^t - \psi n_t^t \pi_t^C) \tag{3.3}$$

$$c_{t+1}^t + e_{t+1}^t n_{t+1}^t \pi_{t+1}^C + \epsilon n_{t+1}^t \pi_{t+1}^C = s_t \tilde{R}_{t+1}$$

$$+ w(1 - \phi n_{t+1}^t - \psi n_{t+1}^t \pi_{t+1}^C) \tag{3.4}$$

Here savings are denoted s_t, $\tilde{R}_{t+1}$ is the gross interest rate, ϵ is a goods cost that accrues for surviving children, and the parent's wage is given by w (assumed to be constant over time). In addition to the goods expense, children are costly in terms of time. Every birth requires fraction ϕ of the time endowment, regardless of whether the child survives or not. Children who survive until adulthood require an additional time input of fraction ψ of total time.

In the parental decision problem, the survival probabilities π_t^A and π_{t+i}^C are taken as given. Since not all young adults survive to the second period of adulthood, the question arises as to what happens to their savings s_t. We assume that there exists a perfect annuity market; in other words, the adults of a given cohort insure each other against the risk of survival. This assumption implies that the interest factor $\tilde{R}_{t+1}$ is given by the risk-free interest factor R_{t+1} divided by the survival probability π_t^A:

$$\tilde{R}_{t+1} = R_{t+1}/\pi_t^A. \tag{3.5}$$

This assumption of a perfect annuity market is equivalent to an assumption of incomplete markets where all accidental bequests are redistributed to the old households of the same generation, in proportion to their savings.

The decision problem of an adult can be solved in closed form. Since a positive level of education can be reached without any spending given that $\theta > 0$, the solution to the individual problem can be either interior or at the corner $e_{t+1}^t = 0$. Since child quality is a normal good, parents will choose a positive amount of education if their wage w is sufficiently high. The threshold for the interior solution is given by:

$$w \geqslant \hat{w}_{t+i} \equiv \frac{\pi_{t+i}^C \gamma (\theta - \epsilon \eta)}{\gamma \eta (\phi + \pi_{t+i}^C \psi)}, \qquad i = 0, 1. \tag{3.6}$$

Notice that this condition provides a threshold for each period's income separately, as opposed to total lifetime income. At first sight, this may seem surprising, because a rise in the other period's income should also increase the demand for education. However, this income effect is exactly offset by a substitution effect, since increasing the other period's income also increases fertility, which raises the cost of providing education.

If the wage condition is satisfied, the interior optimum can be computed explicitly:

$$s_t = \frac{\pi_t^A}{1 + \pi_t^A \beta} \left(\beta - \frac{1}{R_{t+1}} \right) w, \tag{3.7}$$

$$e_{t+i}^t = \frac{\gamma\eta\left[(\phi + \pi_{t+i}^C\psi)w + \epsilon\pi_{t+i}^C\right] - \theta\gamma\pi_{t+i}^C}{\pi_{t+i}^C\gamma(1-\eta)}, \qquad i = 0, 1 \qquad (3.8)$$

$$n_{t+i}^t = \frac{\beta^i\gamma(1-\eta)\left(1 + \frac{\pi_t^A}{R_{t+1}}\right)w}{(1+\gamma)(1+\beta\pi_t^A)\left((\phi + \psi\pi_{t+i}^C)w - \pi_{t+i}^C(\theta - \epsilon)\right)}. \qquad i = 0, 1 \quad (3.9)$$

From the last equation, it is apparent that we need to impose a parameter restriction to guarantee that fertility is positive:

$$\eta < 1.$$

Intuitively, the weight attached to quality in the utility function should not be too large, since otherwise the household would like to have an infinitesimal number of children of infinite quality.

Given the explicit solution for all choice variables, we can infer how private decisions are affected by a number of possible changes in the economic environment. If $\theta > \epsilon$, parents with higher wage have fewer children, and spend more on education:

$$\frac{\partial n_{t+i}^t}{\partial w} < 0, \qquad \frac{\partial e_{t+i}^t}{\partial w} > 0. \qquad i = 0, 1$$

Intuitively, parents with higher wages can afford to spend more on education. At the same time, a high wage implies that time is costly. It is therefore optimal for high-income parents to have fewer children so as to economize on the time cost needed for raising them, but then provide a lot of education. We will see below that for this effect to arise it is essential that parents are able to substitute quantity for quality. If the education choice is at the corner $e_{t+1}^t = 0$, the relation between income and fertility is reversed.

Higher infant longevity implies fewer children and less education:

$$\frac{\partial n_{t+i}^t}{\partial \pi_{t+i}^C} < 0, \qquad \frac{\partial e_{t+i}^t}{\partial \pi_{t+i}^C} < 0. \qquad i = 0, 1$$

However, the number of surviving children $\pi_{t+i}^C n_{t+i}^t$ increases as π_{t+i}^C rises; thus, the decline in births is less than proportional to the increase in longevity. Parents care only about the number of surviving children. If the child survival rate rises, surviving children become cheaper, thus both income and substitution effects are positive and the demand for surviving children has to increase. As far as education is concerned, the income effect is positive but the substitution effect goes in the opposite direction. In our set-up, it appears that the latter dominates, and education is lowered by higher infant longevity. A similar effect is found by Fioroni (2009). According to her, drops in child mortality are detrimental for growth as fertility increases and education declines. This effect disappears with public education systems.

This increase in the number of surviving children is independent of the functional form chosen for utility. The decline in overall fertility n_{t+i}^t follows because the total cost of children is less than proportional to π_{t+i}^C, which given log utility implies that the increase in the number of survivors is less than proportional to the increase in the survival probability. Further analysis of the effect of child mortality on fertility can be found in Boucekkine *et al.* (2009) and Kalemli-Ozcan (2002, 2003).

A change in adult mortality has no effect on education, and an ambiguous effect on fertility. In particular, the effect of higher parental longevity on fertility depends on equilibrium savings:

$$\frac{\partial n_t^t}{\partial \pi_t^A} = R \frac{\partial n_{t+1}^t}{\partial \pi_t^A} > 0 \Leftrightarrow \beta R_{t+1} < 1 \Leftrightarrow s_t < 0.$$

Adult longevity influences fertility only through an income effect that works through savings. If savings are positive, higher adult survival lowers income, since the interest rate R_{t+1} is negatively related to π_t^A (because of the assumption of perfect annuity markets). Higher survival rates therefore lower income and fertility. The opposite result obtains for a household which borrows, because now a decline in the interest rate increases total income. Notice, however, that apart from the direct effect of fertility choice, an increase in the adult survival rate will have an indirect positive effect on fertility because more adults survive to the second period and get to have additional children.

Finally, if the return to schooling increases, parents will have fewer children and spend more on education:

$$\frac{\partial n_{t+i}^t}{\partial \eta} < 0, \qquad \frac{\partial e_{t+i}^t}{\partial \eta} > 0, \qquad i = 0, 1.$$

If the condition (3.6) is violated in either period, the household is at the corner solution, where at least one of the education choices is equal to zero. There are generally three types of corner solution, with either $e_t^t = 0$, or $e_{t+1}^t = 0$, or both. We concentrate on the case where education spending is zero in both periods.

In this case, savings and fertility are given by:

$$\bar{s}_t = \frac{\pi_t^A}{1 + \pi_t^A \beta}\left(\beta - \frac{1}{R_{t+1}}\right)w. \tag{3.10}$$

$$\bar{n}_{t+i}^t = \frac{\beta^i \gamma \left(1 + \frac{\pi_t^A}{R_{t+1}}\right)w}{(1+\gamma)(1+\beta\pi_t^A)\left((\phi + \psi\pi_{t+i}^C)w + \epsilon\pi_{t+i}^C\right)} \cdot \quad i = 0, 1 \tag{3.11}$$

Given the corner solution, the relationship between the parental wage and fertility is reversed relative to the case with positive education spending. Given that $\epsilon > 0$, parents with higher wages now have more children:

$$\frac{\partial \bar{n}_{t+i}^t}{\partial w} > 0, \qquad i = 0, 1$$

The intuition for this result is easy to see by first considering the case $\epsilon = 0$, where the only cost for children is a time cost. The assumption of log utility implies that the parents want to spend a constant fraction of their full income on children. Since with a pure time cost the cost of having a child is exactly proportional to the wage, fertility turns out to be independent of the wage. If now $\epsilon > 0$, there is an additional goods cost, which is more affordable for richer parents, which explains why fertility is positively related to wages in the corner regime.

The effects of adult and child mortality are similar to the results obtained for the interior solution. Higher infant longevity implies lower fertility, but a larger number of surviving children. Higher parent longevity has an uncertain effect on fertility, given by:

$$\frac{\partial \bar{n}_t^t}{\partial \pi_t^A} = R\frac{\partial \bar{n}_{t+1}^t}{\partial \pi_t^A} > 0 \Leftrightarrow \beta R_{t+1} < 1 \Leftrightarrow s_t < 0.$$

Finally, the fertility choice is independent of the weight attached to child quality.

Exercise: Consider that wages increase with age due to experience. Income in the second period is now $xw(1 - \phi n_{t+1}^t - \psi n_{t+1}^t \pi_{t+1}^C)$. Give a condition on x such that $e_t^t = 0$ and $e_{t+1}^t > 0$.

Figure 3.1 shows the relationship between the parental wage and fertility across the corner regime and the interior regime. For low wages, education choice is at a corner, and there is a positive relationship between income and fertility. Fertility converges to zero as the wage approaches zero, since very

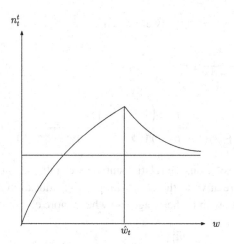

Figure 3.1 Fertility as a function of human capital when $\theta > \epsilon > 0$

poor parents are not able to pay for the goods cost for even a small number of children. Above the threshold for an interior education choice, the quantity-quality tradeoff kicks in, and fertility starts to decline with income.

3.3 Numerical experiments – calibration

We first calibrate the parameters of the model to match the fertility pattern in 1670. We assume that one period lasts 15 years.

A first set of parameters is fixed a priori. The time costs parameters are set to have $\phi + \psi = 0.15$ (Chapter 2) and $(\phi + \psi)/\phi = 4$. Imposing that the ratio of the total parental time cost of a surviving child over that of a non-surviving child has to be equal to 4 is borrowed from Bar and Leukhina (2010b), who use the data on age-specific mortality and the assumption that the instantaneous cost function of raising a child is a decreasing linear function of the child's age to obtain that ratio. We accordingly obtain $\phi = 0.0375$ and $\psi = 0.1125$. The time discount rate and the risk-free interest rate are both set to 1 percent per quarter, which yields $\beta = 0.99^{60}$ and $R = 1.01^{60}$. We already know that equalizing these two rates will imply that adult mortality will not affect fertility rates. Any reasonable departure from this assumption would anyhow lead to small effects.

For wages and survival probabilities, we will use the data we have. We will assume that relative wages and relative survival probabilities do not change over the period 1670–1770, as we do not have enough consistent data to do

Table 3.6. *Results of the calibration procedure*

Parameter		Value
θ	Fixed factor in education	0.253
ϵ	Goods cost of one child	0.234
γ	Taste for children	0.401
η	Return on education	0.453
z	Relative wage: Rouen/Geneva	1.251

otherwise. For relative wages across social classes we take the average of the available data (rental value and poll tax for Rouen, and three observations on dowries for Geneva). For survival probabilities, we take those indicated in Tables 3.2 and 3.3.

For the remaining parameters, θ, ϵ, γ, and η, we assume that they are the same in both cities. We still allow the overall level of wages to differ across cities by a factor z. We calibrate those five parameters so as to match as best as possible the fertility pattern in 1670. Total fertility of a group is the sum of fertility rates conditional on being alive:

$$2\left(n_t^t + n_{t+1}^t\right). \tag{3.12}$$

The net reproduction rate is given by:

$$\pi_t^C n_t^t + \pi_t^A \pi_{t+1}^C n_{t+1}^t. \tag{3.13}$$

In 1670 we have seven observations of the total fertility. We minimize the sum of squared error between the theoretical total fertility and the observed one. We do not impose any a priori on whether a given class is in the corner regime, and we let the calibration procedure decide what is best. The results are presented in Table 3.6.

We first observe that θ is marginally above ϵ, which implies that fertility will almost not depend on wages in the interior regime. Hence, we do not need wage effects to calibrate differential fertility by social class; the infant mortality pattern is enough to do that.

The goods cost of one child can be compared with the wage vectors: $(10, 1.445, 0.724)$ for Geneva and $z \times (10, 4.983, 3.823, 1.016)$ for Rouen. Notice that $z = 1.251$, so the nobles in Rouen are expected to be 25 percent richer than the nobles in Geneva.

The return on education is 0.453, on the low side of the admissible interval for contemporaneous economies (see Chapter 2).

The parameters have not been chosen to match education data. It would still be interesting to compare the implied investment in education $\theta + e$ with the literacy data. To do so, we first need to scale the literacy data to make them of the same magnitude as education in the model. We assume the following relationship:

$$\theta + e = \sigma_0 \text{literacy}^{\sigma_1},$$

where σ_0 and σ_1 are two parameters that we allow to be different in the two cities (this turns out not to matter much). We calibrate the four σ parameters by minimizing the squared deviation from predicted literacy and observed ones in 1670 (1700 for Geneva). This yields for Geneva $\sigma_0 = 2.51$ and $\sigma_1 = 3.75$ and for Rouen $\sigma_0 = 2.22$ and $\sigma_1 = 2.39$.

3.4 Numerical experiments – comparative statics

Figures 3.2 and 3.3 show the results of the calibration and, then, some comparative static analysis. Let us first consider the two first lines, "observations

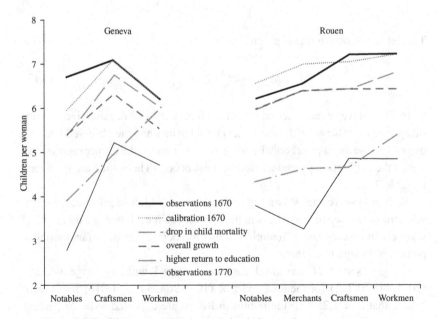

Figure 3.2 Fertility rates: calibration and simulation

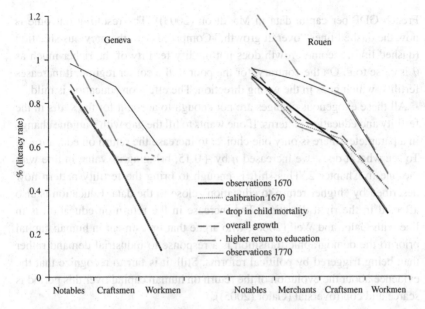

Figure 3.3 Literacy rates: calibration and simulation

1670" and "calibration 1670." The relatively flat fertility pattern, hump-shaped in Geneva, and decreasing with income in Rouen, is reproduced by the calibration. As far as education is concerned, the model is not far from the data (and remember we did nothing to ensure that except rescaling the education expenditures to match the literacy data) except for workmen in Geneva. In fact, both workmen and craftsmen in Geneva are in the corner regime, with θ as their only education, and so the model cannot reproduce that workmen have a very low literacy rate compared with craftsmen.

Consider now the line "observation 1770." The question is, how do we get there from the initial situation? We have first implemented a generalized drop in infant mortality which is consistent with what we know on Geneva as a whole from Perrenoud (1978). All survival probabilities for children were multiplied by 1.163, and this is what leads to the dashed line "drop in child mortality." The distance between the dotted line and the dashed line represents the effect of this overall improvement. The effect is to reduce fertility by a little bit less than one child (more in Geneva than in Rouen) and to reduce very slightly the education investment for those who are not in the corner regime. The effect on fertility is not negligible, but we are still far from the observations in 1770.

Let us now introduce a generalized growth effect, by multiplying all incomes in Geneva by a factor 1.165 and in Rouen by a factor 1.13 (using Swiss and

French GDP per capita data in Maddison (2003)). The resulting outcome is now the dashed lines "overall growth." Compared with the previous situation (dashed line), income growth does not modify fertility of the richer much as θ is close to ϵ. On the contrary, for the poor in the corner regime, it increases fertility, which goes in the wrong direction. The effect on education is mild.

All these exogenous changes are not enough to account for the shifts in the fertility and education patterns. If one wants to fill the gap with a unique change in a parameter, there is only one choice: to increase the return on education η. To see what it does, we increased η by $+0.15$, bringing its value in line with the one in Chapter 2. This shift is enough to bring the fertility pattern now described by "higher return to education" close to the data. Education is also affected in the right direction. The increase in the return on education is in line with Galor and Weil (2000), who argue that investment in human capital prior to the demographic transition is a response to industrial demand rather than being triggered by political reforms. Still, it is fair to recognize that the evidence about the evolution of the return on human capital over this period is scarce and controversial (Galor (2005)).

In our set-up, adult mortality plays a limited role. It affects only the survival of mothers, but has no direct effect on the return on investment in education. A generalization of the current set-up would be to follow Ben-Porath (1967), according to whom the return on investment in education depends on the length of time during which education will be productive, i.e. a longer active life makes initial investment in human capital more profitable. The first authors to integrate this argument in an endogenous growth model are de la Croix and Licandro (1999). Provided that human capital is an engine of growth, an increase in longevity may sustain permanent income growth. This first model is completed and generalized by Boucekkine *et al.* (2002). In particular they introduce for the first time a two-parameter survival function which is now used when one wants to model in a general equilibrium model the decrease in mortality at different ages. To exploit the full possibilities of this model, cohort life tables for the pre-industrial era are needed. Boucekkine *et al.* (2003) use data from Perrenoud (1978), who constructed life tables from 1625 to 1825 on the basis of a wide nominative study in Geneva (Switzerland), and Beltrami's (1951) work based on parish registers to reconstitute age-group dynamics of the Venetian population over the period 1600–1790. The main finding of Boucekkine *et al.* (2003) is that the observed changes in adult mortality from the last quarter of the seventeenth century to the first quarter of the eighteenth century played a fundamental role in launching modern growth. This study thus promotes the view that the early decline in adult mortality is responsible for some part of the acceleration of growth at the dawn of the modern age. All these papers, however, consider fertility as exogenous. The total effect of adult longevity on fertility therefore remains to be evaluated.

The Ben-Porath mechanism has been subject to criticism recently by Hazan (2009) and Hazan and Zoabi (2006). Hazan (2009) shows that the lifetime labor input of American men born in 1840–1970 declined despite the dramatic gains in life expectancy. Hazan further argues that a rise in the lifetime labor supply is a necessary implication of the Ben-Porath type model, which casts doubts on the possibility of such a model explaining the rise in schooling. Hazan's critique applies only when survival curves are rectangular however – see Cervellati and Sunde (2009). Still, life expectancy can raise the return on education even in the absence of any Ben-Porath effect. For example, in Bar and Leukhina (2010a), falling mortality directly raises the return to human capital accumulation by improving knowledge transmission over time, i.e. by raising the productivity of time spent innovating. Another reason the net return on education may have increased is because the cost of education has decreased, through, for example, the provision of schools, as in Boucekkine *et al.* (2007, 2008).

3.5 Additional data

In the first half of the twentieth century, there was some interest in the analysis of differential fertility by occupation and socio-economic class in England. It is agreed that there was an inverse correlation between fertility levels and socio-economic status, and increasing differentials during the late nineteenth century, see, for example, Stevenson (1920). These earlier studies are now backed up by more recent approaches, as in Haines (1989). If we want to inspect differential fertility for earlier periods, however, Census data such as those used in the above mentioned papers are no longer available. A source of information that is available for very long time periods are the genealogical records of the high aristocracy. Such data have been exploited by Hollingsworth (1964) and Peller (1965). In Figure 3.4 we report the index of marital fertility of Wilson and Woods (1991), which applies to the whole population of England and Wales. The level has been adjusted to match the number given in Wrigley and Schofield (1981) (page 254) for the period 1500–1599. We observe that it is almost constant through time, until it started to drop in the last half of the nineteenth century. We also report the fertility rate of British peerage families from Hollingsworth (1964), which include more than 26,000 individuals over more than three centuries. Fertility in this social class first falls then rises in the eighteenth century, then falls again. The gap between this fertility rate and the overall fertility rate in England widens in the nineteenth century and then

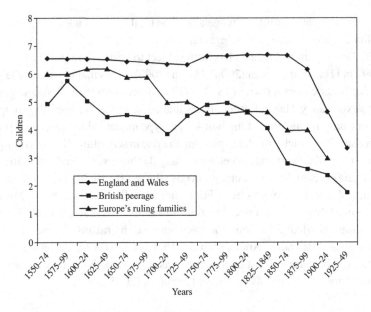

Figure 3.4 Fertility of aristocrats versus whole population

narrows in the twentieth. The third series represents the fertility rate of the very
top class of Europe's families, the 8,500 members of the ruling families studied
by Peller (1965). The highest level of fertility in the ruling families was reached
in 1600–1649. The first suggestion of a decline appeared in 1650–1699. The
decline became more rapid in 1700–1749. The numbers allow Peller (1965) to
conclude that fertility started to decline two centuries earlier than in the general
population.

The question arises as to what degree the fertility choices of ruling families and the peerage are representative of high-income families in general. For
Europe's ruling families, which come from many different backgrounds and
societies, this is hard to establish. The British peerage families, however, were
engaged in a wide range of professions and made up a sizable fraction of the
high-income individuals in England and Wales. Given the lack of other data
sources, we therefore use the British peerage families to proxy for high-income
fertility in England in general, so that the differential between peerage and general fertility can be interpreted as the fertility differential between the rich and
the poor.

We can then ask what we can learn from the behavior of this fertility differential from 1700 (before the Industrial Revolution) until 1950 about the causes of
the demographic transition. Taking into account the fertility differential, three

phases need to be explained. First, from 1700 until 1820, rich and poor fertility increased in unison, with little change in the fertility differential. Next, from 1820 to 1880, poor fertility stayed constant while rich fertility fell, which widened the differential. Finally, after 1880, fertility falls in both groups, and the differential shrinks over time.

Here, too, we can ask whether a parameterized version of the model can account for all three phases described above. In the simplest form of the model, this turns out to be impossible. If we allow for changes in the return on education, however, the model will be able to match the data. Indeed, only changes in the return on education can explain why the differential fertility widened (without relying on unrealistic changes in differential mortality). This indicates that the return on education may have increased significantly in the first phase of the nineteenth century.

3.6 Conclusion

Since the major phase of fertility decline in Europe coincided with big changes in living conditions and social and economic institutions, it has been hard to identify the key cause of fertility decline. In this chapter, we have attempted to learn more on fertility decline by considering forerunners: groups within Europe that experienced substantial fertility decline decades or even centuries before the mass of the population. A key advantage of this approach is that we can compare the forerunners with their neighbors and contemporaries. Linking differences between the forerunners and others to fertility differentials allows a clear view of why fertility started to fall.

In line with the most common explanation for the fertility decline, we concentrate on income, child and adult mortality, and the return on education as potential explanations for fertility differences.

Our main conclusions are twofold. First, differences in wages and mortality rates are important determinants of fertility differentials between social groups before the onset of the demographic transition. Second, only changes in the return on education are a successful explanation for the beginning of the fertility decline.

PART TWO

Education policy

4

Education policy: private versus public schools

The existing literature on the respective merits of public and private education has relied mostly on models with exogenous fertility. The first paper in this field is Glomm and Ravikumar (1992),[1] which contrasts the effects of public and private schooling systems on growth and inequality. In a country with little inequality, a fiscal externality created by public schooling leads to lower growth under public schooling than under private schooling. But, in the long run, public education is better for equality. This is not a very surprising result: as it redistributes resources through school funding, the public regime promotes equality, but introduces a fiscal externality, which hampers growth.

The empirical implications of this result are that one should observe that countries which rely the most on public schools should develop a more equal distribution of income but grow at a slower pace. It is, however, not easy to compare countries which are usually very different along so many dimensions. One way to limit the possible heterogeneity across countries is to look at states or provinces of the same country. For example, in India, there is a wide variation in the share of students going to private schools. Figures 4.1 and 4.2 correlate this share with income inequality and income growth. The correlation with inequality is of the expected sign, although it is not very strong (coefficient of correlation is 0.24). The correlation with growth goes in the wrong direction compared with the result of Glomm and Ravikumar (1992). Across Indian states, it is positive: the states with the higher share of students in public schools grow faster.[2] Of course, those simple correlations do not tell us anything in terms of causality.

This chapter uses some material published in de la Croix and Doepke (2004).

[1] The model of Glomm and Ravikumar (1992) has been extended by Bénabou (1996) to allow for local interactions between agents, such as neighborhood effects and knowledge spillovers.

[2] Sources are Kingdon (2005) for share of students in private schools, primary, Table 3; Krishna (2004) for growth, Table 2; Pal and Ghosh (2007) for rural inequality, Table 3.

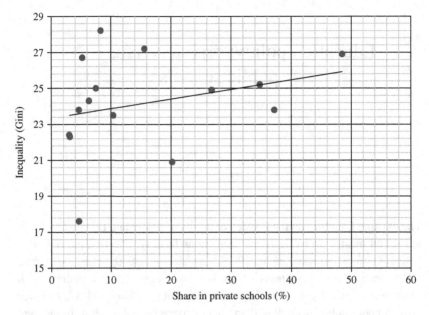

Figure 4.1 Private education and rural inequality circa 2000 across Indian states

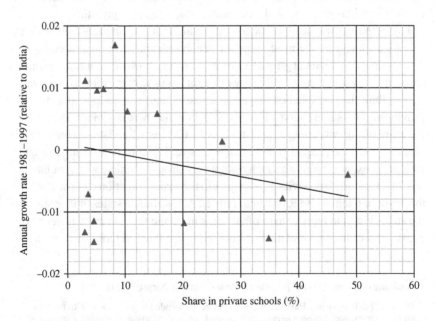

Figure 4.2 Private education and growth circa 2000 across Indian states

In this chapter, we compare the theoretical implications of a public and a private schooling regime for economic growth and the evolution of the income distribution when fertility is endogenous. And we will show that the endogeneity of fertility matters. Our main finding is that while private schooling leads to higher growth when there is little inequality in human capital endowments across families, public schooling can dominate when inequality is sufficiently high. This result is driven by the effects of the schooling regime on fertility differentials within the population.

In the model economy of the previous chapters, parents decide on their number of children and on the education of each child. With private schooling, the model generates a fertility differential between parents with low and high human capital. Parents with low human capital have many children and provide little education to each child. Since the parents who provide the least education have the highest fertility rates, when inequality is high, average education is low. With public schooling, the fertility differential between rich and poor disappears. If inequality in human capital is high, this leads to higher average education levels in the public schooling regime than in the private regime. Comparing the two regimes, growth will be higher with private education when inequality is low, while the opposite holds when inequality is high.

Another role for public education is related to the dynamics of income distribution. Differential fertility introduces a centrifugal force in the economy as witnessed by Proposition 2.3: higher reproduction rates by low-skilled people increase the relative number of the poor and can reduce their relative income. Because public education eliminates the fertility differential between skilled and unskilled, it offsets this centrifugal force.

It is instructive to compare our results to Glomm and Ravikumar (1992), who analyze the choice of an education regime in an endogenous growth model with fixed fertility. They find, as we do, that public schooling can lead to higher growth only if initial inequality is high, but they arrive at this conclusion for different reasons. In their model, the key imperfection favoring private schooling is a fiscal externality, which is not present in our model. Public schooling can dominate in terms of growth if the income distribution is sufficiently unequal and the production function for human capital is sufficiently concave. Concavity also makes public schooling more attractive in our model, but a second key factor in favor of public schooling is the endogenous fertility differential.[3]

---

[3] The long-run impact of existing fertility differentials on educational outcomes and the income distribution has been studied by Fernández and Rogerson (2001) and Mare (1997). Mare (1997) finds that fertility differentials per se are too small in the US to have large effects on average education. Fernández and Rogerson (2001), meanwhile, show that the association of fertility differentials with the degree of marital sorting can lead to sizable long-run effects.

4.1 The model

The model is a simplified version of the one in the previous chapter, without physical capital and with only two groups of households. The private education regime corresponds to the one described previously.

4.1.1 The set-up with private education

The model economy is populated by overlapping generations of people who live for two periods: childhood and adulthood. People are indexed by i and differ only in their human capital endowment h_t^i. Adults care about consumption c_t^i, their number of children n_t^i, and the human capital of children h_{t+1}^i. The utility function is given by:

$$\ln(c_t^i) + \gamma \ln(n_t^i h_{t+1}^i).$$

Raising one child takes fraction $\phi \in (0, 1)$ of an adult's time. An adult has to choose consumption c_t^i, the number of children n_t^i, and education per child e_t. Education is provided by teachers, and we assume that the average human capital of teachers equals the average human capital in the population $\bar{h}_t$. Education e_t^i is measured in units of time of the average teacher, so that the total education cost for n_t^i children is given by $n_t^i e_t^i \bar{h}_t$. The budget constraint for an adult with human capital h_t^i is then given by:

$$c_t^i + n_t^i e_t^i \bar{h}_t = h_t^i (1 - \phi n_t^i). \tag{4.1}$$

Here the price of the consumption good and the wage per unit of human capital are normalized to 1 because production is linear in human capital.

The human capital of the children h_{t+1}^i depends on human capital of the parents h_t^i, average or teacher's human capital $\bar{h}_t$, and education e_t^i:

$$h_{t+1}^i = \mu(\theta + e_t^i)^\eta (h_t^i)^\tau (\bar{h}_t)^{1-\tau}. \tag{4.2}$$

The parameters satisfy $\mu, \theta > 0$ and $\eta, \tau \in (0, 1)$. This accumulation technology assumes diminishing returns to parental human capital, but constant returns to scale in parental human capital and teacher human capital. This assumption is common in the literature (see e.g. de la Croix and Michel (2002), Tamura

---

While the last two papers take policies as given, Knowles (1999b) demonstrates that accounting for endogenous fertility differentials is important for understanding the long-run consequences of redistribution policies. Specifically, direct income transfers tend to increase fertility differentials and can thereby have perverse long-run effects on the income distribution.

(1991)) where the spillover effect of average human capital is found to be crucial for human capital convergence. It corresponds to the endogenous growth case of Chapter 2.

We assume that the population is divided into two groups, A and B, with human capital h_t^A and h_t^B, where A is the group with less human capital: $h_t^A < h_t^B$. The absolute sizes of the groups are given by P_t^A and P_t^B. The law of motion for the group sizes is:

$$P_{t+1}^i = P_t^i n_t^i, \quad i = A, B. \tag{4.3}$$

Their initial relative size is:

$$z_t = \frac{P_t^A}{P_t^B}. \tag{4.4}$$

In this formulation we abstract from inter-group mobility such as in Chapter 1, and in particular from mobility through mating. The extent to which mating can reduce the "inheritability" of skills is limited by the fact that mating is assortative on average.[4] Average human capital is given by:

$$\bar{h}_t = \frac{P_t^A h_t^A + P_t^B h_t^B}{P_t^A + P_t^B}. \tag{4.5}$$

The aggregate production function for the consumption good is linear in the aggregate supply of effective labor:

$$Y_t = L_t,$$

where L_t is given by:

$$L_t = P_t^A \left(h_t^A (1 - \phi n_t^A) - e_t^A n_t^A \bar{h}_t \right) + P_t^B \left(h_t^B (1 - \phi n_t^B) - e_t^B n_t^B \bar{h}_t \right). \tag{4.6}$$

Notice that the education time for all children is subtracted from total labor supply, since time devoted to teaching is not available for goods production. Since the total efficiency units of labor needed for education are fixed, it does not matter who provides the education in equilibrium. For simplicity, we assume

---

[4] See Fernández and Rogerson (2001) and Kremer (1997) on the effects of sorting and assortative mating on long-run inequality, Gokhale et al. (2001) on the interaction between mating processes, the inheritability of skills, and the inter-generational transmission of inequality, and Preston and Campbell (1993) on differential fertility and the distribution of IQ.

without loss of generality that there is an identical share of teachers in both groups. We assume that production is carried out by a competitive firm, which implies that the wage per unit of human capital is 1. Instead of writing out this condition explicitly, we have already incorporated it in the budget constraint.

Definition 4.1 Private education inter-temporal equilibrium
Given initial human capital endowments (h_0^A, h_0^B) and group sizes (P_0^A, P_0^B), an equilibrium with private education consists of sequences of aggregate quantities $\{z_t, \bar{h}_t, L_t\}$, group sizes $\{P_{t+1}^i\}_{i=A,B}$, and decision rules $\{c_t^i, n_t^i, e_t^i, h_{t+1}^i\}_{i=A,B}$ such that:

1. *the households' decision rules $c_t^i, n_t^i, e_t^i, h_{t+1}^i$ maximize utility subject to the constraints (4.1) and (4.2);*
2. *the group populations evolve according to (4.3);*
3. *aggregate variables $z_t, \bar{h}_t$, and L_t are given by (4.4), (4.5), and (4.6).*

4.1.2 Fertility and education choices under private education

We denote the relative human capital of a household as:

$$x_t^i \equiv \frac{h_t^i}{\bar{h}_t}.$$

The solution to the household decision problem can either be interior or at a corner where the household chooses zero education. For a household that has enough human capital such that the condition $x_t^i > \frac{\theta}{\phi\eta}$ holds, there is an interior solution for the optimal education level, and the first-order conditions imply:

$$e_t^i = \frac{\eta\phi x_t^i - \theta}{1 - \eta}, \qquad \text{and:} \qquad (4.7)$$

$$n_t^i = \frac{(1 - \eta)\gamma x_t^i}{(\phi x_t^i - \theta)(1 + \gamma)}. \qquad (4.8)$$

The second-order conditions for a maximum are satisfied. Note that education increases in human capital x^i, while fertility decreases in x^i. This reflects that skilled people invest relatively more in the quality of their children than in their quantity (see Table 1 and the discussion in the introduction). The lowest possible fertility rate is given by:

$$\lim_{x_t^i \to \infty} n_t^i = \frac{\gamma(1 - \eta)}{\phi(1 + \gamma)}.$$

For a household endowed with a human capital such that $x_t^i \leqslant \frac{\theta}{\phi\eta}$ holds, the optimal choice for education e_t^i is zero. The first-order conditions imply:

$$e_t^i = 0, \qquad \text{and:} \qquad (4.9)$$

$$n_t^i = \frac{\gamma}{\phi(1 + \gamma)}. \qquad (4.10)$$

Once the choice for education is zero, fertility in equation (4.10) no longer increases as the human capital endowment falls. To ensure that at least households of type B invest in education, i.e. $e^B > 0 \; \forall \; x^B > 1$, we impose an upper bound on θ in Assumption 4.1.

Assumption 4.1
The parameters satisfy the following condition:

$$\eta\phi > \theta.$$

When Assumption 4.1 does not hold, the amount of human capital one receives even without investing in education is so high that a parent with average human capital ($x = 1$) would choose zero education.

Fertility as a function of relative human capital follows the same pattern as in Figure 1.1. As we will see later, this differential-fertility effect has implications for the advantages of public and private education.

4.1.3 The set-up with public education

In the public education regime, parents do not choose an individual education level for their children. Instead, the government levies a proportional income tax v_t on all adults, and uses the proceeds to finance a common education level $\bar{e}_t$ for all children. Budget balance is observed in every period. The budget constraint for an adult with human capital h_t^i now becomes:

$$c_t^i = (1 - v_t)h_t^i(1 - \phi n_t^i). \qquad (4.11)$$

Notice that parents are allowed neither to provide private education in addition to the common level of public education, nor to opt out of the public education system (as in the next chapter). The human capital of the children h_{t+1}^i is now given by:

$$h_{t+1}^i = \mu(\theta + \bar{e}_t)^\eta (h_t^i)^\tau (\bar{h}_t)^{1-\tau}. \qquad (4.12)$$

Since the government has to observe budget balance, total expenditure on education has to equal total tax receipts at time t. The government's budget constraint is given by:

$$\bar{e}_t \bar{h}_t (P_t^A n_t^A + P_t^B n_t^B) = v_t (P_t^A h_t^A (1 - \phi n_t^A) + P_t^B h_t^B (1 - \phi n_t^B)). \quad (4.13)$$

We assume that v_t and therefore $\bar{e}_t$ are determined in each period by a vote of the adult population. Since we assume logarithmic utility, it will turn out that all adults prefer the same tax rate. Therefore no conflict of interest arises, and the tax is independent of the distribution of human capital.

Definition 4.2 Public education inter-temporal equilibrium

Given initial human capital endowments (h_0^A, h_0^B) and group sizes (P_0^A, P_0^B), an equilibrium with public education consists of sequences of aggregate quantities $\{z_t, \bar{h}_t, L_t\}$, group sizes $\{P_{t+1}^i\}_{i=A,B}$, private decision rules $\{c_t^i, n_t^i, h_{t+1}^i\}_{i=A,B}$, and policy variables $\{v_t, \bar{e}_t\}$, such that:

1. *the households' decision rules c_t^i, n_t^i, h_{t+1}^i maximize utility subject to the constraints (4.11) and (4.12);*
2. *the government's budget constraint (4.13) is satisfied;*
3. *given decision rules, the policy variables maximize the utility of adult households;*
4. *the group populations evolve according to (4.3);*
5. *aggregate variables $z_t, \bar{h}_t,$ and L_t are given by (4.4), (4.5), and (4.6).*

4.1.4 Fertility and policy choices under public education

Once the education level is fixed by public policy, parents no longer face a quality-quantity tradeoff. Therefore the optimal fertility choice is independent of parental human capital. The first-order condition for n_t implies that everyone chooses the same number of children:

$$n_t = \frac{\gamma}{\phi(1+\gamma)}. \quad (4.14)$$

Since fertility is constant, the government budget constraint (4.13) simplifies to:

$$\bar{e}_t \frac{\gamma}{\phi(1+\gamma)} = v_t \left(1 - \frac{\gamma}{1+\gamma}\right),$$

which can be solved to give:

$$\bar{e}_t = \frac{\phi v_t}{\gamma}. \quad (4.15)$$

Using (4.14) and (4.15), the indirect utility of a household with human capital h_t is given by:

$$\ln\left((1-v_t)h_t\left(1-\frac{\gamma}{1+\gamma}\right)\right)+\gamma\ln\left(\frac{\gamma}{\phi(1+\gamma)}\mu(\theta+\phi v_t/\gamma)^\eta (h_t)^\tau (\bar{h}_t)^{1-\tau}\right).$$

The adults choose the tax v_t to maximize utility. The first-order condition for a maximum leads to:

$$v_t = \frac{\gamma(\phi\eta-\theta)}{\phi(1+\gamma\eta)},$$

and the resulting choice for public education is:

$$\bar{e}_t = \frac{\eta\phi-\theta}{1+\gamma\eta}. \tag{4.16}$$

The second-order condition for a maximum is satisfied. Assumption 4.1 guarantees a positive level of public education.

4.2 Comparing private and public education

4.2.1 Long-run dynamics

To study the dynamic behavior of the economy, it is useful to introduce the growth rate g_t of average human capital:

$$g_t = \frac{\bar{h}_{t+1}}{\bar{h}_t}.$$

Along the balanced growth path, g_t is also the growth rate of GDP per capita.

Private education
We first consider the private education regime.

Exercise: Consider the situation where $x_0^A < \theta/(\phi\eta) < x_0^B$. Show that there cannot be a balanced growth path with group A in the corner regime (no education, high fertility) because it would imply that the relative size of this group would go to 1.

Since we are mainly interested in the dynamics around the balanced growth path, we therefore consider cases where the maximization program of all individuals yields interior solutions. Replacing the optimal education choice (4.7) into the accumulation law of human capital (4.2) leads to:

$$x_{t+1}^i = \frac{1}{g_t}\mu \left(\frac{\eta}{1-\eta}\right)^\eta \left(\phi x_t^i - \theta\right)^\eta \left(x_t^i\right)^\tau. \tag{4.17}$$

Using the definitions of relative human capital $x_t^i = h_t^i/\bar{h}_t$ and the population ratio $z_t = P_t^B/P_t^A$, (4.5) can be expressed as:

$$1 = x_{t+1}^A \frac{z_{t+1}}{1+z_{t+1}} + x_{t+1}^B \frac{1}{1+z_{t+1}}.$$

Replacing x_{t+1}^A and x_{t+1}^B using equation (4.17), we obtain an expression for the growth rate of average human capital:

$$g_t = \frac{\mu}{1+z_{t+1}} \left(\frac{\eta}{1-\eta}\right)^\eta \left(z_{t+1}\left(\phi x_t^A - \theta\right)^\eta \left(x_t^A\right)^\tau + \left(\phi x_t^B - \theta\right)^\eta \left(x_t^B\right)^\tau\right). \tag{4.18}$$

The law of motion for the population ratio z_t is obtained by replacing the optimal fertility choice (4.8) into the law of motion for population (4.3):

$$z_{t+1} = \frac{x_t^A(\phi x_t^B - \theta)}{x_t^B(\phi x_t^A - \theta)} z_t. \tag{4.19}$$

Finally, from the definition of average human capital (4.5) we have:

$$x_t^B = 1 + z_t(1 - x_t^A). \tag{4.20}$$

The set of equations (4.17) to (4.20) can be restated as a dynamic system of order two in the variables (x_t^A, z_t). An analysis of this system leads to proposition 4.1.

Proposition 4.1 Balanced growth path with private education
Under Assumption 4.1, there is a balanced growth path of the economy with private education characterized by $x_t^A = x_t^B = 1$, i.e. inequality has vanished. The growth rate of output and human capital is:

$$g^\star = \mu \left(\frac{\eta(\phi - \theta)}{1-\eta}\right)^\eta > 0.$$

This balanced growth path is locally stable if:

$$\tau < 1 - \frac{\eta\phi}{\phi - \theta}.$$

Proof: The set of equations (4.17) to (4.20) can be restated as a dynamic system of order two in the variables (z_t, x_t^A):

$$z_{t+1} = \frac{x_t^A(\phi(1 + z_t(1 - x_t^A)) - \theta)}{(\phi x_t^A - \theta)(1 + z_t(1 - x_t^A))} z_t$$

$$x_{t+1}^A = \frac{(1 + z_{t+1})\left(x_t^A\right)^\tau (\phi x_t^A - \theta)^\eta}{z_{t+1}\left(x_t^A\right)^\tau (\phi x_t^A - \theta)^\eta + (1 + z_t(1 - x_t^A))^\tau(\phi(1 + z_t(1 - x_t^A)) - \theta)^\eta}.$$

The only fixed point of this system is $(\bar{z}, 1)$. Linearizing around this point leads to:

$$\begin{bmatrix} z_{t+1} - \bar{z} \\ x_{t+1}^A - 1 \end{bmatrix} = \begin{bmatrix} 1 & \dfrac{\theta\bar{z}(1 + \bar{z})}{\theta - \phi} \\ 0 & \dfrac{\theta\tau - (\eta + \tau)\phi}{\theta - \phi} \end{bmatrix} \begin{bmatrix} z_t - \bar{z} \\ x_t^A - 1 \end{bmatrix}.$$

The linearized dynamics of x_t^A are autonomous and x_t^A converges to 1 if

$$\frac{\theta\tau - (\eta + \tau)\phi}{\theta - \phi} < 1,$$

that is

$$\tau < 1 - \frac{\eta\phi}{\phi - \theta}.$$

∎

The stability condition imposes an upper limit on the parameter τ. If τ exceeds this limit, the aggregate externality deriving from $\bar{h}_t$ in equation (4.2) is not strong enough to offset the effect of parental human capital h_t^i, and inequality will persist or increase over time.

Public education

We now turn to the case of public education. Since parents with high and low human capital have the same number of children, the relative size of the groups is constant over time:

$$z_{t+1} = z_t = z_0.$$

To analyze the dynamics of the economy, we replace the public education level (4.16) into the accumulation law of human capital (4.2). For type-i households, this leads to:

$$x_{t+1}^i = \frac{1}{g_t} \mu \left(\frac{\eta(\theta\gamma + \phi)}{1 + \gamma\eta} \right)^\eta \left(x_t^i \right)^\tau. \tag{4.21}$$

Combining this with (4.20) gives:

$$1 + z_0(1 - x_{t+1}^A) = \frac{1}{g_t} \mu \left(\frac{\eta(\theta\gamma + \phi)}{1 + \gamma\eta} \right)^\eta \left(1 + z_0(1 - x_t^A) \right)^\tau.$$

Replacing g_t by its value from (4.21), we obtain:

$$x_{t+1}^A = \frac{1 + z_0}{z_0 + \left(\frac{1+z_0}{x_t^A} - z_0 \right)^\tau}. \tag{4.22}$$

The dynamics described by equation (4.22) are monotone, and x_t^A converges to 1 for any $\tau < 1$. Along the balanced growth path, the growth rate can be computed by setting $x^A = 1$ in equation (4.21). The analysis leads to the following proposition:

Proposition 4.2 Balanced growth path with public education
Under Assumption 1, there is a balanced growth path of the economy with public education characterized by $x_t^A = x_t^B = 1$, i.e. inequality has vanished. The growth rate of output and human capital is:

$$g^\circ = \mu \left(\frac{\eta(\theta\gamma + \phi)}{1 + \gamma\eta} \right)^\eta > 0.$$

This balanced growth path is globally stable.

Proof: The relative human capital of low-skilled people evolves according to:

$$x_{t+1}^A = \frac{1 + z_0}{z_0 + \left(\frac{1+z_0}{x_t^A} - z_0 \right)^\tau} \equiv \Phi(x_t^A).$$

We study the dynamics $x_{t+1}^A = \Phi(x_t^A)$ in the interval $[0, 1]$. There are two fixed points, 0 and 1. Moreover, the dynamics are monotone:

$$\Phi'(x_t^A) = \frac{\tau(1+z_0)^2 \left(\frac{x_t^A}{1+z_0(1-x_t^A)} \right)^{1-\tau}}{\left(x_t^A z_0 + \left(x_t^A \right)^{1-\tau} \left(1 + z_0(1 - x_t^A) \right)^\tau \right)^2} > 0.$$

x_t^A thus converges either to 0 or to 1. The local stability of these two points depends on the derivative of Φ:

$$\Phi'(0+) = +\infty \qquad \Phi'(1) = \tau.$$

Since the fixed point at 0 is locally unstable and the dynamics are monotone, the fixed point at 1 is globally stable. ∎

In summary, under both private and public education there exists a balanced growth path in which all inequality has vanished. The stability properties of the two education regimes, however, are different. Under public education, all children receive the same education.[5] Since we assume that the children's human capital increases less than proportionally with the parent's human capital ($\tau < 1$), this implies that inequality decreases over time. From any initial conditions, the economy with public education converges to a balanced growth path in which inequality has disappeared.

In the private regime, education choices differ across the two groups. Children whose parents have an above-average human capital endowment receive above-average education. If the effect of parental human capital on their children's human capital is sufficiently large, the combined effect of parental endowments and education can lead to rising inequality. In that case, the economy does not converge to the balanced growth path, and the income difference between the two groups can grow without bounds.

4.2.2 Implications for growth

On a balanced growth path, both regimes display constant fertility and education, and the choice for education is lower in the public education regime. From (4.7), in the private regime the education choice on the balanced growth path is given by:

$$e = \frac{\eta\phi - \theta}{1 - \eta},$$

[5] Note that, in our framework, the only public education regime is a national education regime. It approximates countries where the central government organizes education, as in the majority of developing countries, and much of Europe. If one considers the possibility that school districts may not be national in scale, convergence can still predominate, either because the difference in education of teachers across school districts is smaller than the differences in education of parents (Tamura (2001)), or because there are knowledge spillovers across districts (de la Croix and Monfort (2000)), or because stratification is slowed down by higher housing rents in rich districts (Bénabou (1996)). If convergence still prevails, it will be at a slower pace than with a national education system because resources put into the regional public education system will rely more heavily on the district income level, and redistribution across regions through taxes will be lower.

while in the public regime education is (4.16):

$$\bar{e} = \frac{\eta\phi - \theta}{1 + \gamma\eta},$$

which is clearly lower. The choice of fertility, meanwhile, is higher with public education. In the private regime, fertility is given by (4.8):

$$n = \frac{1 - \eta}{\gamma}(\phi - \theta)(1 + \gamma), \qquad (4.23)$$

while in the public regime fertility is (4.14):

$$n = \frac{\gamma}{\phi(1 + \gamma)}. \qquad (4.24)$$

Given that Assumption 4.1 holds, (4.24) always exceeds (4.23). The growth rate along the balanced growth path depends directly on education. Therefore, once the balanced growth path is reached, growth is always higher in the private regime. The following proposition summarizes these findings.

Proposition 4.3 Public and private education in the long run
Under assumption 4.1, along a balanced growth path, education and growth are lower under public education than under private education, while fertility is higher.

The reason for the growth rate differential is that in the public regime, parents do not internalize the negative effect of having many children on the education resources per child. Therefore they choose a relatively higher number of children, and education spending per child is smaller than in the private regime.

Even if the economy is not on the balanced growth path, fertility and education are fixed in the public education regime. In the private education regime, however, both choice variables depend on the parents' human capital. Adults with low human capital invest less in education and have a higher number of children. Both effects tend to lower the growth rate of human capital. This opens the possibility for the public regime to temporarily yield higher growth.

Using the production function for human capital (4.2) and equation (4.3), the growth rate g_t of average human capital is given by:

$$
\begin{aligned}
g_t = \frac{\bar{h}_{t+1}}{\bar{h}_t} &= \frac{P_t^A n_t^A h_{t+1}^A + P_t^B n_t^B h_{t+1}^B}{\bar{h}_t(P_t^A n_t^A + P_t^B n_t^B)} \\
&= \mu \frac{z_t n_t^A \left(\theta + e_t^A\right)^\eta \left(x_t^A\right)^\tau + n_t^B \left(\theta + e_t^B\right)^\eta \left(x_t^B\right)^\tau}{z_t n_t^A + n_t^B}. \qquad (4.25)
\end{aligned}
$$

This expression holds for both private and public education, and shows that the growth rate depends on the education choices of groups A and B, and the relative weight of their children in tomorrow's population.

Recall that in the private regime the education choice is given by equations (4.7) and (4.9), i.e.:

$$e_t^i = \max\left\{\frac{\eta\phi x_t^i - \theta}{1 - \eta}, \; 0\right\},$$

while in the public regime education is given by (4.16):

$$e_t^i = \frac{\eta\phi - \theta}{1 + \gamma\eta}.$$

Since group B is defined as the one with higher human capital, we have $x_t^B \geq 1$, and therefore their education is always higher in the private than in the public regime. For group A, the private regime yields higher education only if x_t^A is close to 1. Comparing the two expressions, we find that education will be higher in the private regime if x_t^A is large enough such that the following condition is satisfied:

$$x_t^A \geq \frac{\phi(1 - \eta) + \theta(1 + \gamma)}{\phi(1 + \gamma\eta)}. \tag{4.26}$$

If condition (4.26) is met, the private regime must lead to higher growth than the public regime, since education is higher for both types of parents. If x_t^A is sufficiently low such that (4.26) is violated, which regime results in higher growth depends on the relative population weight of the two groups.

Proposition 4.4 Comparison of public and private regime
Assume that Assumption 4.1 holds, and that the parameters satisfy $\eta + \tau < 1$. Then for a given x_t^A sufficiently low to violate (4.26), there exists a threshold for z_t above which the public education regime yields higher growth than the private education regime.

Proof: Fix an x_t^A violating (4.26). Assume that the relative size z_t of group A goes to infinity while holding x_t^A constant, and notice that x_t^B depends on x_t^A and z_t and is given by (4.20):

$$x_t^B = 1 + z_t(1 - x_t^A),$$

while e_t^B is given by (4.7):

$$e_t^B = \frac{\eta\phi x_t^B - \theta}{1 - \eta}.$$

Thus both x_t^B and e_t^B are asymptotically linear in z_t. The growth rate g_t is given by (4.25):

$$g_t = \mu \left(\frac{z_t n_t^A \left(\theta + e_t^A\right)^\eta \left(x_t^A\right)^\tau}{z_t n_t^A + n_t^B} + \frac{n_t^B \left(\theta + e_t^B\right)^\eta \left(x_t^B\right)^\tau}{z_t n_t^A + n_t^B} \right).$$

Since n_t^i is bounded and we assume $\eta + \tau < 1$, the second term inside the parentheses converges to zero as z_t goes to infinity. The limit is therefore given by:

$$\lim_{z_t \to \infty} g_t = \mu \left(\theta + e_t^A\right)^\eta \left(x_t^A\right)^\tau.$$

Thus in the limit only the education choices of group A will matter for growth. Since we assume that (4.26) is violated, group A chooses higher education under public rather than under private education. Therefore, there is some z_t sufficiently high such that the growth rate of average human capital is higher in the public regime than in the private regime.   ∎

In summary, when the economy is not on the balanced growth path, growth can be higher either in the public or in the private regime. If there is little inequality (x_t^A is close to 1) or if group B makes up a large fraction of the population, the private regime will yield higher growth. If x_t^A is sufficiently low to violate (4.26), and if the relative size z_t of group A is sufficiently large, the public regime will lead to higher growth.

Thus, the question as to which regime leads to higher growth hinges on the initial distribution of income and population. Moreover, as the economy evolves over time, the relative income and size of the two groups change, which can revert the advantages of the two regimes. This possibility is explored in more detail in the next section.

4.3 Growth and inequality over time

We compute the equilibrium for a parameterized version of our economy under private and public education. The key parameter governing dynamics in the model is the elasticity τ of children's human capital with respect to their parents' human capital, and we compute outcomes for a range of values for τ. The remaining parameters have been calibrated to match the balanced growth path of the private education model to US data. Table 4.1 summarizes the result of the calibration exercise that we now describe.

Table 4.1. *Calibration: a summary*

Parameter		Benchmark
Productivity of education	μ	7.860
Return to education	η	0.600
Taste for children	γ	0.169
Time-cost parameter	ϕ	0.075
Innate education level	θ	0.017
Intergenerational transmission of human capital	τ	0, 0.1, 0.2, 0.3

4.3.1 Calibration

The overall productivity μ does not affect decisions and growth rate differentials and can therefore be chosen arbitrarily; we set it such that the balanced growth rate is 2% per year. The elasticity η of human capital with respect to education governs the maximum fertility differential. To prevent inflating the role of fertility differentials, it is important not to choose η too high. A conservative estimate is $\eta = 0.6$, which leads to a maximum fertility ratio of 2.5 (i.e. if minimum fertility is two children per woman, the maximum is five).

As in Chapter 2, the altruism parameter γ is chosen such that the growth rate of population in the balanced growth path is zero. This leads to $\gamma = 0.169$. The time–cost parameter ϕ for having a child is set to $\phi = 0.075$. We choose θ such that in the balanced growth path of the private education regime, total education expenditure as a fraction of GDP equals 7.5%. This implies $\theta = 0.017$.

The remaining parameter τ determines the weight of parental human capital in the production of children's human capital. We leave it unspecified for now and compute outcomes for a range of choices for τ. The threshold for τ below which the private education balanced growth path is stable is $1 - \frac{\eta\phi}{\phi-\theta} = 0.224$. The empirical studies suggest that the stable region of the parameter space is the empirically relevant case. Given our parameter choices, the human capital threshold below which people do not educate their children is $\theta/(\eta\phi) = 0.38$.

4.3.2 Initial conditions and growth

We found in the last section that private education will always lead to higher growth if inequality is low, but public education can dominate if inequality is high. Figure 4.3 shows the range of initial conditions z_0 and x_0^A for which public education leads to higher growth in the parameterized economy, for

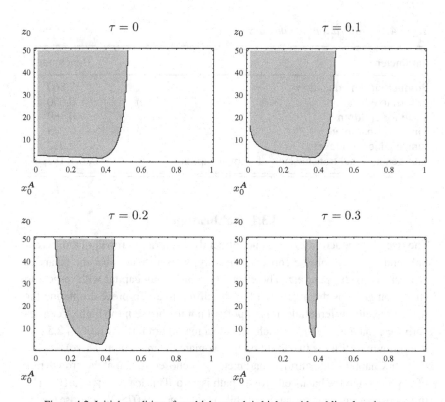

Figure 4.3 Initial conditions for which growth is higher with public education

four different values of τ. In all cases, private education dominates for x_0^A that exceed a value of about 0.6. Below this value, there is a zone in which public schooling dominates, and the size of this zone is decreasing in τ. The range of x_0^A for which public education yields more growth increases in z_0, i.e. public education is more likely to be advantageous when group A is relatively large.

Interestingly, when the relative human capital x_0^A becomes very low, private schooling dominates once again. The reason is that there is a lower limit for the education of group A (at zero) and an upper limit for fertility. Once x_0^A is low enough to reach the corner solution for education and fertility, the only effect of decreasing x_0^A further is to increase x_0^B and therefore the education of group B, which raises growth. This same effect does not arise in the public education regime, since fertility and education are independent of x_0^A and x_0^B.

The influence of τ on the regions is related to the allocation of total education spending on groups A and B. Notice that fertility and education decisions are independent of τ. Therefore the only effect of changing τ on growth is the direct one, through the weight of parental human capital in the production function for h^i_{t+1}. When τ is zero, parental human capital has no direct effect on the children's human capital. For a given amount of total spending, growth is maximized if equal amounts are spent on children of type-A and type-B parents. Since spending is equalized under public schooling, the region of higher growth under public schooling is large when τ is small. When τ is large, the return on education is higher for type-B children, since they benefit more from parental human capital. Education for type-B children is higher under private schooling; thus private education yields higher growth.

4.3.3 Human capital accumulation and inequality dynamics

Figures 4.4 and 4.5 show how human capital and inequality evolve over time under public and private schooling. The only difference between the two figures concerns the value of the parameter τ. The balanced growth path with private

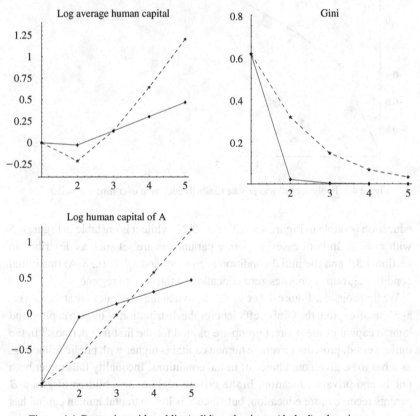

Figure 4.4 Dynamics with public (solid) and private (dashed) education over time – $\tau = 0.22$

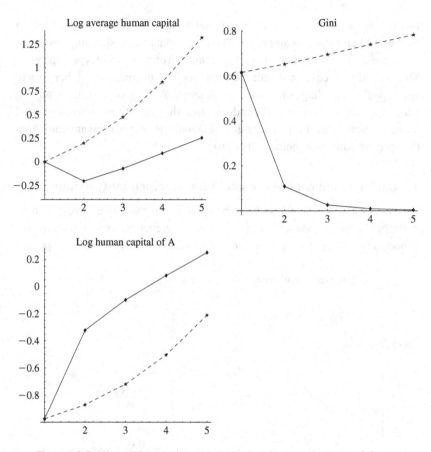

Figure 4.5 Public (solid) and private (dashed) education over time – $\tau = 0.5$

education is stable in Figure 4.4 with $\tau = 0.22$, while it is unstable in Figure 4.5 with $\tau = .5$. In both cases, the other parameters are set such as described in section 4.3.1 and the initial condition is $z_0 = 90$ and $x_0^A = 0.38$. At this initial condition, group A chooses zero education in the private regime.

We first consider Figure 4.4 ($\tau = 0.22$), so that the dynamics are stable. Average human capital, the Gini coefficient for the distribution of human capital, and human capital of the poorest group are plotted for the first five periods.[6] In the initial period, growth of average human capital is higher with public schooling, as it has to be given our choice of initial conditions. Inequality falls under both public and private education. In the private regime, the children of group-B parents receive more education, but since τ is low, parental human capital has

---

[6] The Gini index can be computed as $z_t(1 - x_t^A)/(1 + z_t)$ – see Chapter 1.

little effect and inequality still declines. In the second period, the growth advantage shifts to the private regime, since x^A has increased, and the education and fertility differential is reduced. From the second period on, as x^A approaches 1, average human capital per capita keeps increasing in both regimes, but growth is higher with private education. Inequality is further reduced in each case, with the faster reduction occurring under public education.

If the objective were to maximize growth, the optimal policy would be to start out with public education and switch to private education later on. An unambiguous welfare ranking of the policies is not possible, since at least initially the two groups have opposing interests, and there is no obvious method of accounting for population changes when evaluating welfare. However, given that inequality is reduced faster under public education, it is apparent that if policies were chosen according to a welfare function which places most weight on group A, public education could be maintained longer than in the growth-maximizing policy. This is reflected in the third panel of the figure where the human capital of the poorest group benefits from public education until $t = 3$, i.e. one more period than average human capital.

The graphs in Figure 4.5 show average human capital, inequality, and human capital of group A for $\tau = .5$, a value well above the stability limit. For this value of τ, private schooling always gives higher growth than public schooling. Consequently, average human capital is higher under private schooling from the first period on. However, the higher growth rate comes at the price of increased inequality. Under public schooling, inequality decreases over time, and the economy converges to the balanced growth path without inequality. Under private schooling, x_t^A converges to zero and the Gini coefficient converges to 1. At the same time, fertility is permanently higher for group A, implying that in the limit group A makes up 100 percent of the population, while accounting for zero percent of the income. Thus even though private schooling maximizes growth unambiguously, the tradeoff between growth and inequality is even more stark than before. Given that private schooling implies that an ever decreasing share of the population earns an ever increasing share of income, private schooling would not be chosen (at least not permanently) given any welfare function that places some weight on group A. Indeed, human capital of group A is higher with public education at least during the first five periods.

4.4 Conclusion

Our analysis leads to three main conclusions. First, we find that public schooling can distort the fertility and education choice of parents, in the sense that parents increase fertility once education is provided for free. In doing so, parents do not internalize the negative effect of having many children on the education resources per child. This effect explains that in a balanced growth path in which there is no inequality, the growth rate of income per capita is higher with private education.

Second, when there is inequality, we find that the comparison of growth rates can switch in favor of public education. The reason is that under private education, parents with below-average income substitute child quantity for quality, and therefore have many children and invest little in education per child. This substitution has a double-negative effect on growth: children of poor parents have little human capital, and since poor parents have many children, a lot of weight is placed on children with little human capital when computing the average. This differential-fertility effect is not present under public education, since education is free and all parents have the same number of children.

Third, the same differential-fertility effect which lowers growth under private education can also result in a diverging income distribution. Since poor parents have more children than the average, groups with below-average income make up an increasing share of the population over time. If inter-generational persistence in human capital is high, the income of low-skilled groups declines relative to the average. The result is that an ever decreasing fraction of the population accounts for an ever increasing fraction of total income. This divergence can be prevented by a public education system, since fertility and education are equalized across income groups, so that relative group sizes stay the same and incomes converge.

A robust implication of our analysis is that the merits of different educational systems depend on the initial distribution of income and population. While in this chapter we take funding type (private or public) as given, the results indicate that an optimizing policy maker might be expected to switch from one education regime to another as the income distribution evolves over time. In the next chapter, the choice of policy is endogenized.

5

Education politics and democracy

In this chapter, we develop an analytically tractable framework that integrates political determination of the quality of public schools with private education and fertility decisions. In the previous chapter, the economy was characterized either by private education or by public education. We here provide a set-up where both systems coexist: parents may choose between sending their children to tax-financed public schools and, alternatively, opting out of the public system and providing private education to their children. They also determine their number of children as a function of their income and of the expected quality of schools.

The motivation for investigating the role of public education in an integrated framework comes from the observation that education is one of the main areas of government intervention. Indeed, rather than merely regulating the private sector, the governments of nearly all countries act as major providers of primary and secondary education to their citizens. At the same time, the government is generally not the only provider of education; education systems often display a juxtaposition of public and privately funded institutions. Table 5.1 shows that the degree of private involvement in the provision of education varies a great deal across countries.

Recently, the OECD Program for International Student Assessment (PISA), which assesses the knowledge and skills of 15-year-old students in a cross-section of countries, has sparked an intense debate on the merits of different education systems. A central question in this debate is why education systems differ so much across countries in the first place. Are there particular characteristics that explain the choice of an integrated education system instead of a regime with segregation between public and private schools? Equally important is the question of what the mix of public and private provision of schooling

This chapter uses some material published in de la Croix and Doepke (2009).

Table 5.1. *Share of private resources in total education funding, 2003*

Norway	1.5%
Portugal	1.7%
Turkey	2.7%
France	7.8%
UK	16.4%
Germany	17.0%
Australia	25.9%
US	28.0%
Chile	48.5%

implies for the quality of education. Does the quality of education improve if private schools are allowed to compete with the public sector, or will a system in which the government is the sole provider of education yield the best results?

These questions do not have obvious answers: both public and private schools can yield good or bad results, depending on variables such as school funding and the quality of teachers. Therefore, when assessing different schooling systems we also need to consider how the mix between private and public funding will affect the quality of education that each school provides. These choices, in turn, may look very different depending on the political makeup of a country: the political priorities of a broad-based democracy are different from those of a plutocratic state that is dominated by a small elite.

To analyze these issues, we will rely on probabilistic voting as the political mechanism, which yields a fully tractable theory of education regimes in which voting equilibria are guaranteed to exist. This contrasts with the existing literature on education politics,[1] which relies in most cases on the median voter model. The advantage of the probabilistic voting model, on top of being more tractable, is not to be restricted to democracies, since we can analyze what happens if the political system is biased to the rich.

The second main departure from the existing literature is that we endogenize fertility decisions, which leads to novel implications for uniqueness and efficiency properties of equilibria. As in the previous chapter, by raising their

---

[1] Our chapter relates to different branches of the literature. A number of authors have addressed the choice of public versus private schooling within a majority voting framework (see Bearse *et al.* (2005), Epple and Romano (1996), Glomm and Ravikumar (1998), and Stiglitz (1974)). A recurring theme in this literature is the argument that if there are private alternatives to public schools, voters' preferences may not be single-peaked, so that a majority voting equilibrium may fail to exist.

fertility rate relative to what they would choose if they were paying for their children's education, the public school parents impose a fiscal externality on all taxpayers. This externality is absent if parents send their children to private schools and therefore fully take into account the education cost of the marginal child. Compared with the benchmark model in Chapter 1, the model developed here introduces a new factor determining the tradeoff faced by parents between quality and quantity of children: the quality and the cost of education. It provides a new way to see the relationship between education policy, which affects quality and costs, and the dynamics of population.

5.1 The model economy

In this section we introduce our benchmark model. Compared with the models of the previous chapters, there are several differences. First, we concentrate on today's outcome in a static framework. Second, the distribution of skills is continuous. The advantage of the continuous distribution is that it makes analytics more tractable, but any dynamic extension would be harder (as in Chapter 2). In section 5.5, we use instead a two-point distribution of human capital, and extend the analysis to a dynamic setting where today's children are tomorrow's adults.

5.1.1 Preferences and technology

The model economy is populated by a continuum of households of measure 1. Households are differentiated by their human capital endowment x, where x is the wage that a household can obtain in the labor market. People care about consumption c, their number of children n, and their children's education h. The utility function is given by:

$$\ln(c) + \gamma \left[\ln(n) + \eta \ln(h)\right]. \tag{5.1}$$

Notice that parents care about both child quantity n and quality h. The parameter $\gamma \in \mathbb{R}_+$ is the overall weight attached to children. The parameter $\eta \in (0, 1)$ is the relative weight of quality.[2] As we will see below, the tradeoff between quantity and quality is affected by the human capital endowment of the parent and by the schooling regime.

---

[2] The parameter η cannot exceed 1 because the parents' optimization problem would not have a solution. More specifically, utility would approach infinity as parents choose arbitrarily high levels of education and arbitrarily low levels of fertility. A similar condition can be found in Moav (2005).

To attain human capital, children have to be educated by teachers. The wage of teachers equals the average wage in the population, which is normalized to 1. The important assumption here is that the cost of education is fixed, i.e. all parents face the same education cost regardless of their own wage. The level of the teacher's wage is set to the average wage for convenience. Parents can choose between two different modes of education. First, there is a public schooling system, which provides a uniform education s to every student. Education in the public system is financed through an income tax v; apart from the tax, there are no direct costs to the parents. The schooling quality s and the tax rate v are determined through voting, to be described in more detail later. Parents also have the possibility of opting out of the public system. In this case, parents can freely choose the education quality e, but they have to pay the teacher out of their own income. Since education e is measured in units of time of the average teacher, the total cost of educating n children privately is given by ne. We assume that education spending is tax deductible. While tax deductibility of education expenditures varies across countries, deductibility simplifies the analysis because it implies that taxation does not distort the choice between quantity and quality of children (taxes distorting this choice are studied in Chapters 8 and 9). Apart from the education expenditure, raising one child also takes fraction $\phi \in (0, 1)$ of an adult's time. The budget constraint for an adult with wage x is given by:

$$c = (1 - v) [x(1 - \phi n) - ne]. \tag{5.2}$$

Education is thus either private, e, or public, s. Effective education can be expressed as the maximum of the two: $h = \max\{e, s\}$. Of course, parents who prefer public education will choose $e = 0$.

Substituting the budget constraint (5.2) into the utility function (5.1) allows us to rewrite the utility of a given household as:

$$u[x, v, n, e, s] = \ln(1 - v) + \ln(x(1 - \phi n) - ne) + \gamma \ln n + \gamma \eta \ln \max\{e, s\}.$$

The consumption good is produced by competitive firms using labor as the only input. We assume that the aggregate production function is linear in effective labor units. The production set-up does not play an important role in our analysis; the advantage of the linear production function is that the wage is fixed.

5.1.2 Timing of events and private choices

The level of public funding for education s is chosen by a vote among the adult population. The voters' preferences depend on their optimal fertility and education choices (n and e), which are made before voting takes place. In making these choices, agents have perfect foresight regarding the outcome of the voting process. This timing is motivated by the observation that public education spending can be adjusted frequently, while fertility cannot. Similarly, the choice between public versus private education entails substantial switching costs, especially when educational segregation is linked to residential segregation.[3]

At given expected policy variables v and s, the utility function u is concave in n. Within each group, some agents may choose public schooling, in which case their fertility rate is denoted n^s, while others opt for private education; fertility for those in private schools is denoted as n^e. All parents planning to send their children to the public school choose the same fertility level:

$$n^s = \arg\max_n u[x, v, n, 0, s] = \frac{\gamma}{\phi(1+\gamma)}. \tag{5.3}$$

Fertility is constant because the income and substitution effects exactly offset each other. On the one hand, richer parents would like to have more children, but on the other hand their opportunity cost of raising children is also higher.

The households planning to provide private schooling choose:

$$n = \arg\max_n u[x, v, n, e, s] = \frac{x\gamma}{(1+\gamma)(e+\phi x)},$$

$$e[x] = \arg\max_e u[x, v, n, e, s] = \frac{\eta\phi x}{1-\eta}. \tag{5.4}$$

As in previous chapters, private spending on education depends positively on the wage x. Notice that e is independent of the outcome of the voting process, implying that the timing of choosing e does not affect the results (in contrast, we will see in Section 5.4.1 that the timing of choosing between public and private schooling does matter). Replacing the optimal value for $e[x]$ in the fertility equation we find:

$$n^e = \frac{\gamma(1-\eta)}{\phi(1+\gamma)}. \tag{5.5}$$

Thus, conditional on choosing private schooling, fertility is independent of x as well. From equations (5.3) and (5.5) we see that parents choosing private education have a lower fertility rate.

---

[3] In section 5.4.1 we will explore the implications of alternative timing assumptions.

Lemma 5.1 Constant parental spending on children

For given s, v, and x, parental spending on children (and therefore taxable income) does not depend on the choice of private versus public schooling, and is equal to $\frac{\gamma}{1+\gamma}$ x.

Proof: From the budget constraint (5.2), total spending on children is given by $x\phi n + ne$. Substituting either $n = n^s$ and $e = 0$ or $n = n^e$ and $e = \eta\phi x/(1 - \eta)$ yields that:

$$x\phi n + ne = \frac{\gamma}{1+\gamma}x.$$

Taxable income therefore is:

$$x(1 - \phi n) - ne = \frac{1}{1+\gamma}x.$$

∎

Lemma 5.1 implies that the tax base does not depend on the fraction of people participating in public schooling. This property will be important for establishing uniqueness of equilibrium. The lemma relies on three assumptions: homothetic preferences, tax-deductible education spending, and endogenous fertility. With endogenous fertility, parents choosing private schools have fewer children, keeping their total budget allocation to children in line with those choosing public schools. This is a typical feature of endogenous fertility models.

Exercise: Show that, with fixed fertility, the resources allocated to children with public education would differ from those with private education.

Exercise: Show that, even with fixed fertility, a constant tax base could be achieved through an endogenous labor supply set-up.

A first result is that parents with high human capital are more demanding in terms of expected public education quality. In other words, child quality is a normal good.

Lemma 5.2 Opting-out decision

There exists an income threshold:

$$\tilde{x} = \frac{1 - \eta}{\hat{\eta}\phi\eta} E[s], \qquad \text{with: } \hat{\eta} = (1 - \eta)^{\frac{1}{\eta}}, \qquad (5.6)$$

such that households strictly prefer private education if and only if $x > \tilde{x}$.

Proof: We compute the level x such that a household with income x is indifferent between public and private schooling by solving $u[x, v, n^s, 0, [E](s)] = u[x, v, n^e, e, 0]$:

$$\tilde{x} = \frac{1 - \eta}{\hat{\eta}\phi\eta} [E](s), \qquad\qquad \text{with: } \hat{\eta} = (1 - \eta)^{\frac{1}{\eta}}.$$

$\tilde{x}$ is bigger than zero and depends positively on $[E](s)$. If x is greater (resp. smaller) than $\tilde{x}$, $u[x, v, n^s, 0, [E](s)]$ is smaller (resp. greater) than $u[x, v, n^e, e, 0]$, and the household prefers private (resp. public) education, which proves the lemma. ∎

Here E[s] is expected quality of public schooling. An implication of the above lemma is that if some people with income x choose public schooling, all people with income $x' < x$ will strictly prefer public schooling. Similarly, if at least some people with income x opt out of the public system and choose private education, all households with income $x' > x$ make the same choice.

We assume a uniform distribution of human capital over the interval $[1 - \sigma, 1 + \sigma]$.[4] Accordingly, the associated density function is given by $g(x) = 0$ for $x < 1 - \sigma$ and if $x > 1 + \sigma$, and $g(x) = 1/(2\sigma)$ for $1 - \sigma \leqslant x \leqslant 1 + \sigma$. We denote the fraction of children participating in the public education system as:

$$\Psi = \begin{cases} 0 & \text{if} \quad \tilde{x} < 1 - \sigma, \\ \dfrac{\tilde{x} - (1 - \sigma)}{2\sigma} & \text{if} \quad 1 - \sigma \leqslant \tilde{x} \leqslant 1 + \sigma, \\ 1 & \text{if} \quad \tilde{x} > 1 + \sigma. \end{cases} \tag{5.7}$$

5.1.3 The political mechanism

The public education system operates under a balanced-budget rule:

$$\int_0^{\tilde{x}} n^s \, s \, g[x] \, dx =$$

$$\int_0^{\tilde{x}} v\left(x(1 - \phi n^s)\right) g[x] \, dx + \int_{\tilde{x}}^{\infty} v\left(x(1 - \phi n^e) - e[x]n^e\right) g[x] \, dx, \tag{5.8}$$

---

[4] Arcalean and Schiopu (2010) look at whether our results are changed by assuming a Pareto distribution instead.

with total spending on public education on the left-hand side and total revenues on the right-hand side. After replacing fertility and education by their optimal values, this constraint reduces to:

$$v = \Psi \frac{\gamma}{\phi} s. \tag{5.9}$$

Since the level of schooling and taxes are linked through the budget constraint, the policy choice is one-dimensional.

The level of public expenditures, and hence taxes, is chosen through probabilistic voting. Assume that there are two political parties, p and q. Each one proposes a policy s^p and s^q. The utility gain (or loss) of a voter with income x if party q wins the election instead of p is $u[x, v^q, n, e, s^q] - u[x, v^p, n, e, s^p]$. Instead of assuming that an adult votes for party q with probability 1 every time this difference is positive (as in the median voter model), probabilistic voting theory supposes that this vote is uncertain. More precisely, the probability that a person votes for party q is given by:

$$F\left(u[x, v^q, n, e, s^q] - u[x, v^p, n, e, s^p]\right),$$

where F is an increasing and differentiable cumulative distribution function. This function is plotted in Figure 5.1. It captures the idea that voters care about

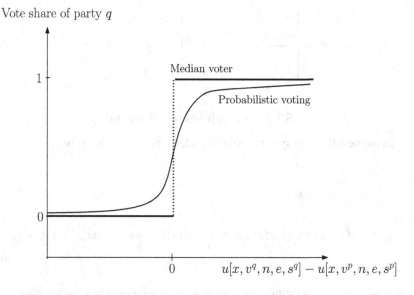

Figure 5.1 Probabilistic voting versus median voter

an "ideology" variable in addition to the specific policy measure at hand, i.e. the quality of public schooling. The presence of a concern for ideology, which is independent of the policy measure, makes the political choice less predictable (see Persson and Tabellini (2000) for different formalizations of this approach). The probability that a given voter will vote for party q increases gradually as the party's platform becomes more attractive. Under standard majority voting, in contrast, the probability of getting the vote jumps discretely from 0 to 1 once party q offers a more attractive platform than party p.

Since the vote share of each party varies continuously with the proposed policy platform, probabilistic voting leads to smooth aggregation of all voters' preferences, instead of depending solely on the preferences of the median voter. Party q maximizes its expected vote share, which is given by $\int_0^\infty g[x]F(\cdot)dx$. Party p acts symmetrically, and, in equilibrium, we have $s = s^q = s^p$. The maximization program of each party implements the maximum of the following weighted social welfare function (this result was first derived by Coughlin and Nitzan (1981)):

$$\int_0^\infty g[x]\,(F)'(0)\,u[x, v, n, e, s]dx.$$

The weight $(F)'(0)$ captures the responsiveness of voters to the change in utility. If there are groups in the population that differ in their responsiveness (their "ideological bias"), the distribution of political power becomes uneven. In particular, a group that has little ideological bias cares relatively more about economic policy. Such groups are therefore targeted by politicians and enjoy high political power. Political power may also depend on other features of the political system, such as voting rights. We will capture the political power of each person by a single parameter $\varpi[x]$. This includes the extreme cases of representative democracy with equal responsiveness, and dictatorship of the rich ($\varpi[x] = 0$ for x below a certain threshold). Accordingly, the objective function maximized by the probabilistic voting mechanism is given by:

$$\Omega[s] \equiv \int_0^{\tilde{x}} u[x, v, n^s, 0, s]\varpi[x]g[x]dx$$

$$+ \int_{\tilde{x}}^\infty u[x, v, n^e, e[x], 0]\varpi[x]g[x]dx. \tag{5.10}$$

The maximization is subject to the government budget constraint (5.8).

We start by assuming that all individuals have the same political power, i.e. $\varpi[x] = 1$, implying that the weight of a given group in the objective function is given simply by its size. The role of this assumption will be investigated further in Section 5.3. We can check that $\Omega[s]$ is strictly concave. Replacing $\tilde{x}$ by $2\sigma\Psi+1-\sigma$ in the objective, taking the first-order condition for a maximum, and solving for s, yields:

$$s = \frac{\eta\phi}{1+\gamma\eta\Psi} \equiv s[\Psi]. \tag{5.11}$$

From this expression we can see that s is decreasing in the participation rate Ψ: when more children participate in public schools, spending per child is reduced. Looking at the corresponding tax rate,

$$v = \frac{\eta\gamma\Psi}{1+\gamma\eta\Psi}, \tag{5.12}$$

we observe that a rise in participation is followed by a less than proportional rise in taxation. Since, by Lemma 5.1, the taxable income is unaffected by increased participation, this translates into lower spending per child. To see the intuition for this result, consider the consequences of increasing Ψ for a given s. In the welfare function maximized by the political system, the increase in Ψ leads to a proportional increase in the marginal benefit of increasing schooling s, since more children benefit from public education. The marginal cost of taxation, in contrast, increases more than proportionally, since the higher required taxes reduce consumption and increase marginal utilities. To equate marginal costs and benefits, an increase in Ψ is therefore met by a reduction in s.

5.1.4 The equilibrium

So far, we have taken the participation rate Ψ as given, and solved for the corresponding voting outcome concerning the quality of public schools. In equilibrium, the choice of whether or not to participate in public schooling has to be optimal. In the definition of equilibrium we will use an earlier result: the incentive to use private schooling is increasing in income (Lemma 5.2). As a consequence, any equilibrium is characterized by an income threshold $\tilde{x}$ such that people choose public education below $\tilde{x}$ and private education above $\tilde{x}$. This leads to the following definition of an equilibrium.

Definition 5.1 Political economy equilibrium with perfect foresight
An equilibrium consists of an income threshold $\tilde{x}$ satisfying (5.6), a fertility rule $n = n^s$ for $x \leqslant \tilde{x}$ and $n = n^e$ for $x > \tilde{x}$, a private education decision $e = 0$ for $x \leqslant \tilde{x}$ and $e = e[x]$ for $x > \tilde{x}$, and aggregate variables (Ψ, s, v) given by equations (5.7), (5.11), and (5.12), such that the perfect foresight

condition holds:

$$E[s] = s. \tag{5.13}$$

Proposition 5.1 Existence and uniqueness of equilibrium
An equilibrium exists and is unique.

Proof: The result follows from an application of the Brouwer fixed point theorem. Given (5.11), the equilibrium expected schooling quality $E[s]$ and actual quality s lie in the interval:

$$E[s], s \in \left[\frac{\eta\phi}{1 + \gamma\eta}, \eta\phi \right]. \tag{5.14}$$

We now define a mapping Δ from $E[s]$ into s which maps this interval into itself. Since an equilibrium requires $E[s] = s$, a unique equilibrium exists if the mapping has a unique fixed point.

Given expected schooling quality $E[s]$, according to Lemma 5.2 and equation (5.7) the fraction of families participating in public education is given by:

$$\Psi(E[s]) = \max \left\{ \min \left\{ \frac{1-\eta}{2\sigma\hat{\eta}\phi\eta} E[s] - \frac{1-\sigma}{2\sigma}, 1 \right\}, 0 \right\}.$$

This function is (weakly) increasing in $E[s]$; the higher the expected quality of public education, the more parents are going to prefer using the public sector.

We can now use (5.11) to map the expected education quality $E[s]$ into the actual education quality s that would result from the political system if fraction $\Psi(E[s])$ of families participated in the public system. This education quality $s = \Delta(E[s])$ is given by:

$$\Delta(E[s]) = \frac{\eta\phi}{1 + \gamma\eta\Psi(E[s])} = \frac{\eta\phi}{1 + \gamma\eta \max \left\{ \min \left\{ \frac{1-\eta}{2\sigma\hat{\eta}\eta} E[s] - \frac{1-\sigma}{2\sigma}, 1 \right\}, 0 \right\}}. \tag{5.15}$$

An equilibrium is characterized by a fixed point of $\Delta(E[s])$, i.e. a schooling level s that satisfies $s = \Delta(s)$, so that the schooling quality s that is expected by the parents is identical to the one actually implemented in the political process. Given (5.15), Δ is a continuous, weakly decreasing function mapping the closed interval given in (5.14) into itself. The mapping therefore crosses the 45-degree line exactly once, and a unique equilibrium exists. ∎

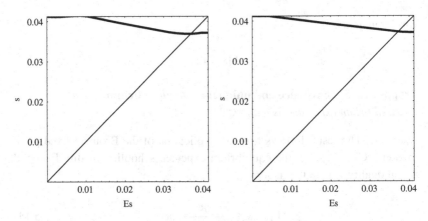

Figure 5.2 The fixed point with $\sigma = 0.5$ (left) and $\sigma = 0.8$ (right)

To see the intuition for the result, notice that participation in public school-ing is a continuously increasing function of expected school quality through equations (5.6) and (5.7). Actual school quality, in turn, is a continuous and decreasing function of participation. Combining these results, we can construct a continuous and decreasing mapping from expected to actual school quality. This mapping has a unique fixed point, which characterizes the equilibrium.

The uniqueness result relies on endogenous fertility. If one assumes, on the contrary, that fertility is exogenous and constant, Lemma 5.1 no longer holds, and the tax basis increases with participation Ψ. If the tax-basis effect is sufficiently pronounced, the actual schooling level will no longer decrease in participation, and the equilibrium mapping may fail to have a unique fixed point.

Figure 5.2 shows two numerical examples of the fixed point mapping. The chosen parameters are: $\gamma = 0.4$, $\eta = 0.55$, $\phi = 0.075$. The implied fertility levels are $n^e = 1$, $n^s = 2.22$. In the left panel, $\sigma = 0.5$, and we have $s = 0.034$ and $\Psi = 1$. In the right panel, $\sigma = 0.8$, and we have $s = 0.037$ and $\Psi = 0.96$.

5.2 Comparing the education regimes

Depending on the equilibrium coverage of the public education system, we have three cases to consider (Table 5.2).

In the fully public regime, all children go to public school. Under segregation, the most skilled parents send their children to private school, while others use public schools. In the fully private regime, everybody attends private schools. We first derive the conditions under which each education regime arises. The following proposition summarizes the results.

Table 5.2. *Typology of education regimes*

Regime	Ψ
Fully public	1
Segregation	$\in (0, 1)$
Fully private	0

Proposition 5.2 Occurrence of education regimes

The fully private regime is not an equilibrium outcome.

Whether public schooling can arise in equilibrium depends on the preference parameters γ and η. Let $\hat{\gamma} = (1 - \hat{\eta} - \eta)/(\hat{\eta}\eta)$.

If $\gamma > \hat{\gamma}$, public education is not an equilibrium outcome and $\Psi < 1/2$ for any σ.

If $\gamma < \hat{\gamma}$, the fully public regime prevails if and only if

$$\sigma \leqslant \hat{\sigma} = \frac{1 - \eta}{(1 + \gamma\eta)\hat{\eta}} - 1.$$

Otherwise, we have segregation with $\Psi > 1/2$.

Proof: We first show that the private regime is not an equilibrium outcome. In *a reductio ad absurdum* argument, we assume the existence of such a case. We start from the optimal value of s given in equation (5.11). From this equation, we observe that as Ψ tends to zero, s tends to $\eta\phi$. With this quality of public schooling, the equilibrium income threshold (from equation (5.6)) is: $\tilde{x}[\eta\phi] = (1 - \eta)/\hat{\eta}$. For private education to be an equilibrium, this threshold should be lower than or equal to lowest income $1 - \sigma$. Given the definition of $\hat{\eta} = (1 - \eta)^{1/\eta}$, we have that $\hat{\eta} < 1 - \eta$, which implies $x[\eta\phi] > 1 > 1 - \sigma$. Hence, with a quality of public schools going to $\eta\phi$, it is always optimal for the poorest person to choose public education. Therefore, the private regime cannot arise in equilibrium.

If the public regime is an equilibrium, it has $\Psi = 1$ and $s = \eta\phi/(1 + \gamma\eta)$ (from equation (5.11)). For this to be an equilibrium, we need the richest person to send his children to public school, which requires $\tilde{x}[\eta\phi/(1 + \gamma\eta)] \geqslant 1 + \sigma$. This condition can be written:

$$\frac{1 - \eta}{\hat{\eta}(1 + \gamma\eta)} \geqslant 1 + \sigma.$$

If $\gamma \geqslant \hat{\gamma} = (1 - \hat{\eta} - \eta)/(\hat{\eta}\eta)$, the right-hand side of the inequality is below 1, and the inequality can never be satisfied. This condition links the taste for children γ to the weight of education η independently of σ. If $\gamma < \hat{\gamma}$, the above inequality can be rewritten as a condition on σ, which is the condition of the proposition.

It remains to be shown that $\gamma < \hat{\gamma} \Leftrightarrow \Psi > 1/2$. $\Psi = 1/2$ implies that the equilibrium is segregated. We solve for the equilibrium value of Ψ, which is given by:

$$\Psi = \frac{-\gamma\hat{\eta}\eta(1-\sigma) - 2\hat{\eta}\sigma + \sqrt{8\gamma\hat{\eta}\eta\sigma\left(1-\hat{\eta}(1-\sigma)-\eta\right) + \left(\gamma\,\hat{\eta}\,\eta(1-\sigma)+2\,\hat{\eta}\,\sigma\right)^2}}{4\gamma\,\hat{\eta}\,\eta\,\sigma}.$$

There is only one value of γ for which this big expression is equal to 1/2, and it is $\hat{\gamma}$. Since Ψ is a continuous function of γ, and we already know that it can be equal to 1 for certain values of σ if $\gamma < \hat{\gamma}$, we conclude that $\Psi > 1/2$ for $\gamma < \hat{\gamma}$ and $\Psi < 1/2$ for $\gamma > \hat{\gamma}$. ∎

Let us first explain why the fully private regime cannot be an equilibrium outcome. When participation is very low ($\Psi \to 0$), high-quality public education can be provided at very low tax levels. The quality of public schools is then sufficiently high ($s \to \eta\phi$) for the poorest parents to prefer public over private education.

To see whether a fully public regime can arise, we have to look at the preferences of the richest person. If this person has a high income relative to the average (high σ), her preferred education quality is sufficiently large relative to what is provided by public schools for private education to be optimal. The effect of inequality on segregation is established in the next proposition. The fully public regime arises only if the income distribution is sufficiently compressed, so that the preferred education level varies little in the population. From now on we restrict attention to the region of the parameter space where the fully public regime can occur for a sufficiently compressed income distribution, and where at any time at least half the population is in public schools.

Assumption 5.1 *The model parameters satisfy:*

$$\gamma < \hat{\gamma} \equiv \frac{1 - \hat{\eta} - \eta}{\hat{\eta}\eta}.$$

Since in nearly all countries participation in public schools far exceeds 50 percent, this is the empirically relevant case. Put differently, using the calibrated parameter values $\eta = 0.6$ and $\phi = 0.075$ from Chapter 2, Assumption 5.1 can be read as a condition on fertility n^s (see equation (5.3)). The condition imposes $n^s < 7.79$ per person, which requires fertility per woman to be smaller than 15.6 children (obviously realistic).

Proposition 5.3 Inequality and segregation

Under Assumption 5.1, an increase in inequality leads to a lower share of public schooling, a higher quality of public schooling, and lower taxes:

$$\frac{\partial \Psi}{\partial \sigma} \leq 0, \quad \frac{\partial s}{\partial \sigma} \geq 0, \quad \frac{\partial v}{\partial \sigma} \leq 0.$$

The inequalities are strict if a positive fraction of parents already uses private schools.

Proof: In the interior regime (segregation), we have from (5.6) and (5.7):

$$\Psi = \frac{\frac{1-\eta}{\hat{\eta}\phi\eta}s - (1-\sigma)}{2\sigma}.$$

Taking the derivative with respect to s, we obtain:

$$\frac{\partial \Psi}{\partial \sigma} = \frac{2\sigma - 2\left[\frac{1-\eta}{\hat{\eta}\phi\eta}s - (1-\sigma)\right]}{2\sigma} = \frac{1}{\sigma}\left(\frac{1}{2} - \Psi\right).$$

Hence,

$$\text{If } \Psi \in (0, 1), \quad \frac{\partial \Psi}{\partial \sigma} > 0 \Leftrightarrow \Psi < \frac{1}{2}. \tag{5.16}$$

In the public regime,

$$\Psi = 1, \Rightarrow \partial\Psi/\partial\sigma = 0. \tag{5.17}$$

Proposition 5.2 together with (5.12), (5.16), and (5.17) imply Proposition 5.3. ∎

Higher income inequality leads to lower participation in public schools and to more segregation (Ψ closer to 1/2) if the majority of the population is in public schools. Intuitively, in this case an increase in inequality raises the income of the marginal person (who was indifferent between private and public schooling before the increase in inequality). As a consequence, the preferred level of education increases, and this person now strictly prefers private schooling. The lower participation in public schooling after an increase in inequality also implies that the tax rate goes down. Thus, despite the increased demand for redistribution, everybody is taxed less as more parents opt out of the public schooling system.

The preferences of households at the income threshold $\tilde{x}$ are linked to the relative quality of public versus private schooling. At the threshold, households are indifferent between both types of schools. This implies that the quality they receive from public schools is lower than the quality of private schools, since the gap between the two has to compensate for higher costs of private education.[5]

5.3 Political power and multiple equilibria

In this section, we relax the earlier assumption that each member of the population carries equal weight in the voting process. We will see that if political power is concentrated among high-income individuals, multiple equilibria can arise.

As a particularly simple form of variable political power, we consider outcomes with a minimum-income restriction for voting. There is now a threshold $\bar{x}$ such that only individuals with income $x \geqslant \bar{x}$ are allowed to vote. All individuals above the threshold continue to carry equal weight in the voting process. This formulation captures property restrictions on voting, which were common in the early phases of many democracies. Similar cases of political exclusion can also arise from literacy requirements, age restrictions on voting (given that young people tend to be relatively poor), citizenship restrictions (assuming that recent immigrants are poorer on average than the native population), and political mechanisms other than voting (such as lobbying and bribery) that favor the rich in both democracies and non-democracies.

The objective function of the political system is now given by:

$$\Omega[s] \equiv$$
$$\int_{\bar{x}}^{\max\{\bar{x},\tilde{x}\}} u[x, v, n^s, 0, s]g[x]dx + \int_{\max\{\bar{x},\tilde{x}\}}^{\infty} u[x, v, n^e, e[x], 0]g[x]dx. \tag{5.18}$$

---

[5] This result is consistent with the literature devoted to the estimation of the relative quality of private education, correcting for the effect of higher social class of the pupils in the private sector. Most of the results suggest that controlling for sample selectivity reduces the achievement advantage of private school students over public school students, but does not eliminate it. See Kingdon (1996) for India, Bedi and Garg (2000) for Indonesia, Alderman *et al.* (2001) for Pakistan, and Neal (1997) for Catholic US schools. Some other studies find no difference between private and public school performances (see Goldhaber (1996)).

Replacing $\tilde{x}$ by $2\sigma\Psi + 1 - \sigma$ in the objective, taking the first-order condition for a maximum and solving for s yields:

$$\text{If } \Psi \geqslant \frac{\tilde{x} - (1 - \sigma)}{2\sigma}, \quad s = \frac{\eta\phi\left((1 - \sigma) - \tilde{x} + 2\sigma\Psi\right)}{\Psi\left(\gamma\eta\left((1 - \sigma) - \tilde{x} + 2\sigma\Psi\right) + (1 + \sigma) - \tilde{x}\right)}.$$

(5.19)

$$\text{If } \Psi < \frac{\tilde{x} - (1 - \sigma)}{2\sigma}, \quad s = 0.$$

Hence, with a biased political system, corner solutions with a schooling quality of zero may arise. The equilibrium schooling quality s satisfies:

$$s = \max\left\{\frac{\eta\phi\left(1 - \sigma - \tilde{x} + 2\sigma\Psi\right)}{\Psi\left(1 + \sigma - \tilde{x} + \gamma\eta\left(1 - \sigma - \tilde{x} + 2\sigma\Psi\right)\right)}, 0\right\}.$$

(5.20)

The corresponding tax rate is still given by (5.12). A few properties of (5.20) are of interest here. First, we have $s = 0$ for $\Psi \leq \tilde{x} - (1 - \sigma)/2\sigma$. Second, we have:

$$s = \max\left\{\frac{\eta\phi}{\frac{(1+\sigma-\tilde{x})\Psi}{(1-\sigma-\tilde{x}+2\sigma\Psi)} + \gamma\eta\Psi}, 0\right\} \leq \frac{\eta\phi}{1 + \gamma\eta\Psi},$$

where the right-hand side is the schooling level that arises with equal political power as given by (5.11). Finally, for $\Psi = 1$ we have:

$$s = \frac{\eta\phi}{1 + \gamma\eta},$$

just as in the case with equal political power. In the new formulation with variable voting power, the existence of an equilibrium can still be proven. However, the equilibrium is no longer necessarily unique. Further, it is no longer true that the fully private regime never exists (as we showed in proposition 5.2 for the democratic case of an even distribution of political power). In fact, in the biased political system, pure private schooling is always an equilibrium outcome.

As soon as $\tilde{x}$ is smaller than $\bar{x}$, i.e. all voters expect to send their children to private schools, the chosen school quality is zero. Intuitively, these voters care only about taxes, and not about the quality of public schools that they do not use. As a consequence, private schooling becomes attractive to all parents.

Exercise: Suppose now that individuals below the threshold had positive but sufficiently low weight $\varpi < 1$ in the political mechanism. Compute the equilibrium schooling quality. Show that proposition 5.4 below still holds for ϖ small. Derive a threshold value for ϖ such that proposition 5.4 holds.

To show that multiple equilibria can arise, we concentrate on the parameter space where fully public schooling is the unique equilibrium when $\bar{x} = 0$. We establish that in this case there are at least three equilibria for $\bar{x} > 1 - \sigma$.

Proposition 5.4 Multiplicity of equilibria for $\bar{x} > 1 - \sigma$
If $\bar{x}$, γ, and σ satisfy the conditions

$$\bar{x} > 1 - \sigma, \quad \gamma < \hat{\gamma}, \quad and \quad \sigma \leqslant \hat{\sigma} = \frac{1 - \eta}{(1 + \gamma\eta)\hat{\eta}} - 1,$$

there are at least three equilibria. One is a fully private regime, one is a fully public regime, and one features segregation.

Proof: As in the proof of proposition 5.1, we will proceed by analyzing the mapping from expected schooling quality E[s] into actual quality s. Given (5.20), a schooling quality of zero is now possible, so that E[s] and s lie in the following interval:

$$E[s], s \in [0, \eta\phi]. \tag{5.21}$$

We now define a mapping $\bar{\Delta}$ from E[s] into s, which maps this interval into itself. Since an equilibrium requires E[s] = s, any equilibrium corresponds to a fixed point of the mapping.

Given expected schooling quality E[s], according to lemma 5.2 and equation (5.7) the fraction of families participating in public education is given by:

$$\Psi(E[s]) = \max\left\{\min\left\{\frac{1 - \eta}{2\sigma\hat{\eta}\phi\eta} E[s] - \frac{1 - \sigma}{2\sigma}, 1\right\}, 0\right\}. \tag{5.22}$$

This function is (weakly) increasing in E[s]; the higher the expected quality of public education, the more parents are going to prefer using the public sector.

We can now use (5.20) to map the expected education quality E[s] into the actual education quality s that would result from the political system if fraction $\Psi(E[s])$ of families participated in the public system. This education quality $s = \bar{\Delta}(E[s])$ is given by:

$$\bar{\Delta}(E[s]) = \max\left\{\frac{\eta\phi\left(1 - \sigma - \bar{x} + 2\sigma\Psi(E[s])\right)}{\Psi(E[s])\left(\gamma\eta\left(1 - \sigma - \bar{x} + 2\sigma\Psi(E[s])\right) + 1 + \sigma - \bar{x}\right)}, 0\right\}. \tag{5.23}$$

An equilibrium is characterized by a fixed point of $\bar{\Delta}(E[s])$, i.e. a schooling level s that satisfies $s = \bar{\Delta}(s)$, so that the schooling quality s that is expected by the parents is identical to the one actually implemented in the political process. Given $\Psi(E[s])$ and the properties of (5.20) stated in the text, $\bar{\Delta}$ is a continuous function mapping the closed interval given in (5.21) into itself. Due to the Brouwer fixed-point theorem, at least one equilibrium exists. Also notice that $\Psi = 0$ is always an equilibrium, since $\bar{\Delta}(E[0]) = 0$.

Now assume that conditions $\gamma < \hat{\gamma}$ and $\sigma < \hat{\sigma}$ are satisfied. We want to establish that in this case pure public schooling $\Psi = 1$ is an equilibrium. In (5.23), the schooling quality corresponding to $\Psi = 1$ is $s = \eta\phi/(1 + \gamma\eta)$. The first term inside the minimization in (5.22) satisfies for this s:

$$
\frac{1-\eta}{2\sigma\hat{\eta}\phi\eta}s - \frac{1-\sigma}{2\sigma} = \frac{1-\eta}{2\sigma\hat{\eta}(1+\gamma\eta)} - \frac{1-\sigma}{2\sigma}
$$

$$
\geq \frac{1}{2\left(\frac{1-\eta}{\hat{\eta}(1+\gamma\eta)} - 1\right)}\left(\frac{1-\eta}{\hat{\eta}(1+\gamma\eta)} - \left(2 - \frac{1-\eta}{(1+\gamma\eta)\hat{\eta}}\right)\right)
$$

$$
= \frac{1}{\frac{1-\eta}{\hat{\eta}(1+\gamma\eta)} - 1}\left(\frac{1-\eta}{\hat{\eta}(1+\gamma\eta)} - 1\right) = 1,
$$

where $\gamma < \hat{\gamma}$ guarantees that the right-hand side of the first equation is positive, and the inequality follows from $\sigma \leq \hat{\sigma}$. The public education quality $s = \eta\phi/(1 + \gamma\eta)$ is therefore mapped into $\Psi(s) = 1$, which, in turn, implies $\bar{\Delta}(E[s]) = s$. Therefore, if pure public schooling is an equilibrium under an equal division of political power, it is still an equilibrium with a voting threshold $\bar{x} < 1 - \sigma$. Since pure private schooling is always an equilibrium, we have at least two equilibria in this case. Next, notice that the slope of $\bar{\Delta}(s)$ is zero at $s = 0$, since for sufficiently small s we still have $\Psi = 0$. Also, at $s = \eta\phi/(1 + \gamma\eta)$ the slope of $\bar{\Delta}(s)$ is zero as well, since given $\sigma < \hat{\sigma}$ we have $\Psi = 1$ in a neighborhood of $s = \eta\phi/(1 + \gamma\eta)$. Given that $\bar{\Delta}(s)$ is continuous, it has to cross the 45-degree line at least once more in between those values, implying the existence of a third equilibrium, which features segregation. ∎

In Figure 5.3 we take the same parameter values as in Figure 5.2 and we set $\sigma = 0.5$ and $\bar{x} = 0.7$, which implies that the bottom 20 percent have no political power. There are now three fixed points: $s = 0$, $s = 0.017$, and $s = 0.037$, with participation $\Psi = 0$, $\Psi = 0.3$, and $\Psi = 1$.

The possibility of multiple equilibria exists because we assume that people have to decide on fertility and public versus private schooling before the vote

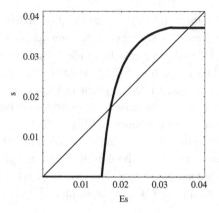

Figure 5.3 The fixed point with multiple equilibria ($\sigma = 0.5$, $\bar{x} = 0.7$)

on the quality of public education takes place. If all decisions were taken simultaneously, the voting process would lead to the same outcome as the weighted
social planning problem, which is generically unique. Pre-commitment generates multiplicity in this setting, but not in the version with equal political
weights.

Multiplicity arises because there is now a strategic complementarity between
the education choices of skilled people through the quality of public schools.
When everyone with political power uses private schools, a given individual
does not want to switch to the public system, since the quality of the public
schooling is low. If, however, all voters were to switch together to the public
system, they would vote for a much higher quality of public schools, in which
case it would be rational to stay in the public system. As each member of a
group attaches a particular importance to the decisions of the other members of
the same group, multiple equilibria arise. The rationale for multiplicity is well
explained by Shell (2008):

> The market economy is a social system. In attempting to optimize her
> own actions, each agent must attempt to predict the actions of the other
> agents. A, in forecasting the market strategy of B, must forecast B's
> forecasts of the forecasts of others including those of A herself. It is not
> surprising that this process may generate uncertainty in outcomes even
> in the extreme case in which the fundamentals are non-stochastic.

Provided that there is a strong concentration of political power, the model
can account for the fact that some countries with similar general characteristics

choose very different educational systems.[6] The next proposition shows that despite the possibility of multiple equilibria, the coverage of public schooling is never higher in societies dominated by the rich than it is in democracies.

Proposition 5.5 Coverage of public education as a function of $\bar{x}$

Let Ψ_0 be the equilibrium coverage of public education for a threshold $\bar{x} = x_0$, and v_0 the corresponding tax rate. If Ψ_1 and v_1 are an equilibrium coverage and a tax rate for a $\bar{x} = x_1 > x_0$, then we have:

$$\Psi_1 \leqslant \Psi_0,$$

$$s_1 \leqslant s_0,$$

$$v_1 \leqslant v_0.$$

Proof: We have established previously that:

$$\max\left\{\frac{\eta\phi}{\frac{(1+\sigma-\bar{x})\Psi}{(1-\sigma-\bar{x}+2\sigma\Psi)} + \gamma\eta\Psi}, 0\right\} \leq \frac{\eta\phi}{1+\gamma\eta\Psi},$$

where the left-hand side is the schooling level that arises for a given Ψ as given by (5.20), and the right-hand side is the level that arises with equal political power as given by (5.11). Since the reverse mapping from a given schooling quality into Ψ does not depend on the distribution of political power, this inequality implies that the mappings Δ and $\bar{\Delta}$ defined in the proofs of propositions 5.1 and 5.4 satisfy $\bar{\Delta}(s) \leq \Delta(s)$. Equilibria in the two environments correspond to levels of s that satisfy $s = \bar{\Delta}(s)$ and $s = \Delta(s)$, respectively. It was established in the proof of proposition 5.1 that $\Delta(s)$ is weakly decreasing and crosses the 45-degree line only once from above. Since $\bar{\Delta}(s) \leq \Delta(s)$, it then follows that $\bar{\Delta}$ cannot cross the 45-degree line above the unique crossing point for $\Delta(s)$, so that we have $\bar{s} \leq s$. Finally, the relationship between s and v does not depend on the distribution of political power, and taxes are monotonically increasing in s, so that we have $\bar{v} \leq v$.   ■

---

[6] A number of authors have derived similar multiplicity results in other applications of voting models. In Saint-Paul and Verdier (1997) there is majority voting on a capital income tax. If political power is unequally distributed, and is biased in favor of households having better access to world capital markets, expectations-driven multiple equilibria can arise. In a dynamic majority voting framework, Hassler *et al.* (2003) assume that young agents base their education decisions on expectations over future redistribution. Self-fulfilling expectations can lead to either high or low redistribution equilibria. Finally, there are other political economy models that do not have indeterminacy of equilibrium but display multiple steady states (see, for example, Bénabou (2000) or Doepke and Zilibotti (2005)). Initial conditions, as opposed to self-fulfilling expectations, determine which steady state the economy approaches.

While we have established the results of this section for the extreme case where households with an income below $\bar{x}$ do not wield any political power, the results generalize to an environment where these households have some positive weight in the political system, but lower than the weight of households with income above $\bar{x}$. In particular, it is easy to establish that, for any $\bar{x}$, a fully private regime exists if the weight of low-income people is sufficiently small. As before, if in this case the unique equilibrium in the model with an even distribution of political power is pure public schooling, at least three equilibria exist when the poor have less political power.

5.4 Alternative timing assumptions

So far we have assumed that the level of government spending on education is determined after private households have decided whether to send their children to private or public schools. In this section we analyze two alternative timing assumptions.

5.4.1 Outcomes with full government commitment

We first assume that voters elect a government which pre-commits to a given overall spending level on education, while households can make their schooling choice conditional on this spending. Even though under each timing assumption people have perfect foresight, we will see that timing makes an important difference. For the following analysis, we return to the assumption of an even distribution of political power, i.e. $\bar{x} = 0$.

In the new timing, the government sets the tax rate at the beginning of the period. Since the tax base is independent of the schooling choice, this is equivalent to determining total spending on public education. After the tax is set, parents choose fertility and public versus private education for their children. Public schooling per child will then be given by the ratio of pre-committed total spending to the number of children in public schools. Since the government has perfect foresight, the problem can be solved backwards by first determining individual decisions as a function of policies, and then choosing policies taking this dependency into account.

Since fertility choices conditional on schooling are not affected by taxes, fertility rates will be, as above, determined by equations (5.3) and (5.5). Private education spending is also unaffected by the new timing of decisions and is given by equation (5.4). The participation decision is determined by the threshold defined in lemma 5.2, which is now defined in terms of actual schooling quality s:

$$\tilde{x}[s] = \frac{1-\eta}{\hat{\eta}\phi\eta}\, s. \tag{5.24}$$

We also redefine the endogenous fraction of children participating in the public education system as a function of actual quality:

$$\Psi[s] = \begin{cases} 0 & \text{if} \quad \tilde{x}[s] < 1-\sigma, \\ \dfrac{\tilde{x}[s] - (1-\sigma)}{2\sigma} & \text{if} \quad 1-\sigma \leqslant \tilde{x}[s] \leqslant 1+\sigma, \\ 1 & \text{if} \quad \tilde{x}[s] > 1+\sigma. \end{cases} \tag{5.25}$$

From equation (5.9), the link between taxes and expenditures is given by:

$$v = \Psi[s]\frac{\gamma}{\phi}\, s. \tag{5.26}$$

The objective function modeling the voting process is the same as before, but Ψ and $\tilde{x}$ are now endogenous:

$$\Omega[s] \equiv \int_0^{\tilde{x}[s]} u[x,v,n^s,0,s]g[x]dx + \int_{\tilde{x}[s]}^\infty u[x,v,n^e,e[x],0]g[x]dx. \tag{5.27}$$

The structure of the problem is similar to a standard Ramsey (1927) problem, where the government chooses optimal taxes taking into account the reaction of private agents. Once again three regimes are possible: fully public ($\Psi[s] = 1$), segregation ($1 > \Psi[s] > 0$), and fully private ($\Psi[s] = 0$). In the segregation case, the first-order condition for optimization is as follows:

$$\int_0^{\tilde{x}[s]} \left(\frac{\partial u}{\partial v}\frac{\partial v}{\partial s} + \frac{\partial u}{\partial s}\right)g[x]dx + \int_{\tilde{x}[s]}^\infty \left(\frac{\partial u}{\partial v}\frac{\partial v}{\partial s} + \frac{\partial u}{\partial s}\right)g[x]dx$$

$$+ \int_0^{\tilde{x}[s]} \frac{\partial u}{\partial v}\frac{\partial v}{\partial \Psi}\frac{\partial \Psi}{\partial s}g[x]dx + \int_{\tilde{x}[s]}^\infty \frac{\partial u}{\partial v}\frac{\partial v}{\partial \Psi}\frac{\partial \Psi}{\partial s}g[x]dx = 0.$$

The first line of this optimality condition is the same as the one we get in the problem without commitment. The second line is a new term which arises from the endogenous dependency of Ψ on s. This term is always negative. The new negative term implies that under government commitment, the optimal s is lower than under no-commitment, as long as the solution for Ψ is interior.

Intuitively, the government now takes into account that a marginal increase in s increases the number of families using public schools. On the margin this lowers the value of the objective function, since the marginal family is just indifferent between private and public schooling, but imposes a fiscal burden on the rest of the population once it switches from private to public school.

In the fully private and public regimes, participation $\Psi[s]$ is locally independent of s, as long as the marginal family strictly prefers its current schooling choice. The additional term is therefore zero, and hence the optimal schooling choice of s does not depend on government commitment. Proposition 5.6 summarizes the result.

Proposition 5.6 Equilibrium with commitment
An equilibrium with commitment exists. Public school quality is lower than or equal to the level reached without commitment. The inequality is strict if participation Ψ satisfies: $0 < \Psi < 1$.

Existence is guaranteed because the objective function is continuous on a compact set. The equilibrium is not guaranteed to be unique, however, because the objective function is not globally concave. In particular, it has kinks at the values of s corresponding to $\tilde{x}[s] = 1 - \sigma$ and $\tilde{x}[s] = 1 + \sigma$. However, multiplicity occurs only for knife-edge cases.

Exercise: Plot the objective function $\Omega(s)$ given in (5.27) where v has been substituted by its value from (5.26) and parameters are those used for Figure 5.2.

If we extend this model to concentrated political power as in section 5.3, we no longer get generic multiplicity of equilibria. Under the original timing, multiple equilibria arose as self-fulfilling prophecies. With government commitment, the government moves first and chooses the generically unique equilibrium that maximizes the objective function.

5.4.2 Outcomes with partial government commitment

We finally consider another possible timing, in which parents choose fertility first, then government commits to school quality, and then parents decide whether to send their child to public or private school. This is probably the most realistic timing. Indeed, as far as fertility decisions are concerned, the realistic assumption is that households move before the government does. Children generally enter school at age six, so that at the very minimum, six years pass from the fertility decision until schooling actually begins. It is hard to imagine that the government commits to a schooling quality more than six years ahead of time, without any possibility of later adjustments.

In this intermediate case, when households choose fertility, they do so under perfect foresight regarding the future quality of schools. There will be an income threshold $\hat{x}$ below which people have large families (corresponding to the expectation of public schooling). The objective of the voting process takes three different forms depending on how the threshold for private education $\tilde{x}[s]$ compares with the threshold for small families $\hat{x}$. For $\hat{x} < \tilde{x}[s]$, it is given by:

$$\Omega[s] = \int_0^{\hat{x}} u[x, v, n^s, 0, s]g[x]dx + \int_{\hat{x}}^{\tilde{x}[s]} u[x, v, n^e, 0, s]g[x]dx$$

$$+ \int_{\tilde{x}[s]}^{\infty} u[x, v, n^e, e[x], 0]g[x]dx,$$

for $\hat{x} = \tilde{x}[s]$, we have:

$$\Omega[s] = \int_0^{\tilde{x}[s]} u[x, v, n^s, 0, s]g[x]dx + \int_{\tilde{x}[s]}^{\infty} u[x, v, n^e, e[x], 0]g[x]dx,$$

(5.28)

and for $\hat{x} > \tilde{x}[s]$, we have:

$$\Omega[s] = \int_0^{\tilde{x}[s]} u[x, v, n^s, 0, s]g[x]dx + \int_{\tilde{x}[s]}^{\hat{x}} u[x, v, n^s, e[x], 0]g[x]dx$$

$$+ \int_{\hat{x}}^{\infty} u[x, v, n^e, e[x], 0]g[x]dx.$$

If $\hat{x} \neq \tilde{x}[s]$, as in the previous case the first-order condition for optimality has an additional term related to the marginal impact of s on $\tilde{x}[s]$. In equilibrium, however, agents have perfect foresight, and $\hat{x} = \tilde{x}[s]$ will hold. Consider the s that maximizes the objective function holding $\tilde{x}[s]$ constant at $\hat{x}$, as in our original timing. In equation (5.28), in a neighborhood around this s the marginal effect of a change in s on $\tilde{x}$ is zero. The reason is that agents below $\hat{x}$ have chosen large families in expectation of using public schools, whereas families above $\hat{x} = \tilde{x}[s]$ have chosen small families in expectation of private schooling. Families close to the threshold therefore strictly prefer their expected schooling choice to the alternative. Thus for $\hat{x} = \tilde{x}[s]$ which occurs in equilibrium, the first-order condition is as in our original timing. If the solution is interior, this implies that the outcome has to be the same.

Hence, it is sufficient that parents commit to a fertility level before the government decision to retrieve the results derived previously.

5.5 A dynamic extension

In this section, we propose a two-group version of the model, which will allow us to study some dynamic aspects.

5.5.1 The model economy

There are two types of people, skilled and unskilled. The two types are indexed by i and differ only in their wage w^i. The utility function and budget constraint are given by equations (5.1) and (5.2).

The aggregate production function is linear in both labor inputs. Using A for unskilled and B for skilled, we have:

$$Y_t = w^A L^A + w^B L^B.$$

Here w^A and $w^B > w^A$ are the marginal product of each type. We can normalize $w^A = 1$ without loss of generality. The total input of the groups is given by L^A and L^B. The input of workers of type i is smaller than the total population P^i, since some adults work as teachers.

It is convenient to define the relative wage of a family of type i as $x^i = w^i/\bar{w}$. Relative wages are related to the size of the two groups. Denoting the sizes of the groups relative to group A by:

$$z^A = 1, \quad z^B = \frac{P^B}{P^A}, \tag{5.29}$$

the average wage is given by:

$$\bar{w} = \frac{\sum_{i=A,B} P^i w^i}{\sum_{i=A,B} P^i} = \frac{1 + z^B w^B}{1 + z^B}, \tag{5.30}$$

which allows us to compute:

$$x^B = \frac{w^B(1 + z^B)}{1 + z^B w^B} \in [1, w^B]. \tag{5.31}$$

We see from this equation that the wage of skilled people relative to the average, x^B, varies from w^B to 1 when z^B varies from 0 to infinity. Equation (4.5) also implies the following relation between x^B, x^A, and z^A:

$$x^A = 1 + z^B(1 - x^B) \in [1/w^B, 1]. \tag{5.32}$$

5.5.2 Private choices

All the private choices can be directly translated from Section 5.1.2. Both the
skilled and unskilled parents planning to send their children to the public school
choose the same fertility level given by (5.3). The households planning to
provide private schooling behave as described in (5.4). Lemmas 5.1 (constant
parental spending on children) and 5.2 (opting-out decision) hold. We denote
the utility of a type i household as $u^i[v, n, e, s]$.

5.5.3 The political mechanism

We denote the endogenous percentage of children of each group participating
in the public education system as Ψ^A and Ψ^B. The public education system
operates under a balanced-budget rule:

$$
s \sum_{i=A,B} z^i \Psi^i \hat{n}^i \bar{w} =
$$
$$
v \sum_{i=A,B} z^i \left(x^i(1 - \phi\Psi^i \hat{n}^i - \phi(1 - \Psi^i)\tilde{n}^i) - (1 - \Psi^i)\tilde{n}^i e^i \right) \bar{w}. \quad (5.33)
$$

The level of public expenditure, and hence taxes, is chosen through probabilistic voting. The maximization program of each party implements the
maximum of the following weighted social welfare function:

$$
\Omega[s] \equiv \sum_{i=A,B} z^i \varpi^i \left(\Psi^i u^i[v, \hat{n}, 0, s] + (1 - \Psi^i)u^i[v, \tilde{n}, e^i, 0] \right). \quad (5.34)
$$

The maximization is subject to the government budget constraint (5.33).

Assuming that all individuals have the same political power, taking the first-
order condition for a maximum and solving for s yields:

$$
s = \frac{\eta\phi(1 + z^B)}{1 + z^B + \gamma\eta(\Psi^A + z^B\Psi^B)} \equiv s[\Psi^A, \Psi^B]. \quad (5.35)
$$

From this expression we can see that s is decreasing in both participation rates
Ψ^A and Ψ^B. Looking at the corresponding tax rate,

$$
v = \frac{\eta\gamma(\Psi^A + z^B\Psi^B)}{1 + z^B + \gamma\eta(\Psi^A + z^B\Psi^B)}. \quad (5.36)
$$

5.5.4 The equilibrium

Definition 5.2 Political equilibrium with two types of agents

An equilibrium is a vector of individual variables $(\hat{n}^i, \tilde{n}^i, e^i, \Psi^i)_{i=A,B}$ and aggregate variables (s, v) such that equations (5.3)–(5.12) hold, and the following conditions are satisfied:

$$\forall i, \; if \; \begin{cases} \Psi^i = 1 & : \quad u^i[v, \hat{n}, 0, s] \geqslant u^i[v, \tilde{n}, e^i, 0] \\ 1 > \Psi^i > 0 & : \quad u^i[v, \hat{n}, 0, s] = u^i[v, \tilde{n}, e^i, 0] \\ \Psi^i = 0 & : \quad u^i[v, \hat{n}, 0, s] \leqslant u^i[v, \tilde{n}, e^i, 0]. \end{cases} \tag{5.37}$$

The first constraint says that if public education yields higher utility for group i, everyone in group i uses the public education system. The second constraint says that for group i to split between the two types of schools they need to be indifferent between them. The third constraint applies when group i prefers private education.

Denote the coverage of public education as $\Psi = \Psi^A + \Psi^B \in [0, 2]$. An implication of Lemma 5.2 is that Ψ^A and Ψ^B satisfy the following relationships:

$$(\Psi^B > 0) \Rightarrow (\Psi^A = 1)$$
$$(\Psi^A < 1) \Rightarrow (\Psi^B = 0),$$

and are therefore uniquely determined by Ψ.

Hence potential equilibria can be indexed by Ψ. We can now define the function:

$$\Delta^i[\Psi] = u^i[v, \hat{n}, 0, s] - u^i[v, \tilde{n}, e^i, 0],$$

which expresses the difference of utilities between public and private education for group i as a function of Ψ, where s and v depend on Ψ. $\Delta^i[\Psi]$ is not well defined at $\Psi = 0$, since here measure zero of agents use public schooling, so that positive public schooling can be provided at zero taxes. We therefore extend the function as follows:

$$\Delta^i[0] = \lim_{\Psi \to 0} \Delta^i[\Psi].$$

Extended this way, the function $\Delta^i[\Psi]$ is continuous. We can now define a mapping F from (Δ^A, Δ^B) to the interval $[0, 2]$, which gives the set of values

Table 5.3. *Education regimes with two types of households*

Regime	Ψ	Ψ^A	Ψ^B
Public	2	1	1
Partial segregation (1)	$\in (1, 2)$	1	$\in (0, 1)$
Segregation	1	1	0
Partial segregation (2)	$\in (0, 1)$	$\in (0, 1)$	0

for Ψ consistent with Δ^A and Δ^B in equilibrium:

$$F(\Delta^A, \Delta^B) = \begin{cases} 2 & \text{for} \quad \Delta^A > 0, \Delta^B > 0 \\ [1, 2] & \text{for} \quad \Delta^A > 0, \Delta^B = 0 \\ 1 & \text{for} \quad \Delta^A > 0, \Delta^B < 0 \\ [0, 1] & \text{for} \quad \Delta^A = 0, \Delta^B < 0 \\ 0 & \text{for} \quad \Delta^A < 0, \Delta^B < 0. \end{cases}$$

The combined mapping $F(\Delta^A, \Delta^B)$ maps the interval $[0, 2]$ into itself, and equilibria are given by fixed points of this mapping. The existence and uniqueness of the equilibrium can now be proved following the lines of Section 5.1.4.

Indeed, both differences $u^i[v, \hat{n}, 0, s] - u^i[v, \tilde{n}, e^i, 0]$ are monotonically decreasing in Ψ^A and Ψ^B because v drops out and s depends negatively on Ψ^A and Ψ^B. This will ensure uniqueness of equilibrium.

5.5.5 Comparing the education regimes

As there are always some parents who choose public education for their children, depending on the coverage of the public education system, this leaves four cases to be considered.

In the public regime, all children go to public school. Under segregation, all skilled parents send their children to private school, while unskilled parents use public schools. In the two partial segregation regimes, either the skilled (1) or the unskilled (2) parents are indifferent between public and private schools (Table 5.3). We now turn to the question under which condition each education regime arises. Proposition 5.7 summarizes the results.

Proposition 5.7 Occurrence of education regimes
Whether public schooling can arise in equilibrium depends on the preference parameters γ and η. Let $\hat{\eta} = (1 - \eta)^{1-\frac{1}{\eta}}$ and $\hat{\gamma} = \hat{\eta}/\eta$.
If $\gamma > \hat{\gamma}$, public education is not an equilibrium outcome. Segregation arises if the conditions

$$x^B > \frac{\hat{\eta}(1 + z^B)}{1 + z^B + \gamma\eta} \tag{5.38}$$

and

$$x^B \geqslant \frac{1 + z^B}{z^B} \left(1 - \frac{\hat{\eta}}{1 + z^B + \gamma\eta} \right) \tag{5.39}$$

are satisfied. Partial segregation (1) (skilled are indifferent) arises if (5.38) is violated, and partial segregation (2) (unskilled are indifferent) arises if (5.39) is violated.

If $\gamma < \hat{\gamma}$, partial segregation (2) (unskilled are indifferent) never arises. Public education is an equilibrium if

$$x^B \leqslant \frac{\hat{\eta}}{1 + \gamma\eta} \tag{5.40}$$

holds, segregation arises if (5.38) is satisfied, and partial segregation (1) arises if both (5.40) and (5.38) are violated.

Proof: For the public regime to be an equilibrium, a skilled person should weakly prefer public schooling to private schooling, given the tax rate and schooling level that prevail in this regime. If this condition is satisfied for a skilled parent, the same follows for an unskilled parent. The constraint takes the form:

$$u^B \left[v, \hat{n}, 0, s \right] \geqslant u^B [v, \tilde{n}, e^B, 0].$$

After substituting v, $\hat{n}$, s, $\tilde{n}$, and e^B by their equilibrium values, the condition leads to (5.40).

Thus, the relative income of skilled workers x^B should be below a certain threshold for them to stay in the public schools. Two cases can be distinguished. If this threshold is larger than 1, the public regime will emerge if x^B lies between 1 and this threshold. If the threshold is lower than 1 (for example, if γ is large), then the public regime cannot arise in equilibrium.

For the segregated regime to arise in equilibrium, two participation constraints have to be met. First, the skilled persons should have no incentive to go to public schools, and second, the unskilled persons should have no incentive to go to private schools. The first constraint can be written as:

$$u^B \left[v, \hat{n}, 0, s \right] \leqslant u^B [v, \tilde{n}, e^B, 0].$$

After substituting v, $\hat{n}$, s, $\tilde{n}$, and e^B by their equilibrium values, the constraint leads to (5.38). Hence x^B has to be sufficiently large for the skilled persons to stay in the private schools. Intuitively, the gain from private schooling is a function of the income of the parent, with the gain the greater the greater the income. The right-hand side of (5.38) tends to the one of equation (5.40) (public regime) as z^B goes to zero. It is increasing in z^B and concave, and tends to $\hat{\eta} > 1$ as z^B goes to infinity. When $\gamma > \hat{\gamma}$, the constraint never binds for small z^B, but it can always be binding for large z^B since $\hat{\eta} > 1$. More precisely, when $\gamma > \hat{\gamma}$, the right-hand side of equation (5.38) starts below the line $x^B = 1$ for low z^B, crosses the line at the point:

$$z^B = \frac{\hat{\eta} - (1 + \gamma \eta)}{1 - \hat{\eta}}, \tag{5.41}$$

and then goes to $\hat{\eta}$.

The second constraint (unskilled parents do not choose private school) can be written as:

$$u^A \left[v, \hat{n}, 0, s \right] \geqslant u^A [v, \tilde{n}, e^A, 0].$$

After substituting v, $\hat{n}$, s, $\tilde{n}$, and e^A by their equilibrium values, and replacing x^A using equation (5.32), the constraint leads to (5.39). Here again the threshold $\hat{\gamma}$ plays a central role. If $\gamma > \hat{\gamma}$, the right-hand side of equation (5.39) starts from $+\infty$ at $z^B = 0$, decreases, crosses the axis $x^B = 1$ at the point given in equation (5.41), and then converges to 1 from below as z^B goes to $+\infty$. Since the right-hand sides of equations (5.38) and (5.39) cross the axis $x^B = 1$ at the same point, the two conditions cannot be violated at the same time. For $\gamma < \hat{\gamma}$, the constraint (5.39) never binds.

In the two partial segregation regimes, either the skilled or the unskilled parents are indifferent between public and private schooling. We first consider the case where the skilled are indifferent:

$$u^B \left[v, \hat{n}, 0, s \right] = u^B [v, \tilde{n}, e^B, 0].$$

The equilibrium values for Ψ^B, s, and v are obtained by solving a system of three equations including the indifference condition, $s = s[1, \Psi^B]$, and budget constraint (5.33). We obtain:

$$s = \frac{\eta\phi x^B}{\hat{\eta}},$$

$$v = 1 - \frac{x^B}{\hat{\eta}},$$

$$\Psi^B = \frac{(1 + z^B)(\hat{\eta}/x^B - 1) - \gamma\eta}{\gamma\eta z^B}. \tag{5.42}$$

For partial segregation to occur in equilibrium, the only condition is that the value for Ψ^B in (5.42) is between 0 and 1. It is also necessary that unskilled parents strictly prefer public schooling, but since the skilled are indifferent this condition is automatically satisfied. We therefore need to check only that Ψ^B is between 0 and 1. Using equation (5.42), the constraint $0 < \Psi^B < 1$ holds if:

$$\frac{\hat{\eta}(1 + z^B)}{1 + z^B + \gamma\eta} > x^B > \frac{\hat{\eta}}{1 + \gamma\eta}.$$

This inequality is satisfied when the participation constraints (5.40) and (5.38) are simultaneously violated.

In the second type of partial segregation, it is the unskilled parents who are indifferent between the two types of schools:

$$u^A\left[v, \hat{n}, 0, s\right] = u^A[v, \tilde{n}, e^A, 0].$$

As above, the equilibrium values Ψ^A, s, and v are obtained by solving a system of three equations including the indifference condition, $s = s[\Psi^A, 0]$, and budget constraint (5.33). We obtain:

$$s = \frac{\eta\phi x^A}{\hat{\eta}},$$

$$v = 1 - \frac{x^A}{\hat{\eta}},$$

$$\Psi^A = \frac{(1 + z^B)(x^A - 1/\hat{\eta})}{\gamma\eta}. \tag{5.43}$$

We only need to verify that the skilled always prefer private schooling when the unskilled are indifferent. Using equations (5.32) and (5.43), the constraint

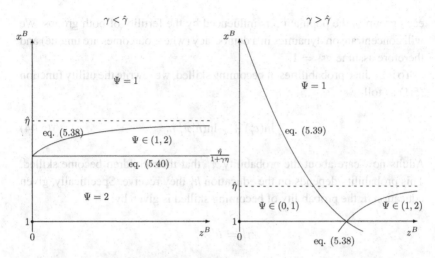

Figure 5.4 The education regimes

$\Psi^A < 1$ holds if:

$$x^B < \frac{1+z^B}{z^B}\left(1 - \frac{\hat{\eta}}{1+z^B+\gamma\eta}\right).$$

This inequality is satisfied when the participation constraint (5.39) is violated.   ■

Figure 5.4 depicts the conditions under which each education regime arises. Two cases can be distinguished depending on the value of γ. If $\gamma < \hat{\gamma}$, then a country with low inequality (low x^B) will choose a public education regime. A country with high inequality will opt for segregation. In between there is a zone in which there is a public sector in which all unskilled and some skilled participate. If $\gamma > \hat{\gamma}$, the public regime is never an equilibrium. Again, high inequality leads to segregation. Moreover, if the share of skilled households in the population is low (low z^B), unskilled people are indifferent between using public and private schools, so that the private sector serves children from both groups.

5.5.6 The dynamics of education regimes

Let us now consider how education feeds back into income and population dynamics. Two dynamic links are key for this relationship. First, a child's probability of becoming skilled depends on its education. Second, the weight of each group in the population is influenced by the fertility of both groups. We will concentrate on dynamics in a democracy (where outcomes are unique) and therefore assume $\varpi^i = 1$.

To introduce probabilities of becoming skilled, we rewrite the utility function (5.1) as follows:

$$\ln(c_t^i) + \gamma \ln(n_t^i \pi_t^i). \tag{5.44}$$

Adults now care about the probability π_t^i that their children become skilled. This probability depends on the education h_t^i they receive. Specifically, given education h, the probability of becoming skilled is given by:

$$\pi_t^i = \mu^i\, h_t^\eta.$$

If we plug this function into (5.44) we recover the original form of the utility function (5.1) up to a constant. We denote the complement probability $1 - \pi_t^i$ as $\bar{\pi}_t^i$. Note that equation (5.4) can be used to define an upper bound on μ^i such that the probabilities belong to $(0, 1)$. Since x^i is bounded above by w^i, μ^i should belong to $[0, \left((1 - \eta)/(\eta\phi w^i)\right)^\eta]$. The parameter η now measures the elasticity of success with respect to the educational investment. Writing probabilities as a function of education, the population evolves according to:

$$P_{t+1}^A = \left[\hat{n}\Psi_t^A \bar{\pi}^A(s_t) + \tilde{n}(1 - \Psi_t^A)\bar{\pi}^A(e_t^A)\right] P_t^A$$

$$+ \left[\hat{n}\Psi_t^B \bar{\pi}^B(s_t) + \tilde{n}(1 - \Psi_t^B)\bar{\pi}^B(e_t^B)\right] P_t^B \tag{5.45}$$

$$P_{t+1}^B = \left[\hat{n}\Psi_t^A \pi^A(s_t) + \tilde{n}(1 - \Psi_t^A)\pi^A(e_t^A)\right] P_t^A$$

$$+ \left[\hat{n}\Psi_t^B \pi^B(s_t) + \tilde{n}(1 - \Psi_t^B)\pi^B(e_t^B)\right] P_t^B. \tag{5.46}$$

In the previous sections we have seen that all decision problems in the model are static in nature. An inter-temporal equilibrium is therefore a sequence of time-t equilibria held together by the laws of motion of the state variables. Existence and uniqueness of time-t equilibria imply the same properties for inter-temporal equilibria.

Definition 5.3 Political economy inter-temporal equilibrium

Given initial conditions $(P_0^i)_{i=A,B}$, an inter-temporal equilibrium is a sequence of time-t equilibria with $\{P_t^i\}_{t\geqslant 0,\ i=A,B}$ satisfying equations (5.45)–(5.46) at all dates $t > 0$.

Proposition 5.8 Existence and uniqueness of inter-temporal equilibria
Given initial conditions $\{P_0^i\}_{i=A,B}$, an inter-temporal equilibrium exists and is unique.

We now analyze the dynamic behavior of the economy. The evolution of the population is described by equations (5.45)–(5.46). Rewriting the law of motion in terms of z_t^B gives:

$$z_{t+1}^B = \frac{\hat{n}\Psi_t^A \pi^A(s_t) + \tilde{n}(1 - \Psi_t^A)\pi^A(e_t^A) + \left[\hat{n}\Psi_t^B \pi^B(s_t) + \tilde{n}(1 - \Psi_t^B)\pi^B(e_t^B)\right]z_t^B}{\hat{n}\Psi_t^A \bar{\pi}^A(s_t) + \tilde{n}(1 - \Psi_t^A)\bar{\pi}^A(e_t^A) + \left[\hat{n}\Psi_t^B \bar{\pi}^B(s_t) + \tilde{n}(1 - \Psi_t^B)\bar{\pi}^B(e_t^B)\right]z_t^B}$$

$$\equiv \Gamma(z_t^B). \tag{5.47}$$

Proposition 5.9 Global dynamics
The dynamics described by $z_{t+1}^B = \Gamma(z_t^B)$ are bounded, and always admit a steady state in $\mathbb{R}_+$.

Proof: We compute the limits of the function Γ defined in equation (5.47) when z_t^B goes to zero and to infinity; both $\Gamma(0)$ and $\lim_{z \to \infty} \Gamma(z)$ are strictly positive and finite. Since Γ is a continuous function on $\mathbb{R}_+$ and converges to finite values on the border of its definition set, it is bounded from above. Hence, dynamics of z_t^B are bounded. Since $\Gamma(0) > 0$ and $\Gamma(z) < z$ for large z, there is at least one $\bar{z}$ such that $\Gamma(\bar{z}) = \bar{z}$ and $\bar{z}$ is a steady state.   ∎

The dynamics of z^B do not always converge to the steady state whose existence is guaranteed by the proposition. Since $\Gamma(0) > 0$ and $\Gamma(z) < z$ for large z, there is always a steady state $\bar{z}$ for which $\Gamma'(\bar{z}) < 1$. There are examples where the steady state is locally stable ($-1 < \Gamma'(z) < 1$), and other examples where $\Gamma'(z) < -1$ and the steady state is unstable. In the latter case, deterministic ever-lasting fluctuations may occur. Figure 5.5 provides such an example.[7] The lower panel depicts the law of motion; it has two increasing segments and one decreasing. The upper panel shows the education regime that each z_t^B corresponds to. The declining schedule in the upper panel depicts the mapping (5.31) from z_t^B into x_t^B. We see that the declining part of the law of motions corresponds to values for z_t^B, which gives rise to the partial segregation regime. The increasing segment of the law of motion above the 45-degree line corresponds to segregated education and the increasing segment below the 45-degree line arises under public education. The steady state (thick dot) lies in the decreasing segment and is locally unstable. Instead there exists a limit cycle of period 2 (hollow dots) to which dynamics converge. The economy reverts back and forth

---

[7] The parameters are: $\eta = 0.4$, $\phi = 0.075$, $\gamma = 0.2$, $w^B = 3$, $\mu^B = 1.7$, and $\mu^A = 0.75$.

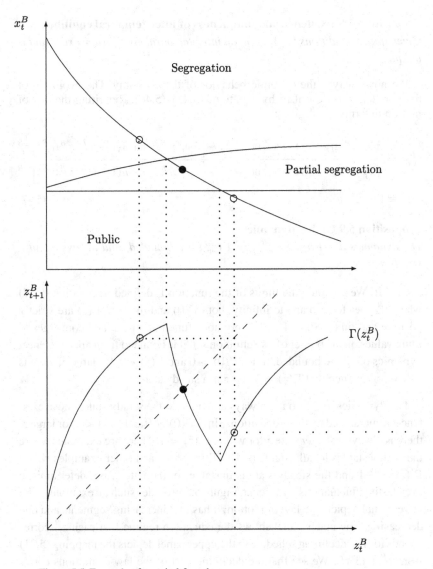

Figure 5.5 Example of a period-2 cycle

between the public and the segregation regime, suggesting periodic swings in the balance between the public and private provision of education.

Further insights on dynamics can be obtained within the public regime. We now provide conditions under which a locally stable steady state exists in this regime. To specialize to public education, we replace Ψ_t^A and Ψ_t^B in equation

(5.47) by 1, and s_t by its optimal value $s[1, 1]$:

$$z_{t+1}^B = \frac{\pi^A(s[1, 1]) + \pi^B(s[1, 1])z_t^B}{\bar{\pi}^A(s[1, 1]) + \bar{\pi}^B(s[1, 1])z_t^B}.$$ (5.48)

Equation (5.48) can be solved for a unique positive steady state:

$$z^B = \frac{\pi^A(s[1, 1])}{1 - \pi^B(s[1, 1])}.$$ (5.49)

Using equation (5.31), the corresponding level of x^B is:

$$x^B = \frac{w^B\left(1 - (\mu^B - \mu^A)(s[1, 1])^\eta\right)}{1 - (\mu^B - \mu^A w^B)(s[1, 1])^\eta}.$$ (5.50)

We now provide a condition for a steady state inside the public regime and show that it is always locally stable.

Proposition 5.10 Dynamics with public education

If:

$$w^B < \frac{\hat{\eta}\left(1 - \mu^B(s[1, 1])^\eta\right)}{(1 + \gamma\eta)\left(1 - \mu^B(s[1, 1])^\eta\right) + \mu^A(1 + \gamma\eta - \hat{\eta})(s[1, 1])^\eta},$$

the dynamics of the public regime admit a steady state given by equations (5.49) and (5.50), which is locally stable.

Proof: The upper bound on w^B is defined by the participation constraint (5.40). Linearizing (5.48) around the steady state, we find that the condition

$$|(\mu^B - \mu^A)s[1, 1]^\eta| < 1$$

is a necessary and sufficient condition for local stability. Since $\mu^B s[1, 1]^\eta < 1$ and $\mu^A s[1, 1]^\eta < 1$, this condition always holds. ∎

If the skill premium w^B is too large, there is no steady state in the public regime. Otherwise, if an economy starts in the public regime not too far away from the steady state, it will converge to the steady state. Convergence is monotonous if $\mu^B > \mu^A$, i.e. if children of skilled parents have a higher probability of becoming skilled than children of unskilled parents for a given level of education. This stability result is consistent with the fact that countries having a public regime tend to stay in this regime (see Chapter 6). In the remaining education regimes, analytic solutions for steady states and stability are not available. Private spending e_t^A and e_t^B and public spending s_t will all depend on z_t^B, which makes equation (5.47) depend on higher powers of z_t^B.

5.6 Extensions to an ethnic dimension

We analyzed above the choice of public spending on education when voters differ in income. Then we looked at how this choice maps into segregation, where segregation means a situation where rich and poor do not attend the same type of school. An interesting extension would be to consider another dimension of heterogeneity, such as ethnicity or religion. Let us call this dimension "type." When the distribution of income and the distribution of types are correlated, which seems to be the case in many countries (the extreme example being probably Namibia, see Weiland (2011)), we can readily apply our results on segregation by income to segregation by type. Two factors are key in determining whether some groups will resort to private schools: income inequality and democracy.

Dottori and Shen (2008) extend the model of this chapter by considering a migrant population which is not entitled to vote. Their conclusions could be applied in a context where there is a poor population of an ethnic minority which is excluded from the political system. When the size of this low-skilled minority is large, they find that wealthy households from the majority group are likely to opt out from public into private schools. Four main effects of the presence of the minority are taken into account: (1) greater congestion in public school; (2) lower average tax base for education funding; (3) reduced low-skilled wage and so more low-skilled majority households' dependence on public education; (4) higher skill premium, which induces high-skilled majority households to privately invest in their children's education and hence weakens their support to finance public school. Moreover, with endogenous fertility, the opting-out decision taken by some majority parents results in a fertility differential between majority and minority households: the minority will grow in size but become relatively poorer and poorer.

In general, introducing the ethnic variable into the model would lead to at least one important conclusion. It should still be true that parents sending their children to private schools have fewer children – because they face a tradeoff between quality and quantity of children through their budget constraint. This is important for the dynamics of population described in the introduction. The ethnic group that relies on public school multiplies faster – and its population share in the economy thus increases over time.

Taking ethnicity into account, it would be relevant to introduce peer effects into the production of education. This means that people like to send their children to schools populated by children of the same "type." This would reinforce the strategic complementarities introduced above. When everyone of a given type with political power uses private schools, a given individual does not want to switch to the public system since both the quality of the public schooling is low and the other people of their type are not in public schools. We may therefore expect peer effects to enlarge the scope for multiple equilibria. Vicious and virtuous circles would be stronger in a divided society.

5.7 Conclusion

The degree of private involvement in the provision of education varies a great deal across countries, ranging from fully public systems as in some European countries to segregated systems as in parts of the US. In this chapter, we try to understand how countries choose the mix of public and private education and how the presence of private schools affects the quality of public education.

First, we conclude that high inequality maps into a segregated education system. In our model's segregated system, the quality of public schools is sufficiently low to induce rich households to pay for private schools to enhance the education of their children. When inequality is low, meanwhile, the rich decide to send their children to public schools, so that they avoid paying for education twice (first through taxes, second through private schools).

Second, we find that as long as the poor have equal weight in the political system, a larger share of private schooling is associated with a higher quality of public schooling. While total tax revenue declines as the share of private schooling increases, the number of students who use public schools declines even faster, implying that the funding level per student increases.

Turning to the role of political power, we find that the quality and extent of public schooling generally increase with the political weight of the poor. In addition, in societies that are dominated politically by the rich, multiple equilibria in the determination of education spending may arise. When the rich are in charge, there is a complementarity between the number of rich people participating in public schools and their quality. For given initial conditions, such a country may have either a high-quality public schooling system in which many or all of the rich participate, or a low-quality system with all the rich using private schools.

6

Empirical evidence

The theory developed in Chapter 5 makes predictions about how the quality and extent of private and public schooling are determined at the aggregate level, and about how schooling and fertility choices vary across households within a given political entity. In this chapter, we compare these predictions to data. We start by focusing on state-level variation in the extent and quality of public education in the United States. This setting is well suited to examining the predictions of our theory for democratic countries, since all US states operate within the same overall political framework, while exhibiting considerable variation in schooling policies as well as the distribution of income. Moreover, we are able to link state-level evidence to household data from the US Census to assess the micro implications of our theory. We then extend the analysis to cross-country data, which allows us to probe the theory's predictions for non-democratic countries. Here we use data from the OECD and the World Bank on public and private education spending, as well as micro data from the OECD Program for International Student Assessment (PISA).

6.1 Inequality, fertility, and schooling across US states

Our model predicts that in a democracy, the choice of public versus private schooling and the level of funding of public schooling are driven by income inequality (see Proposition 5.3). In particular, a state with higher income inequality should exhibit a higher share of private schooling, lower overall spending on public schooling, but higher public education spending per student. In addition, the model predicts that a high-inequality state will have a

This chapter uses some material published in de la Croix and Doepke (2009).

relatively low fertility rate, because parents who send their children to private school economize on fertility. In this section, we examine whether these predictions hold up across US states.

We computed state-level measures of income inequality, average fertility, and the share of private schooling from the 2000 US Census.[1] We correlate these variables with a number of measures of the spending on and the quality of public schooling. In line with the set-up of our theory, we focus on financial measures. As an overall spending measure, we use public education spending per capita in each state (this corresponds to the tax rate v in the model). For the quality of public education (corresponding to the variable s in the model), we consider three alternative measures. "Total current expenditure per student" is a measure of total spending for day-to-day operation of schools, which includes all expenditures of public schools apart from debt repayments, capital outlays, and programs outside of preschool to grade 12. One concern with this broad measure is that it includes some items that may not have a direct educational impact. Therefore, we also use the variable "Total instruction expenditure per student," which includes only expenditures associated directly with student–teacher interaction such as teacher salaries and benefits, textbooks and other teaching supplies, and purchased instructional services. Finally, as an alternative measure of the quality of instruction, we use "Mean teacher salary," an estimate of the average annual salary of teachers in public elementary and secondary schools.[2]

Table 6.1 shows how income inequality (i.e. the Gini coefficient on household income by state) and the share of private schooling correlate with fertility and measures of education spending and quality across states.[3] The correlations are in line with the predictions of Proposition 5.3. In particular, the correlation between inequality and the share of private schooling is positive, whereas the correlation between inequality and per-capita spending on public education is negative.

Taken by themselves, these results might seem to suggest that more inequality leads to less redistribution in the sense of lower support for public education.

---

[1] The data are from the 1 percent sample of the 2000 US Census, made available at www.ipums.org by Ruggles *et al.* (2004).

[2] The expenditure measures are from the National Center for Education Statistics, "Revenues and Expenditures for Public Elementary and Secondary Education", School Year 2000–2001. The teacher salary data is provided by the National Education Association.

[3] "Gini Coefficient" is computed on 1999 household income by state (data from 2000 US Census). "Share in Private School" is the number of households with at least half of their school-age children in private school as a fraction of the total number of households with at least one child in school (data from 2000 US Census). "Number of Children" is the average number of children per household in the same data set, where children are counted only if the head of household is their parent and if they are currently living in the household.

Table 6.1. *Public schooling across US states: correlations*

	Gini coefficient	Private school share
Private school share	0.39 (2.98)	
Public spending per capita	−0.45 (−3.55)	−0.10 (−0.68)
Public spending per student	0.26 (1.86)	0.52 (4.31)
Public instruction spending per student	0.18 (1.25)	0.49 (3.92)
Mean teacher salary in public schools	0.25 (1.78)	0.57 (4.80)
Average number of children	−0.47 (−3.75)	−0.40 (−3.03)

t-Statistics in parentheses.

However, this is not the case when we consider the quality of public education rather than overall spending. All three measures of the quality of public education are positively correlated with inequality.[4] This verifies the third part of Proposition 5.3.

The surprising finding that the correlation coefficients of education spending per capita and education spending per student are of opposite sign can be accounted for by the effect of private schooling on the quality of public schooling. As inequality rises, more students use private schools, which makes it more affordable to offer a high-quality education to those still in public schools. This effect can be seen even more clearly when we correlate education quality with the share of students in private school (second column of Table 6.1). For all three measures, the correlation is positive and highly significant. Hence, the theoretical implication that as the share of private schooling increases, the quality of the public school should increase as well seems to be well supported in the US data.

To establish that these correlations do not rely on some outliers, we do a graphical analysis of the variables. Figure 6.1 shows a cross plot of the share of private schooling and education spending per capita across US states. The relationship is essentially flat, with a slight negative slope in the regression line. However, even though states with a high share of private education don't exhibit higher education spending per capita (i.e. relative to the state's population), they can still spend more on a per-student basis, precisely because relatively fewer students use the public schools. Figure 6.2 shows that the relationship between

---

[4] The correlation is significant at the 10 percent level for total expenditure per student as well as mean teacher salary.

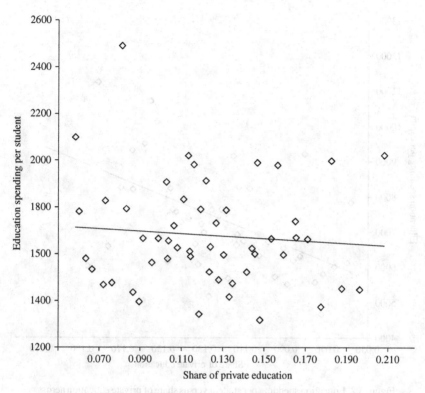

Figure 6.1 Education spending per capita versus share of private education across states

private schooling and education spending per student in public schools across US states is indeed clearly positive.

The finding has important implications for the relationship of inequality and redistribution. If one looked only at aggregate spending, one might think that more inequality leads to less redistribution, as posited by Bénabou (2000), among others. However, the per-person transfer to poorer households (i.e. the education quality provided to households using public schools) does in fact go up. This increase is possible because more inequality leads to more targeted transfers, as richer households opt out of the public system.

The last row of Table 6.1 examines predictions for fertility rates. We find that states with more inequality and a higher share of private schooling have a lower fertility rate. This outcome is in accordance with our model: parents economize on the number of children if the direct cost of education is high.

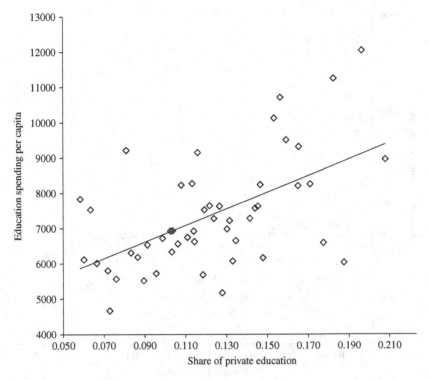

Figure 6.2 Education spending per student versus share of private education across states

6.2 Determinants of fertility and public versus private schooling at the household level

We now examine more closely the inner workings of our model with the help of micro data from the US Census. We want to establish whether the model paints a realistic picture of the interaction between household income, private choices on education and fertility, and the quality of public schooling. This will be useful to assess whether our model indeed provides a plausible mechanism for generating the observed macro correlations. Here, we draw on data on household income, family size (i.e. the household head's own children living in the household), public versus private schooling (for school-age children), and a number of demographic controls from the 1 percent sample of the 2000 US Census.

In the model, a household's decisions on fertility and private versus public schooling depend on two variables: income and the quality of public schooling (see Lemma 5.2 and the preceding discussion). In particular, richer households are predicted to be more likely to choose private schools and to have lower fertility rates. The strength of the income effect depends on the quality of public schooling; for example, if public schooling is of very high quality, even fairly rich households will use public schools. To examine these predictions, Tables 6.2 and 6.3 show regressions of family size and private schooling on household income and a number of controls.[5] We use an ordered logit specification for the fertility choice and a logit specification for the private education choice. All regressions contain dummy variables for the age of the household head as well as for the state of residence (the effect of further controls is discussed below).

The first column of each table presents results for regressions that include only household income in addition to the standard controls. As predicted by the theory, an increase in income is associated with a higher probability of using private schooling and lower fertility.[6] However, in this specification the relationship between household income and fertility is not significant at conventional levels. The remaining columns focus on the joint effect of household income and the quality of public schooling in determining private choices. Each regression contains an additional interaction term of household income with one of our three measures of the quality of public schooling. Notice that schooling quality is measured at the state level, not the household level.[7] In essence, we are still estimating a micro relationship between household income and private choices, but we allow the slope of this relationship to vary systematically across states with a high and a low quality of public education. We find that in both regressions and for all three measures of the quality of public schooling, the estimated coefficient on the interaction term is of the opposite sign to the coefficient on income, which implies that the effect of income on household choices diminishes as the quality of public schooling goes up. When the interaction term is included, all parameter estimates are highly significant, with the one exception of the fertility regression using mean teacher salary as a quality measure.

[5] In order to be able to include households that report zero income, we add $10 to household income before taking logs. The results are qualitatively the same if we shift up incomes by $100 or $500 instead.

[6] The positive effect of income on the probability of private schooling has also been documented by Cohen-Zada and Justman (2003) and Epple *et al.* (2004); see also Nechyba (2006). However, these studies do not consider fertility choices and the interaction of the quality of public schooling across states with income effects.

[7] The fact that schooling quality is a state-level variable also precludes using it in the regression directly, because our regressions already contain state dummies. As a robustness test, we also carried out regressions without state dummies and schooling quality as an included variable, with overall similar results.

Table 6.2. *Estimation results: households' fertility behavior*

		Measure of quality of public education		
		Total expenditure per student	Instruction expenditure per student	Mean teacher salary
Log household income		−0.808 (−3.15)	−0.685 (−3.08)	−0.688 (−1.09)
Interaction income × quality		0.089 (3.15)	0.080 (3.07)	0.063 (1.07)
Total income effect at average quality		−0.013 (−1.11)	−0.012 (−1.11)	−0.012 (−1.11)
		−0.013 (−1.27)	−0.013 (−1.26)	−0.013 (−1.13)

Ordered logit regression of number of children on income and quality of public education. t-statistics in parentheses (standard errors are clustered by state). Data from 2000 US Census. 453,296 observations (households with children). State and age of household dummies in all regressions.

Table 6.3. *Estimation results: households' education behavior*

| | Measure of quality of public education | | |
	Total expenditure per student	Instruction expenditure per student	Mean teacher salary
Log household income	0.557 (17.98)	4.021 (5.69)	3.280 (5.90)	4.894 (2.38)
Interaction income × quality		−0.388 (−4.94)	−0.323 (−4.96)	−0.406 (−2.09)
Total income effect at average quality	0.557 (17.98)	0.569 (28.65)	0.568 (27.01)	0.565 (21.76)

Logit regression of choice of private schooling on income and quality of public education. t-statistics in parentheses (standard errors are clustered by state). Data from 2000 US Census. 311,625 observations (households with children in school). State and age of household dummies in all regressions. Choice of private schooling variable takes the value 1 if at least half of the school-age children in the household attend private schools.

The size of the interaction terms implies substantial variation in the steepness of the income–fertility and income–private schooling relationships across states with a low and high quality of public schooling. In the states with the highest quality of public education, these relationships are essentially flat. This is exactly what one would expect based on the theory: states with high-quality public schooling are close to a fully public regime, i.e. most parents use public schools regardless of income, and fertility varies little across income groups.

The regression results are robust with respect to a number of changes to the specification of the model. We explored sensitivity to racial composition by estimating the regressions separately by race and by including race dummies; we checked urban/rural differences by including a metropolitan area dummy; and we ran the regressions on restricted samples limiting the age range of the included households. Generally, the sign and significance of the interaction term in the two regressions are robust to these changes, as are the sign and significance of the total income effect in the education equation. The sign of the total income effect in the fertility regression turns out to be more sensitive. In particular, for black and Hispanic households the total income effect is strongly negative, whereas for white households it is positive. However, when we restrict the sample to the ages 25–45, the total income effect once again is negative and significant. This suggests that for older white people, the slope of the relation between fertility and income can be reversed. However, even in the case of a positive slope, the sign of the interaction term remains the same.

6.3 Schooling over time

We now turn to the determinants of education systems across countries. Compared with our analysis of education in US states, cross-country data pose additional challenges. There are substantial differences in the level of development and in unobserved variables such as the political system, religious values, etc. across countries which could have independent effects on the variables of interest. The literature contains few empirical studies on the determinants of the mix between public and private education across countries. One exception is James (1993), who regresses private enrollments shares for fifty countries around 1980 on a number of determinants, and concludes that cultural factors such as religious competition and linguistic heterogeneity play an important role. However, the small number of observations compared with the number of explanatory variables casts some doubt on the robustness of the results. Here we do not intend to do full justice to the arising empirical issues but to focus

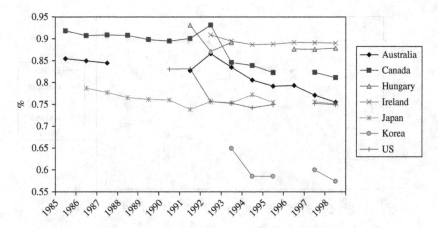

Figure 6.3 Share of public education over time – declining cases

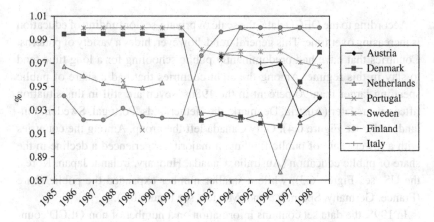

Figure 6.4 Share of public education over time – high and constant cases

on documenting the fundamental correlations and micro relationships implied by our theory.

The OECD provides internationally comparable data on the relative proportions of public and private investment in education for the period 1985–1998 – see Figures 6.3–6.5. In most countries, private-sector expenditure is comprised mainly of household expenditures on tuition and other fees. The exception is Germany, where nearly all private expenditure is accounted for by contributions from the business sector to the system of apprenticeship at the upper secondary level. For primary and lower secondary education, there is little private funding in Germany.

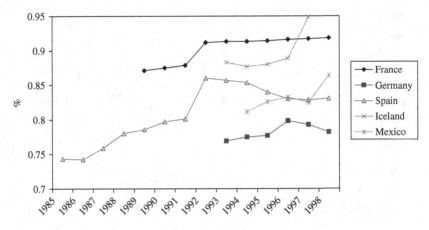

Figure 6.5 Share of public education over time – increasing cases

According to the OECD data, the scale of private-sector funding of education is increasing over time. This general trend, however, hides a variety of patterns. Countries that have had predominantly public schooling for a long time tend to stay in this regime. Among the eight countries that had a share of public spending larger than 90 percent in the 1980s, seven are still in this situation fifteen years later (Austria, Denmark, the Netherlands, Portugal, Sweden, Finland, Italy, see Figure 6.4). Only Canada left the group. Among the countries with a lower share of public funding, a majority experienced a decline in the share of public education (Australia, Canada, Hungary, Ireland, Japan, Korea, the US, see Figure 6.3), while a smaller number expanded the public share (France, Germany, Spain, Iceland, Mexico, see Figure 6.5).

In 1998, the data set contains information on a number of non-OECD countries (Israel, Uruguay, the Czech Republic, Turkey, Argentina, Indonesia, Chile, Peru, Philippines, and Thailand). With observations on thirty-one countries, we can investigate whether inequality is a good predictor of private funding. Computing the correlation between the Gini coefficient for income inequality in 1970 (from Deininger and Squire (1996)) and the share of private funding in 1998, we find that the correlation is positive and strong with a coefficient of 0.44 (t-stat $= 2.64$).[8] The correlation increases to 0.55 (t-stat $= 3.55$) if we consider only the primary and secondary levels of education. Figure 6.6 presents the cross plot of the private share in primary and secondary education with the Gini coefficient.

---

[8] We use the Gini coefficient in 1970 to address possible reverse causality from schooling to inequality.

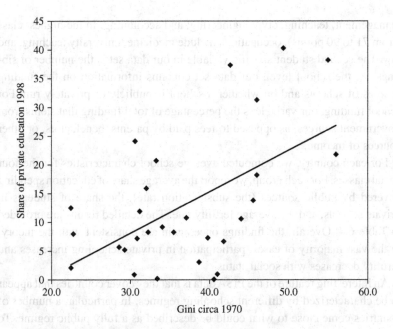

Figure 6.6 Inequality and education systems across countries

6.4 Inequality, fertility, and schooling across countries

We turn next to micro data from the OECD program PISA, collected in the year 2000 on 15-year-old students in the principal industrialized countries. It includes a student questionnaire gathering information about the student's family and a school questionnaire covering information on the extent of public funding and the public or private administration of schools. We focus on four variables in the PISA database. The International Socioeconomic Index (ISEI) captures the attributes of occupations that convert parents' education into income. It was obtained by mapping parents' occupational codes onto an index of occupational status, developed by Ganzeboom *et al.* (1992). This index provides a rough measure of household income and human capital (unfortunately, household income itself is not contained in the database). Using the index, students are assigned to one of four social classes. Typical occupations in the lowest class (between 16 and 35 points on the ISEI scale) include small-scale farmer, metalworker, mechanic, taxi or truck driver, and waiter/waitress. Between 35 and 53 index points, the most common occupations are bookkeeping, sales, small business management, and nursing. As the required skills increase, so does the status of the occupation. Between 54 and 70 points, typical occupations are marketing management, teaching, civil engineering, and accounting. In the highest class (from 71 to 90 points), occupations include medicine, university teaching, and law. The second student-specific variable in our data set is the number of siblings. At the school level, our data set contains information on the funding sources of schools and on whether a school is publicly or privately run. For school funding, our variable is the percentage of total funding that stems from government sources, as opposed to fees paid by parents, benefactors, or other sources of income.

For each country, we computed average school characteristics for the four social classes. For each group, we report the average share of education spending covered by public sources (the subsidization rate), the share of students in private schools, and the average fertility rate. The detailed results are provided in Table 6.4. Overall, the findings once again are consistent with the theory: in the vast majority of cases, participation in private schooling increases and fertility decreases with social status.

An interesting feature of the PISA data is that they cover countries that appear to be characterized by different schooling regimes. In particular, a number of countries come close to what could be described as a fully public regime. To investigate the effects of having a fully public schooling regime, we define countries as fully public if the difference in the subsidization rate between the highest and lowest social class is less than 5 percent. This group includes Hungary, the Czech Republic, Denmark, Finland, Germany, Iceland, Latvia, the Netherlands, Norway, Russia, and Sweden. Table 6.4 also provides the proportion of students attending private schools. The school type is determined by the question "Is your school a public or a private school?" Here public schools are those managed by a public education authority, a government agency, or a governing board that is appointed either by the government directly or elected by public franchise. The remaining countries are classified as being in the segregation regime. We also consider separately the five countries with the highest difference in the public subsidization rate of the lowest and the highest social class (Austria, Australia, Brazil, Mexico, and Spain). In this group, the difference between the subsidization rate of schools attended by members of the top and bottom social classes averages 25 percent.

Table 6.5 provides a number of statistics for the groups of countries with different education regimes. Not surprisingly, in the fully public group the level of public subsidization is particularly high, with an average of 96 percent. These countries are also characterized by low-income inequality (average Gini: 24.7), and the fertility differential between the bottom and top social classes is only 0.36. In all the countries we find that the fertility of the lowest social class exceeds the fertility of the highest social group. In a majority of countries, the

Table 6.4. *PISA data: education, fertility, and social status (1)*

Country	Social status	Number of observations	Subsidization rate	Percent in private schools	Fertility
Australia	16–35	939	76.95	NA	3.30
	36–53	1777	72.33	NA	3.05
	54–70	1607	65.04	NA	2.94
	71–90	542	58.77	NA	2.83
Austria	16–35	874	95.52	4.46	2.81
	36–53	2213	91.60	9.26	2.58
	54–70	992	86.19	16.23	2.40
	71–90	276	80.62	26.09	2.63
Belgium	16–35	1558	89.21	68.87	3.01
	36–53	2388	88.08	75.63	2.59
	54–70	1573	85.46	81.25	2.66
	71–90	516	84.76	83.33	2.75
Brazil	16–35	1699	87.93	2.35	3.67
	36–53	831	79.52	10.59	3.36
	54–70	926	66.77	23.00	3.07
	71–90	125	41.60	49.60	2.86
Canada	16–35	6502	90.36	0.00	3.07
	36–53	9536	89.94	0.00	2.84
	54–70	9006	87.83	0.00	2.81
	71–90	2302	85.12	0.00	2.86
Czech Republic	16–35	1064	93.07	7.33	2.81
	36–53	2741	94.06	6.20	2.48
	54–70	1141	94.71	6.22	2.32
	71–90	309	95.25	6.47	2.19
Denmark	16–35	883	95.11	20.50	3.05
	36–53	1445	94.75	23.18	2.81
	54–70	1130	94.42	24.78	2.88
	71–90	271	94.50	25.46	2.87
Finland	16–35	1010	99.84	1.58	3.26
	36–53	1911	99.85	3.30	2.94
	54–70	1453	99.83	3.51	2.86
	71–90	381	99.78	4.72	2.88
France	16–35	1191	78.29	22.50	3.14
	36–53	1443	75.57	21.83	2.62
	54–70	929	73.36	20.67	2.61
	71–90	268	69.29	26.12	2.89

Table 6.4. *(cont.) PISA data: education, fertility, and social status (2)*

Country	Social status	Number of observations	Subsidization rate	Percent in private schools	Fertility
Germany	16–35	887	97.89	2.03	2.77
	36–53	1970	97.84	3.40	2.46
	54–70	1105	96.56	6.52	2.38
	71–90	357	96.11	7.84	2.46
Greece	16–35	1278	85.63	1.10	2.68
	36–53	1447	87.02	2.07	2.44
	54–70	1074	82.60	4.38	2.31
	71–90	280	72.52	15.71	2.24
Hungary	16–35	1022	85.76	3.82	2.74
	36–53	2070	86.68	4.01	2.42
	54–70	1281	88.20	3.51	2.30
	71–90	261	90.18	6.13	2.38
Iceland	16–35	572	99.58	0.00	3.80
	36–53	1300	99.52	0.62	3.46
	54–70	926	99.10	1.30	3.37
	71–90	364	98.82	1.92	3.46
Ireland	16–35	990	94.68	50.71	3.94
	36–53	1463	91.43	63.98	3.52
	54–70	1040	87.83	72.21	3.33
	71–90	183	81.23	78.69	3.25
Italy	16–35	1391	79.47	2.16	2.45
	36–53	1995	74.50	5.81	2.30
	54–70	896	74.53	5.80	2.22
	71–90	281	71.17	6.05	2.34
Korea	16–35	1554	53.63	47.23	2.46
	36–53	1840	48.12	50.00	2.25
	54–70	803	46.47	49.69	2.18
	71–90	96	42.19	45.83	2.20
Mexico	16–35	1607	44.74	3.17	4.33
	36–53	1134	40.15	17.20	3.74
	54–70	619	34.52	33.60	3.39
	71–90	222	29.87	49.55	2.95
Netherlands	16–35	480	94.93	72.92	3.09
	36–53	739	94.59	77.00	2.80
	54–70	807	93.86	76.70	2.79
	71–90	153	94.85	71.90	2.86

Table 6.4. *(cont.) PISA data: education, fertility, and social status (3)*

Country	Social status	Number of observations	Subsidization rate	Percent in private schools	Fertility
New Zealand	16–35	643	84.82	0.78	3.56
	36–53	1275	81.16	3.61	3.20
	54–70	1041	78.20	5.86	3.07
	71–90	339	73.19	12.39	2.86
Norway	16–35	418	99.57	0.72	3.40
	36–53	1737	99.71	0.63	2.98
	54–70	1148	99.53	1.13	2.99
	71–90	538	99.39	1.12	2.95
Poland	16–35	1052	94.78	0.38	3.07
	36–53	1449	92.08	2.00	2.75
	54–70	564	91.24	4.08	2.49
	71–90	156	82.51	13.46	2.45
Portugal	16–35	1843	89.10	7.27	2.67
	36–53	1501	86.67	6.46	2.33
	54–70	747	83.58	8.17	2.23
	71–90	278	77.73	7.55	2.28
Russia	16–35	1594	94.19	0.00	2.91
	36–53	2742	93.38	0.00	2.71
	54–70	1135	92.94	0.00	2.66
	71–90	828	94.15	0.00	2.44
Spain	16–35	2078	90.92	24.01	2.60
	36–53	2020	82.93	42.48	2.36
	54–70	902	73.21	55.21	2.40
	71–90	387	59.13	68.22	2.50
Switzerland	16–35	1290	98.28	2.56	2.93
	36–53	2398	96.20	5.50	2.58
	54–70	1351	93.73	8.44	2.54
	71–90	582	89.72	13.40	2.68
United Kingdom	16–35	1858	98.24	0.65	3.44
	36–53	3166	96.50	2.46	2.99
	54–70	2276	89.99	8.92	2.82
	71–90	856	84.93	14.02	2.82
United States	16–35	584	94.01	4.11	3.80
	36–53	840	92.42	5.12	3.54
	54–70	899	92.84	5.01	3.10
	71–90	202	87.18	7.92	3.02

Table 6.5. *Statistics for countries with different education regimes*

	Number of countries	Gini in the 1980s	Share of public funding	Funding difference between poor and rich	Fertility differential between poor and rich
Fully public regime	11	24.7	0.96	0.00	0.36
Segregation regime	18	34.6	0.81	0.14	0.47
Top 5 most segregated	5	44.6	0.69	0.25	0.69
Correlation with Gini			−0.58 (3.65)	0.76 (5.96)	0.53 (3.21)

t-Statistics in parentheses.

relationship between fertility and social status is monotonically decreasing; in some countries, it is U-shaped.

In contrast, the group of countries in the segregation regime has an average Gini of 34.6 and a fertility differential of 0.47. The five countries with the highest level of segregation also top the list in terms of inequality and differential fertility: the average Gini coefficient is 44.6 in this group, and the fertility differential between the bottom and top social classes amounts to 0.59. The last row of Table 6.5 presents correlation coefficients between the Gini coefficient and the other variables across all countries in the data set. As predicted by the theory, in countries with higher income inequality average public funding is lower, the subsidization rate is more sensitive to social class, and fertility differentials are larger.[9]

6.5 Public education spending and democracy

We now turn to the implication of our theory concerning the effect of democracy on education politics. Given that data on private spending on education are available for only a few countries, we focus on public spending on education as a fraction of GDP. Here we have a sample of 158 countries covering the period 1970–2002 (with some missing observations; data from World Bank Development Indicators). We divide the sample into three groups, based on their level of democracy. As a democracy indicator, we use the political-rights index from the Freedom in the World Country Ratings. The index lies on a 1–7 scale, with 1 representing the highest degree of freedom. We assign the countries into three groups, where "free" countries have an index of 1, "partially free" have values from 2 to 4, and "non-free" countries have values from 5 to 7.

Table 6.6 displays the mean and variance of public spending on education for the three groups of countries. The mean of spending is increasing with democracy, whereas the variance is decreasing. Figure 6.7 presents a density estimation of the entire distribution of public spending as a share of GDP for the three groups. The density for partially free and non-free countries displays a lower mean and a higher variance. Two-tailed tests of whether the differences are significant are provided in Table 6.7. The mean in democratic (free) countries is significantly different from the one in the two other groups. The variance in the non-free countries is significantly higher than in the partially free countries, where the variance is higher than in the free group. These findings are in line with

[9] One concern here is a reverse causality link whereby school segregation leads to more inequality. The problem is mitigated by the fact that we use Gini coefficients measured twenty years before the observed schooling outcomes.

Table 6.6. *Public education spending and the democracy index*

Democracy index	Observations	Mean	Variance
Free (= 1)	1020	4.96	3.08
Partially free ($1 < x \leqslant 4$)	836	4.11	7.07
Non-free ($4 < x \leqslant 7$)	644	4.07	8.33

Table 6.7. *Public education spending in democracies and non-democracies*

	Mean difference test		Variance ratio test	
	Partially free	Non-free	Partially free	Non-free
Free	0.85 (0.00)	0.89 (0.00)	0.44 (0.00)	0.37 (0.00)
Partially free		0.03 (0.82)		0.85 (0.03)

Note: Mean and variance tests. p-values in parentheses.

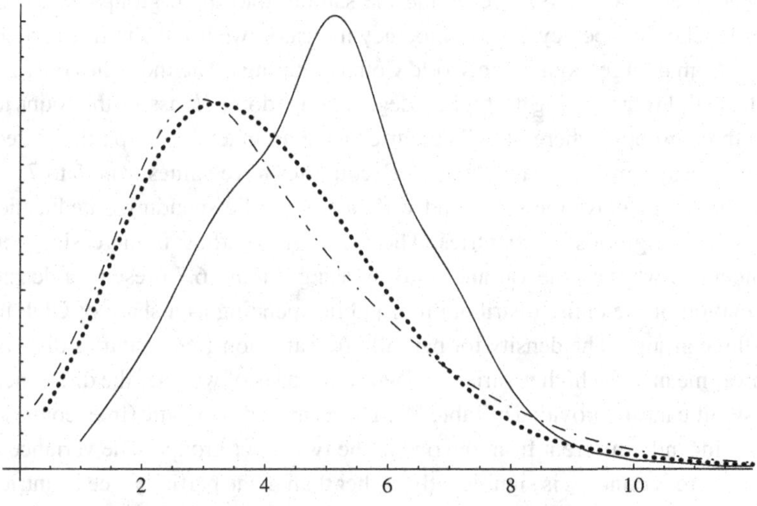

Legend: Free (solid line), partially free (dots), non-free (dashes).
Note: Density estimation using the NonParametrix.m packag by Bernard Gress, 2004

Figure 6.7 Density of public education spending (percent of GDP)

the predictions of our theory for the case of an uneven distribution of political power (see Propositions 5.4 and 5.5). Our mechanism is not the only possible explanation for the observed high variance in public education spending in non-democracies, but it is encouraging that the predictions of the model are in line with data along this dimension also.

6.6 Conclusion

The main predictions of our theory are consistent with a set of stylized facts on public and private schooling in the US as well as in a cross-section of countries. For the US, we document that states with higher inequality have a larger share of private schooling and lower overall spending on public schooling, but a higher quality of public schooling. At the micro level, fertility is decreasing and the probability of using private schools is increasing in income. Moreover, the slope of the income–fertility relationship is flatter in states with a higher quality of public schooling. We obtain similar findings in cross-country data. Using micro data from the OECD PISA program, we confirm that in a large set of countries, high-income households are more likely to use private education, while these households' fertility rates are lower. Comparing across countries, high inequality is associated with a larger share of private schooling.

Concerning the role of political power, we turn to the relationship between democracy and education funding. If we interpret democracies as countries with an even distribution of political power, while non-democracies are biased to the rich, the model of Chapter 5 implies that there is more scope for variation in education systems in non-democracies than in democracies. Indeed, using a cross-section of 158 countries, we find that the variance of public spending across countries is smaller for democracies than for non-democracies.

PART THREE

Sustainability

7

Environmental collapse and population dynamics

The sustainability of societies is questioned in a book by Diamond (2005). His main idea is that non-cooperative behavior may lead economies to collapse. If we have to translate his notion of sustainability into economic terms, we have to cast it in terms of existence of equilibrium.

Definition 7.1 Sustainability *A policy is sustainable if the corresponding intertemporal equilibrium with positive population and resources exists.*

Policy should be understood in a broad sense, including the type of institutions and markets which prevail. The use of "intertemporal" stresses the dynamic nature of sustainability. Let us compare our definition to the original definition of sustainability by the Brundtland Commission (1987): Development is sustainable if "[it] meets the needs of the present without compromising the ability of future generations to meet their own needs." While this definition seems pretty clear, at least in immediate terms of intergenerational justice, it turns out to be quite hard to incorporate in the corpus of economic theory in a rigorous way.

Roughly speaking, sustainability involves two types of issues. On the one hand, sustainability insists on the importance of perpetuity, of not jeopardizing the capacity of the Earth or of humankind to go ahead with existing. On the other hand, it embodies a concern as to the intergenerational path to be followed by our societies: is our consumption such that future generations will be able to have the same level of consumption as well? Are we going to transfer them a planet in a worse state? Is growth in whichever of its forms sustainable at all? In short, there are two ideas: could we make sure that humanity continues and are we being fair towards each of the coming generations? Our definition above addresses well the perpetuity issue, as the existence of equilibrium guarantees positive

This chapter uses some material published in de la Croix and Dottori (2008).

population and resources from now on to infinity. However, it abstracts from any notion of intergenerational justice. "Sustainability as a theory of justice" is left aside. Notice nevertheless that "just and sustainable" equilibria would be a subset of our "sustainable" equilibria.

In this chapter, we show how some institutions (policy) may lead to unsustainable outcomes using a picturesque allegory: Easter Island. The collapse of Easter Island's civilization has fascinated historians, sociologists, anthropologists, and biologists, and, since the seminal article by Brander and Taylor (1998), economists. Easter Island's tragedy is a good starting point to think about sustainability, and the interaction between population and the environment.

Brander and Taylor (1998) explain Easter Island's collapse assuming that the fertility rate increases with the use of renewable resource (i.e. harvesting), while the increased exploitation of resources necessary to feed people encounters decreasing returns. Following Brander and Taylor (1998), the economic literature on Easter Island has usually assumed mechanistic dynamics of population growth, following a Malthusian approach according to which fertility is regulated by nutrition. In such a world, the birth rate is increasing with material living standards, while material living standards and natural resources decline as population increases.[1] In other sciences, population dynamics often follow a "predator–prey" logic, which is very close to the Malthusian approach. (See, for example, Fletcher *et al.* (2011).)

Another characteristic of the current literature is that highly myopic behavior is often postulated to explain what, from an external viewpoint, looks like irrational over-exploitation of resources leading to the collapse of the society.

We propose an alternative story involving non-cooperative bargaining between clans to share the crop. Each clan's bargaining power depends on its threat level when fighting a war. The biggest group has the highest probability of winning. A clan's fertility is determined ex ante by each group. In the quest for greater bargaining power, each clan's optimal size depends on that of the other clan, and a population race follows. This race may exhaust the natural resources and lead to the ultimate collapse of the society. In addition to well-known natural factors, the likelihood of a collapse turns out to be greater when the cost of war is low, the probability of succeeding in war is highly responsive to the number of fighters, and the marginal return to labor is high.

---

[1] Clark's (2007) first chapters contain a rich description of how this Malthusian logic applies to all pre-1800 societies.

The chapter makes a methodological contribution in that it is the first fertility model to include strategic complementarities between groups' fertility decisions.[2]

7.1 Historical evidence

Easter Island had a rising population and a prosperous civilization until about the fifteenth century, after which it declined sharply. By the eighteenth century, when the island was discovered by European explorers, the population had been decimated. Easter Island is therefore an example of how a closed system can collapse, but what exactly happened is still unresolved.

Data on Easter Island are available from archaeological studies,[3] but they generally lack precision. The timing of events is also far from certain, and sources disagree to a considerable extent. The best-accredited theory is that less than 100 people arrived on Easter Island from the Marquesas Islands around CE 400. Thereafter the population began to increase; however, according to Cohen (1995), the population remained relatively low until CE 1100, when the increase accelerated. The peak was probably reached around CE 1400–1600 at over 10,000 (perhaps as high as 20,000 – see Brander and Taylor (1998)), Reuveny and Maxwell (2001). Figure 7.1 displays the likely evolution of population over time.

In the sixteenth century there was a decline of food consumption with likely episodes of cannibalism around CE 1600 and a big population crash during the seventeenth century. A new religion and a new political order settled down after mid 1600. When Easter Island was discovered by Europeans in CE 1722, estimated population amounted to 3000. At the end of the eighteenth century a reliable estimate is of about 2000. Since the nineteenth century there have been many exogenous shocks (kidnapping for the slave market, epidemics due to foreign germs, etc.) and the island can no longer be considered a closed system.

As far as natural resources are concerned, island forest was at its carrying capacity when the first settlers arrived. Cutting trees would have begun almost immediately in order to have firewood and land for agriculture, and to make canoes. The process of deforestation was reinforced during the *moai* construction period since trees were cut to facilitate the transportation of the statues. The

[2] In his conclusion, Lagerlöf (2006) evokes a mechanism close to ours, suggesting that if population size is an input in land acquisition, clans have an extra motive for high fertility. Good and Reuveny (2007) mention that in some episodes population growth was enhanced by the need for a large army.

[3] For more details see Flenley and Bahn (2003), Keegan (1993), Ponting (1991).

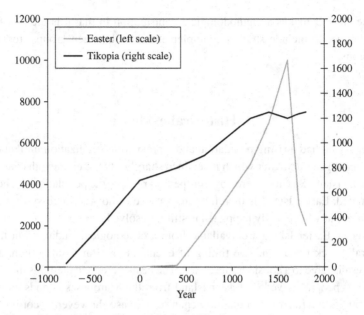

Figure 7.1 Population of Easter Island and Tikopia

rate of deforestation reached its peak around CE 1400, and the forest clearance was probably completed by CE 1600. In CE 1722 when the island was discovered by Europeans, there were basically no trees. The fifteenth century is rated to be the period of maximum deforestation. Figure 7.2 illustrates the deforestation process by reporting the occurrence of forest pollen as a percentage of total pollen over time (from Flenley *et al.* (1991)). The deforestation had a clear impact on human life, having "led to leaching and soil erosion, more wind damage, increased soil evaporation and a reduction in crop yields" (Flenley and Bahn (2003), pp. 191–192).

We also have some data on *moai* carving from Van Tilburg and Mach (1995). There were 887 statues on Easter Island, weighing on average 13.78 tons (that is the number of known statues; there are certainly more buried in sediments). The largest *moai* once erected weighs 82 tons. They were constructed between the twelfth and the sixteenth centuries. The fact that *moai* carving ceased around CE 1600 is confirmed by Dalton and Coats, when "the tools of the artisan were replaced with tools of war, such as the *mataa* (apparently a dagger or spearhead)."[4]

---

[4] Dalton and Coats (2000) p. 491.

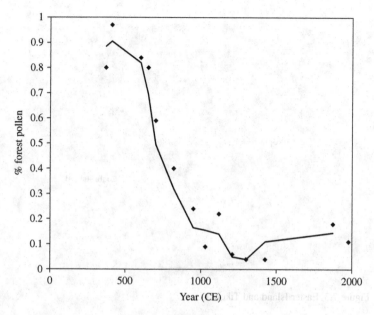

Figure 7.2 Forest coverage on Easter Island

Tikopia is another small island in the Pacific Ocean that provides an interesting contrast (Figure 7.3 shows both islands on the globe). It is similar to Easter Island in many ways, but no collapse occurred and a long-lasting society with relatively stable population evolved. The population reached 1200 in the eleventh century and stayed approximately constant from then on; the environment remains well preserved. Tikopians managed to control population growth (unlike Easter Islanders), thus avoiding the over-exploitation of resources.

Tikopia is located in the far east of the Solomon Islands; culturally and linguistically its people are of Polynesian stock.[5] A small group of Polynesians, probably from the East, settled on Tikopia about BCE 900 and lived by slash-and-burn agriculture. Around BCE 100 the economy began to change – "initially high yields from the wild resources of land and sea were seriously reduced by the pressure of harvesting"[6] – and the people began to rear pigs intensively to compensate for the drastic decline in birds and seafood. After a second wave of immigration from West Polynesia, the population reached

[5] For an in-depth study of Tikopian society see Firth (1936), Kirch (1986), and Kirch and Yen (1982).
[6] Kirch and Yen (1982) p. 354.

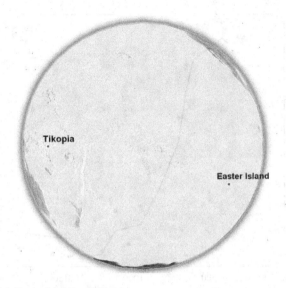

Figure 7.3 Easter Island and Tikopia

1200 and then remained roughly constant (see Figure 7.1). An important decision was taken around the late seventeenth century: to eliminate pigs, which were becoming too costly to feed in terms of resources.

Over-population was avoided by somewhat conscious mechanisms (Kirch (1997)). Several practices can be related to such a purpose: celibacy, prevention of conception, abortion, infanticide, sea voyaging by young males, expulsion of some segment of the population, etc. Firth (1967) reports the existence of a traditional ritual cycle ("the work of the gods") which encoded the ideology of zero-population growth.[7] Kirch and Yen (1982) refer to "a range of social and ritual controls [that] served to maintain population levels" (p. 355).

7.2 The model

The model presented here differs from the ones of the preceding chapter. First, we abstract from education. Second, we introduce a new motive to have children: old-age support. Third, the equilibrium is a Nash Equilibrium rather than a competitive equilibrium.

---

[7] Kirch (1997) rates the text of this ritual as "a remarkable document, unambiguously reflecting the Tikopia ideology of zero-population growth" (p. 40).

7.2.1 Preferences and technology

We consider an overlapping generations framework where agents live for two periods. Every agent belongs to a clan. In each period, the timing of decisions is as follows. Each clan chooses its fertility rate, taking the other's fertility rate as given, and having perfect foresight. A Nash(–Cournot) Equilibrium in fertility rates follows, characterized by a match between the strategy actually played and the strategy expected by the other group. The crop is then shared, following a non-cooperative bargaining process between clans.

Clans were organized along the lines of a genealogical tree. Clan members have a common ancestor, often a son or grandson of the traditional original settler of the island (Sahlins (1955)). For the sake of simplicity we assume that there are only two clans, and that all individuals belong to either one or the other, with no possibility of changing clan membership.

Group i at time t consists of $N_{i,t}$ adults. In the first period the adults are young, they work, they support their parents' consumption and they make fertility choices; in the second part of their lives they consume what their children provide for them. A representative adult belonging to group i receives utility from both periods of consumption and bears a disutility cost from child rearing. For analytical tractability, we assume that households are risk neutral, i.e. preferences are represented by a linear utility function (all results with positive risk aversion are in section 7.6):

$$U_{i,t} = c_{i,t} + \beta d_{i,t+1} - \lambda n_{i,t} \tag{7.1}$$

where $c_{i,t}$ and $d_{i,t+1}$ are the first- and second-period consumption respectively, $n_{i,t}$ is the number of children per adult in group i at time t, $\beta > 0$ is the psychological discount factor, and $\lambda > 0$ is the marginal disutility of child rearing.

In order to ensure marginal decreasing benefits to procreation, we assume that supporting parents costs a fraction $\chi/(1 + n_{i,t-1})$ of young adults' total income $y_{i,t}$. To simplify we assume that $\chi \in (0, 1)$ results from an exogenous social norm.[8] Hence the parent receives a total of:

$$\chi \frac{n_{i,t-1}}{(1 + n_{i,t-1})} y_{i,t}.$$

This formulation introduces the idea that each additional child will bring some additional resources to the parents, but the returns are not constant, since the

---

[8] In the literature on old-age support (Ehrlich and Lui (1991)), the compensation rate χ is determined through self-enforcing implicit contracts. At equilibrium, the value of χ typically depends on longevity and the availability of capital markets.

fraction each child pays decreases with the number of siblings. The chosen formulation makes the support from children a concave function of the number of children. The assumption of decreasing returns in support from children is important to avoid the possibility of offsetting decreasing returns in production just by increasing fertility. Therefore the budget constraint in the first period is:

$$c_{i,t} = \left(1 - \frac{\chi}{1 + n_{i,t-1}}\right) y_{i,t}. \tag{7.2}$$

In the second part of their life, agents are economically supported by their children. Hence the budget constraint is:

$$d_{i,t+1} = n_{i,t} \frac{\chi}{1 + n_{i,t}} y_{i,t+1}. \tag{7.3}$$

The population evolves for each group according to the law of motion:

$$N_{i,t+1} = n_{i,t} N_{i,t}. \tag{7.4}$$

In each period, crop Y_t is obtained according to the production function:

$$Y_t = A(R_t) L^\alpha (N_{1,t} + N_{2,t})^{1-\alpha}$$

where $L = 1$ is the fixed amount of land and $A(R_t)$ is the total factor productivity (TFP) which depends on the stock of natural resources R_t available at time t. The function $A()$ may reflect exogenous conditions determining differences between productivity on Tikopia and Easter Island.

The dynamics of the stock of resources is taken from Matsumoto (2002) as:

$$R_{t+1} = (1 + \delta - \delta R_t / K - b(N_{1,t} + N_{2,t})) R_t, \quad R_0 > 0 \text{ given} \tag{7.5}$$

where $K > 0$ is the carrying capacity, i.e. the maximum possible size of the stock of resources, $\delta > 0$ is the intrinsic growth rate of natural resources, and $b > 0$ is a coefficient weighting the effect of human absorption of resources. Equation (7.5) results from the difference between a logistic "natural" growth rate and a negative human impact on resources. It has the following property:

$$\lim_{t \to \infty} (N_{1,t} + N_{2,t}) = 0 \quad \Rightarrow \quad \lim_{t \to \infty} R_t = K.$$

Let us denote by s group 1's share of the total crop. The representative adult's income can be written as a function of their clan's share as:

$$y_{1,t} = s_t Y_t / N_{1,t};$$
$$y_{2,t} = (1 - s_t) Y_t / N_{2,t}.$$

In the absence of strong property rights and input markets, groups bargain to reach an agreement on crop sharing: if they did not, a war could take place. The bargaining power of each group is affected by its relative size. Therefore under perfect foresight each group has an incentive to increase its fertility in order to increase its threat level in the future. Before studying the bargaining problem analytically let us discuss the two main assumptions on which the mechanism we propose is built.

First, fertility is fixed before the bargaining begins, as a social norm. We may question whether it is not too extreme to assume that clans control their members' fertility. In our framework there is no division between the subjects who are involved in bargaining (the clans) and those who actually have children (all agents are perfectly equal within the clans). In reality the number of children could in fact have been to some extent a social norm: Erickson and Gowdy (2000) refer to archaeological evidence for Tikopia in support of "the adoption of cultural beliefs that incorporated the ethic of zero population growth."

Second, the probability of success in war is ultimately determined by the relative number of individuals able to fight, i.e. young people: when two groups conflict, using basically the same labor-intensive war technology, it is plausible to expect that the bigger group is more likely to win. There is good evidence for episodes of conflict on Easter Island (Keegan (1993), Ponting (1991)), but Diamond (2005) also reports clashes on Tikopia.

7.2.2 The bargaining problem

The outcome of non-cooperative bargaining can be modeled by maximizing a symmetric Nash product (Binmore *et al.* (1986)):

$$(U_{1,t} - \bar{U}_{1,t})^{1/2}(U_{2,t} - \bar{U}_{2,t})^{1/2}$$

where $U_{i,t}$ is the pay-off of group i and $\bar{U}_{i,t}$ is the fall-back pay-off for group i if no agreement is reached. Using equations (7.1), (7.2), and (7.3), the indirect lifetime utilities of a representative member of the current young generation at time t are respectively:

$$U_{1,t} = \left(1 - \frac{\chi}{1 + n_{1,t-1}}\right)\frac{s_t Y_t}{N_{1,t}} + \beta\frac{n_{1,t}\chi}{1 + n_{1,t}}\frac{s_{t+1}Y_{t+1}}{N_{1,t+1}} - \lambda n_{1,t};$$

$$U_{2,t} = \left(1 - \frac{\chi}{1 + n_{2,t-1}}\right)\frac{(1 - s_t)Y_t}{N_{2,t}} + \beta\frac{n_{2,t}\chi}{1 + n_{2,t}}\frac{(1 - s_{t+1})Y_{t+1}}{N_{2,t+1}} - \lambda n_{2,t}.$$

The fall-back pay-off $\bar{U}_{i,t}$ is represented by the utility of a failed agreement. If the parties do not come to an arrangement, they fight. In other words, we can see the emergence of war as a threat to induce compliance. When a war happens, the income is an expected value, since it depends on the probability of the group winning the war. We allow for the possibility that, during the war, a fraction $\omega \in [0, 1)$ of the total crop is wasted. This is likely to occur because fighting often brings about a depletion of resources, or missed production; at the very least the resources are consumed in fighting and so do not provide the usual utility. Moreover, we assume that when a clan wins a war, it appropriates the total crop and that war entails no human loss. This assumption allows the extreme possibility of the extermination of a group (which was probably not the intention of the clans and was also unrealistic in such societies, considering the available weapons and war technology) to be avoided. There is evidence (see Owsley *et al.* (1994)) that struggles very seldom entailed mortal wounds, given the kinds of weapons used, and few fatalities were attributable directly to violence. Hence we assume, like Maxwell and Reuveny (2005), that war does not imply a cost in terms of human life. Since war plays the role of a fall-back outcome that never occurs in the bargaining equilibrium, permitting human loss would simply alter the bargaining power quantitatively without adding substantive insights.

We denote the probability of group 1 winning the war by π_t^ω. We assume that the form of the function $\pi_t^\omega = p(N_{1,t}, N_{2,t})$ relating the winning probability to group sizes satisfies the properties specified in an axiomatic approach by Skaperdas (1996) for contest success functions:

$$p(N_{1,t}, N_{2,t}) = \frac{N_{1,t}^\zeta}{N_{1,t}^\zeta + N_{2,t}^\zeta} \in (0, 1). \tag{7.6}$$

The parameter $\zeta \geqslant 1$ is related to the sensitivity of the probability of winning a war to the size of the clan. It has to be greater than or equal to 1 to guarantee the convexity of the maximization problem. The higher ζ, the greater the influence of the size of the group, so that ζ captures the decisiveness of groups' relative size. The main implication of this is that the ratio of winning probabilities of any two players depends on the ratio of their efforts.

Exercise: An alternative functional form that is frequently used is the logistic:

$$\pi^\omega = \frac{\exp[\zeta(F_1 - F_2)]}{1 + \exp[\zeta(F_1 - F_2)]}$$

where F_i denotes the effort made by group i. This formulation implies that it is the difference between efforts that determines the probability of success. What functional form can we impose on $F()$ to retrieve equation (7.6)?

The fall-back utility of group 1 can be written as:

$$\bar{U}_{1,t} = \pi_t^\omega \left[\left(1 - \frac{\chi}{1+n_{1,t-1}} \right) \frac{(1-\omega)Y_t}{N_{1,t}} \right] + \beta \frac{n_{1,t}\chi}{1+n_{1,t}} \frac{s_{t+1}Y_{t+1}}{N_{1,t+1}} - \lambda n_{1,t}.$$

Notice that fertility has already been chosen when groups bargain, therefore the disutility of child-rearing is not affected by the outcome of the bargaining. Second-period consumption depends on expectations about the next period agreement (s_{t+1}) and output (Y_{t+1}). Perfect foresight is assumed. Notice that the outcome of the bargaining today has no influence on the bargaining tomorrow. The utility net of fall-back is:

$$U_{1,t} - \bar{U}_{1,t} = \left(1 - \frac{\chi}{1+n_{1,t-1}} \right) \left(s_t - \pi_t^\omega(1-\omega) \right) \frac{Y_t}{N_{1,t}};$$

$$U_{2,t} - \bar{U}_{2,t} = \left(1 - \frac{\chi}{1+n_{2,t-1}} \right) \left(1 - s_t - (1-\pi_t^\omega)(1-\omega) \right) \frac{Y_t}{N_{2,t}}.$$

Abstracting from multiplicative constant terms, the net utilities become:

$$U_{1,t} - \bar{U}_{1,t} = s_t - \pi_t^\omega(1-\omega);$$
$$U_{2,t} - \bar{U}_{2,t} = 1 - s_t - (1-\pi_t^\omega)(1-\omega).$$

Using these values the bargaining problem simplifies to:

$$s_t \equiv \arg\max \left[s_t - \pi_t^\omega(1-\omega) \right]^{1/2} \left[1 - s_t - (1-\pi_t^\omega)(1-\omega) \right]^{1/2}. \quad (7.7)$$

Proposition 7.1 Bargaining outcome as a function of population
The bargaining share of the crop for clan 1 is:

$$s_t = \frac{\omega}{2} + \frac{N_{1,t}^\zeta}{N_{1,t}^\zeta + N_{2,t}^\zeta}(1-\omega). \quad (7.8)$$

The following comparative statics results are derived:

$$\frac{\partial s_t}{\partial \omega} = 1/2 - \pi_t^\omega \geqslant 0 \quad \textit{iff } \pi_t^\omega \leqslant 1/2;$$

$$\frac{\partial s_t}{\partial \zeta} = \frac{N_{1,t}^\zeta N_{2,t}^\zeta (1-\omega) \ln\left(\frac{N_{1,t}}{N_{2,t}}\right)}{(N_{1,t}^\zeta + N_{2,t}^\zeta)^2} \geqslant 0 \quad \textit{iff } N_{1,t} \geqslant N_{2,t}.$$

Proof: The first-order condition for Problem (7.7) yields equation (7.8). The second-order condition for a maximum, $[-\omega^2/4]^{-1} < 0$, is satisfied. ∎

An increase in the dead-weight loss ω reduces the fall-back of both groups, but in an asymmetric way depending on the groups' relative size. As equation (7.8) shows, s_t turns out to be a weighted sum of the exogenous contractual power $1/2$ and the endogenous force, due to the likelihood of winning the war, π_t^ω; therefore an increase in the relative weight of the former increases s_t if and only if $1/2 > \pi_t^\omega$. Finally, an increase in the sensitivity of the probability of victory to the numbers of fighters involved determines the advantage of the group with the bigger size.

7.2.3 The fertility choice

Let us now turn to the choice of fertility made by adults at time t. The variable part of the utility, for clans 1 and 2 respectively, is given by:

$$\frac{\beta \chi n_{1,t}}{1+n_{1,t}} \left[\frac{\omega}{2} + \frac{(N_{1,t}n_{1,t})^\varsigma (1-\omega)}{(N_{1,t}n_{1,t})^\varsigma + (N_{2,t}n_{2,t})^\varsigma} \right]$$

$$\times \frac{A(R_{t+1})(N_{1,t}n_{1,t} + N_{2,t}n_{2,t})^{1-\alpha}}{N_{1,t}n_{1,t}} - \lambda n_{1,t}$$

and

$$\frac{\beta \chi n_{2,t}}{1+n_{2,t}} \left[1 - \frac{\omega}{2} - \frac{(N_{1,t}n_{1,t})^\varsigma (1-\omega)}{(N_{1,t}n_{1,t})^\varsigma + (N_{2,t}n_{2,t})^\varsigma} \right]$$

$$\frac{A(R_{t+1})(N_{1,t}n_{1,t} + N_{2,t}n_{2,t})^{1-\alpha}}{N_{2,t}n_{2,t}} - \lambda n_{2,t}.$$

At this point it is worth noting the channels through which endogenous fertility affects utility. There are two kinds of benefits from having more children: a higher old-age support and a strategic motive which operates through an increase in the probability of succeeding in war, and hence through the clan's threat-value in bargaining. Then there are two costs from having children: a direct disutility cost from rearing them, and greater pressure on crops in the next period, as the crops have to be divided among more people.

The first-order conditions for clans 1 and 2 are given by:

$$\frac{1-\omega}{1+n_{1,t}} \frac{\partial \pi_{t+1}^\omega}{\partial n_{1,t}} + \frac{(1-\alpha)N_{1,t}s_{t+1}}{(1+n_{1,t})(N_{1,t}n_{1,t} + N_{2,t}n_{2,t})}$$

$$= \frac{s_{t+1}}{(1+n_{1,t})^2} + \frac{\lambda}{\beta \chi} \frac{N_{1,t}}{Y_{t+1}}; \tag{7.9}$$

$$-\frac{1-\omega}{1+n_{2,t}}\frac{\partial\pi_{t+1}^{\omega}}{\partial n_{2,t}}+\frac{(1-\alpha)N_{2,t}(1-s_{t+1})}{(1+n_{2,t})(N_{1,t}n_{1,t}+N_{2,t}n_{2,t})}$$

$$=\frac{1-s_{t+1}}{(1+n_{2,t})^2}+\frac{\lambda}{\beta\chi}\frac{N_{2,t}}{Y_{t+1}} \qquad (7.10)$$

where s_{t+1} is obtained from equation (7.8), while from equations (7.4) and (7.6) we have:

$$\pi_{t+1}^{\omega}=\frac{(N_{1,t}n_{1,t})^{\zeta}}{(N_{1,t}n_{1,t})^{\zeta}+(N_{2,t}n_{2,t})^{\zeta}}.$$

At optimum the marginal benefit from increasing fertility (the left-hand side of equations (7.9) and (7.10)) equals the marginal cost (the right-hand side). The benefit is represented by the increase in consumption in the second period, due to the larger clan's share and the larger total contribution of their offspring; the cost is represented by the reduction in crop per capita (due to decreasing marginal returns) and the cost of child rearing.

Each group's optimal fertility rate turns out to depend on expectations about the other group's fertility: in this sense we can talk of fertility reaction functions. We assume that when clans choose their own fertility rate they take the other group's one as given, i.e. they behave à la Cournot. A necessary condition for a population race to occur is that fertility reaction functions must have a positive slope, so that it is best for each group to respond to increases in the other group's fertility rate by having more children itself.

Although there is no explicit solution to equations (7.9) and (7.10), we can characterize the solution for a particular parameter configuration as satisfying Assumption 7.1.

Assumption 7.1 *Parameters satisfy* $\zeta=1$, $\omega=0$, $\lambda=0$, *and* $\alpha=1$.

Assumption 7.1 tells us that π_t^{ω} is equal to the proportion of fighters who belong to group 1, there is no dead-weight loss with war, and no disutility from child rearing. Finally $\alpha=1$ means that at every period the island yields a given amount of food depending solely on the stock of natural resources. In this scenario Proposition 7.2 holds.

Proposition 7.2 Population race as a Nash Equilibrium
Under Assumption 7.1:

- *the fertility reaction functions have positive slopes;*

- *the Nash Equilibrium is:*

$$n^*_{1,t} = \sqrt[3]{\frac{N_{2,t}}{N_{1,t}}}, \quad n^*_{2,t} = \sqrt[3]{\frac{N_{1,t}}{N_{2,t}}} \; ; \tag{7.11}$$

- *the Nash Equilibrium is stable.*

Proof: Setting $\omega = 0, \zeta = 1, \lambda = 0, \alpha = 1$ in equations (7.9) and (7.10) we obtain the reaction functions:

$$n_{1,t} = \sqrt{\frac{N_{2,t}}{N_{1,t}} n_{2,t}} \quad \text{and} \quad n_{2,t} = \sqrt{\frac{N_{1,t}}{N_{2,t}} n_{1,t}} \tag{7.12}$$

which show that the best fertility rate for each group is to increase as the other group's fertility increases. At the Nash Equilibrium, there is no incentive for either group to change its fertility rate, given the other group's fertility rate; this amounts to solving the system in equation (7.12), which yields the results in equation (7.11). This solution represents a maximum as:

$$U''_{i,t} = -\frac{2AN_{j,t}\left(2N_{i,t} + \sqrt[3]{\frac{N^4_{i,t}}{N_{j,t}}} + \sqrt[3]{N^2_{i,t}N_{j,t}}\right) R_{t+1}\beta\chi}{\left(N_{j,t} + \sqrt[3]{N^2_{i,t}N_{j,t}} + 2\sqrt[3]{N_{i,t}N^2_{j,t}}\right)^3} < 0.$$

At equilibrium the slopes of the reaction functions are:

$$\frac{\partial n_{i,t}}{\partial n_{j,t}} = \frac{1}{2}\left(\frac{N_{j,t}}{N_{i,t}}\right)^{2/3}.$$

To demonstrate the stability of the Nash Equilibrium, we compute the inverse reaction function of group 2 as $n_{1,t} = n^2_{2,t}(N_{2,t}/N_{1,t})$. The slope of this curve at equilibrium is $(N_{1,t}/N_{2,t})^{2/3}$, which is always greater than for group 1. This ensures that in the $\{n_{2,t}, n_{1,t}\}$ space group 1's reaction function intersects Group 2's from above and the equilibrium is stable. The equilibrium can be reached through adjustments along the reaction functions. ∎

The finding that fertility reaction functions have positive slopes means that there is a strategic complementarity between group sizes, and therefore between the groups' fertility rates as implied by the population race mechanism. It is interesting to observe how the fertility changes if we allow the parameters to be perturbed. The results are summarized in Corollary 7.1 and are illustrated graphically in Figure 7.4.

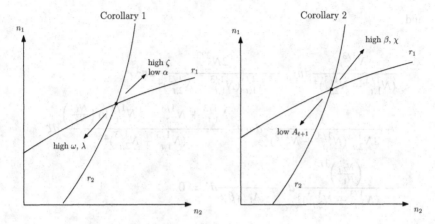

Figure 7.4 Fertility reaction functions (r_1, r_2) and comparative statics

Corollary 7.1 *In the neighborhood of the Nash Equilibrium obtained under Assumption 7.1, the following comparative statics hold:*

$$\frac{\partial n_{i,t}}{\partial \omega} < 0,$$

$$\frac{\partial n_{i,t}}{\partial \zeta} > 0,$$

$$\frac{\partial n_{i,t}}{\partial \lambda} < 0,$$

$$\frac{\partial n_{i,t}}{\partial \alpha} < 0.$$

Proof: Total differentiation of equations (7.9) and (7.10) at the Nash Equilibrium under Assumption 7.1 yields:

$$-\frac{2N_{1,t}^{2/3}}{(N_{1,t}^{1/3} + N_{2,t}^{1/3})^4 N_{2,t}^{1/3}} dn_{1,t} + \frac{N_{2,t}^{1/3}}{(N_{1,t}^{1/3} + N_{2,t}^{1/3})^4} dn_{2,t}$$

$$-\frac{1}{2N_{1,t}^{1/3}(N_{1,t}^{1/3} + N_{2,t}^{1/3})^2} d\omega + \frac{N_{1,t}^{1/3} + N_{2,t}^{1/3} + \frac{1}{3}N_{1,t}^{1/3}\ln\left(\frac{N_{2,t}}{N_{1,t}}\right)}{(N_{1,t}^{1/3} + N_{2,t}^{1/3})^4} d\zeta$$

$$-\frac{\left(\frac{N_{1,t}}{N_{2,t}}\right)^{1/3}}{(N_{1,t}^{1/3} + N_{2,t}^{1/3})^3} d\alpha - \frac{1}{A_{t+1}\beta\chi} d\lambda = 0$$

and

$$\frac{N_{1,t}^{1/3}}{(N_{1,t}^{1/3} + N_{2,t}^{1/3})^4} dn_{1,t} - \frac{2N_{2,t}^{2/3}}{N_{1,t}^{1/3}(N_{1,t}^{1/3} + N_{2,t}^{1/3})^4} dn_{2,t}$$

$$- \frac{1}{2N_{2,t}^{1/3}(N_{1,t}^{1/3} + N_{2,t}^{1/3})^2} d\omega + \frac{N_{1,t}^{1/3} + N_{2,t}^{1/3} + \frac{1}{3}N_{2,t}^{1/3} \ln\left(\frac{N_{1,t}}{N_{2,t}}\right)}{(N_{1,t}^{1/3} + N_{2,t}^{1/3})^4} d\zeta$$

$$- \frac{\left(\frac{N_{2,t}}{N_{1,t}}\right)^{1/3}}{(N_{1,t}^{1/3} + N_{2,t}^{1/3})^3} d\alpha - \frac{1}{A_{t+1}\beta\chi} d\lambda = 0.$$

These expressions can be written in matrix form as:

$$\begin{pmatrix} 1 & -\frac{1}{2}\left(\frac{N_{2,t}}{N_{1,t}}\right)^{2/3} \\ -\frac{1}{2}\left(\frac{N_{1,t}}{N_{2,t}}\right)^{2/3} & 1 \end{pmatrix} \begin{bmatrix} dn_{1,t} \\ dn_{2,t} \end{bmatrix}$$

$$= \begin{pmatrix} \frac{N_{2,t}^{1/3}}{2N_{1,t}}\left[\left(\frac{N_{2,t}}{N_{1,t}}\right)^{1/3} + 1 + \frac{1}{3}\ln\left(\frac{N_{2,t}}{N_{1,t}}\right)\right] & -\frac{(N_{1,t}^{1/3} + N_{2,t}^{1/3})^2 N_{2,t}^{1/3}}{4N_{1,t}} \\ \frac{N_{1,t}^{1/3}}{2N_{2,t}}\left[\left(\frac{N_{1,t}}{N_{2,t}}\right)^{1/3} + 1 + \frac{1}{3}\ln\left(\frac{N_{1,t}}{N_{2,t}}\right)\right] & -\frac{(N_{1,t}^{1/3} + N_{2,t}^{1/3})^2 N_{1,t}^{1/3}}{4N_{2,t}} \end{pmatrix}$$

$$\begin{pmatrix} -\frac{(N_{1,t}^{1/3} + N_{2,t}^{1/3})^4 N_{2,t}^{1/3}}{2A_{t+1}N_{1,t}^{2/3}\beta\chi} & -\frac{1}{2}\left[1 + \left(\frac{N_{2,t}}{N_{1,t}}\right)^{1/3}\right] \\ -\frac{(N_{1,t}^{1/3} + N_{2,t}^{1/3})^4 N_{1,t}^{1/3}}{2A_{t+1}N_{2,t}^{2/3}\beta\chi} & -\frac{1}{2}\left[1 + \left(\frac{N_{1,t}}{N_{2,t}}\right)^{1/3}\right] \end{pmatrix} \begin{bmatrix} d\zeta \\ d\omega \\ d\lambda \\ d\alpha \end{bmatrix}. \qquad (7.13)$$

The left coefficient matrix is positive definite and can be inverted to give:

$$\begin{pmatrix} \frac{4}{3} & \frac{2}{3}\left(\frac{N_{2,t}}{N_{1,t}}\right)^{2/3} \\ \frac{2}{3}\left(\frac{N_{1,t}}{N_{2,t}}\right)^{2/3} & \frac{4}{3} \end{pmatrix}.$$

Pre-multiplying both sides of equation (7.13) by this matrix gives:

$$
\begin{bmatrix} dn_{1,t} \\ dn_{2,t} \end{bmatrix} = \left(\begin{array}{c} \frac{1}{3} + \left(\frac{N_{2,t}}{N_{1,t}} \right)^{\frac{1}{3}} \left[1 + \frac{1}{9} \ln \left(\frac{N_{2,t}}{N_{1,t}} \right) \right] + \frac{2}{3} \left(\frac{N_{2,t}}{N_{1,t}} \right)^{\frac{2}{3}} \\ \frac{1}{3} + \left(\frac{N_{1,t}}{N_{2,t}} \right)^{\frac{1}{3}} \left[1 + \frac{1}{9} \ln \left(\frac{N_{1,t}}{N_{2,t}} \right) \right] + \frac{2}{3} \left(\frac{N_{1,t}}{N_{2,t}} \right)^{\frac{2}{3}} \end{array} \right.
$$

$$
\begin{array}{cc}
- \dfrac{(N_{1,t}^{\frac{1}{3}} + N_{2,t}^{\frac{1}{3}})^2 [(1/2)(N_{1,t}^2 N_{2,t})^{\frac{1}{3}} + N_{2,t}]}{3 N_{1,t} N_{2,t}^{\frac{2}{3}}} & - \dfrac{(N_{1,t}^{\frac{1}{3}} + N_{2,t}^{\frac{1}{3}})^4 (N_{1,t}^{\frac{1}{3}} + 2 N_{2,t}^{\frac{1}{3}})}{3 A_{t+1} N_{1,t}^{\frac{2}{3}} \beta \chi} \\[2em]
- \dfrac{(N_{1,t}^{\frac{1}{3}} + N_{2,t}^{\frac{1}{3}})^2 [N_{1,t} + (1/2)(N_{1,t} N_{2,t}^2)^{\frac{1}{3}}]}{3 N_{1,t}^{\frac{1}{3}} N_{2,t}} & - \dfrac{(N_{1,t}^{\frac{1}{3}} + N_{2,t}^{\frac{1}{3}})^4 (2 N_{1,t}^{\frac{1}{3}} + N_{2,t}^{\frac{1}{3}})}{3 A_{t+1} N_{2,t}^{\frac{2}{3}} \beta \chi}
\end{array}
$$

$$
\left. \begin{array}{c} -\dfrac{1}{3} \left[1 + \left(\dfrac{N_{2,t}}{N_{1,t}} \right)^{\frac{1}{3}} \right] \left[2 + \left(\dfrac{N_{2,t}}{N_{1,t}} \right)^{\frac{1}{3}} \right] \\[2em] -\dfrac{1}{3} \left[1 + \left(\dfrac{N_{1,t}}{N_{2,t}} \right)^{\frac{1}{3}} \right] \left[2 + \left(\dfrac{N_{1,t}}{N_{2,t}} \right)^{\frac{1}{3}} \right] \end{array} \right) \begin{bmatrix} d\zeta \\ d\omega \\ d\lambda \\ d\alpha \end{bmatrix}. \tag{7.14}
$$

The effects are all unambiguous: the effects of ω, λ, and α are negative whereas the effect of ζ is positive. ∎

We observe that equilibrium fertility decreases with ω. Indeed, when a war has a high potential cost, the importance of military power in determining the outcome of the bargaining decreases, and this reduces the strength of the strategic motive for fertility. If ζ increases, the fertility rates at equilibrium also increase: when the bargained share is equal to the probability of success, then, if this probability becomes more sensitive to the relative size of the clans, it is best to increase the size of each clan. As expected, an increase in the disutility of child rearing decreases fertility because having children entails a (greater) disutility cost. Finally, when returns to labor are greater (α is lower), it is optimal to increase fertility because the negative impact on crop per capita is less.

Notice that, when evaluating the marginal effects under Assumption 7.1, β and χ have no effect. If we evaluate their effects in different configurations, further insights can be gained as long as the reaction functions continue to have positive slopes. In particular we have Corollary 7.2, below.

Corollary 7.2 *If the fertility reaction functions have positive slopes, the following comparative statics hold:*

$$\frac{\partial n_{i,t}}{\partial \beta} \geqslant 0,$$

$$\frac{\partial n_{i,t}}{\partial \chi} \geqslant 0,$$

$$\text{if } \{\alpha = 1, \zeta = 1\} \quad \frac{\partial n_{i,t}}{\partial A_{t+1}} \geqslant 0.$$

Proof: Let us denote equations (7.9) and (7.10) by Φ and Ψ respectively. If we differentiate with respect to β and χ we obtain the following equations, whose sign is unambiguous:

$$\frac{\partial \Phi}{\partial \beta} = \frac{\partial \Psi}{\partial \beta} = \frac{\lambda}{\beta^2 \chi};$$

$$\frac{\partial \Psi}{\partial \chi} = \frac{\partial \Psi}{\partial \chi} = \frac{\lambda}{\beta \chi^2}.$$

When the reaction functions both have positive slopes, the effect of a change in parameters on the equilibrium fertility can be assessed by looking directly at the shift in Φ and Ψ.

Keeping $\alpha = 1$ and setting $\zeta = 1$, it is possible to compute each reaction function explicitly, obtaining long expressions. Plugging these expressions into the derivatives of Φ and Ψ with respect to A_{t+1} evaluated at $\alpha = 1$ and $\zeta = 1$, the following equations hold after simplification:

$$\left.\frac{\partial \Phi}{\partial A_{t+1}}\right|_{\alpha=1,\zeta=1} = \frac{\lambda}{A_{t+1}\beta\chi};$$

$$\left.\frac{\partial \Psi}{\partial A_{t+1}}\right|_{\alpha=1,\zeta=1} = \frac{\lambda}{A_{t+1}\beta\chi}.$$

Again, provided the reactions functions have positive slopes, we can see that the effect of A_{t+1} on fertility rates is positive in the neighborhood of $\zeta = 1$ and $\alpha = 1$. ∎

Both χ and β are associated with greater importance of the role of children as old-age support. Therefore they have the common effect of making the cost of child rearing, and hence of enhancing fertility, relatively more bearable.[9]

[9] They have zero effect only when such a cost is not present.

Total factor productivity A_{t+1} is not a parameter as it depends on the current stock of resources; nevertheless it is exogenous to clans' fertility choices and can be dealt with in a comparative statics set-up. It has a positive effect that can be seen as an income effect, making more children affordable for a given disutility of child rearing.[10]

Figure 7.4 summarizes Corollaries 1 and 2. It is worth remarking that Corollary 1 evaluates the parameters at the Nash Equilibrium under Assumption 7.1, whereas the parameters in Corollary 2 have zero effect at that configuration, but have the effects already discussed when evaluated elsewhere (as long as the fertility reaction functions have positive slopes and the specific restrictions given in Corollary 2 are satisfied).

7.2.4 Dynamics

We can now assess the dynamics of the model under Assumption 7.1. The dynamics of the population is obtained by inserting equation (7.11) into equation (7.4) to give:

$$N_{i,t+1} = N_{i,t} \sqrt[3]{\frac{N_{j,t}}{N_{i,t}}}.$$

Denoting $\ln x$ by $\hat{x}$, the population dynamics is determined by a system of two linear difference equations:

$$\hat{N}_{i,t+1} = \hat{N}_{i,t}\, 2/3 + \hat{N}_{j,t}/3.$$

The solution is given by:

$$\hat{N}_{i,t} = \frac{\hat{N}_{1,0} + \hat{N}_{2,0}}{2} + \frac{3^{-t}}{2}(\hat{N}_{i,0} - \hat{N}_{j,0}).$$

and, at steady state, the population of the two clans is equal and given by the geometric average of the two initial population levels:

$$\bar{N}_i = \bar{N}_j = \sqrt{N_{1,0}} \sqrt{N_{2,0}}. \tag{7.15}$$

The dynamics of the stock of resources is provided by equation (7.5), which has a steady state:

$$\bar{R} = K\left(1 - \frac{b(\bar{N}_i + \bar{N}_j)}{\delta}\right). \tag{7.16}$$

---

[10] When $\lambda = 0$ we have a zero effect.

A positive steady state exists if and only if $\bar{N}_i + \bar{N}_j < \delta/b$. We can write this as a condition on the initial populations to give the following proposition:

Proposition 7.3 Sustainable initial populations

- *If a strictly positive steady state for resources exists, then it is stable.*
- *Under Assumption 7.1:*
  - *a positive stable steady state exists if and only if the initial populations are not too high:*

$$2b\sqrt{N_{1,0}}\sqrt{N_{2,0}} < \delta.$$

  - *at steady state $\bar{\pi}^\omega = 1/2$ and $\bar{s} = 1/2$.*

Proof: The steady state for equation (7.16) is strictly positive if and only if:

$$\frac{b(N_i + N_j)}{\delta} < 1. \tag{7.17}$$

The first derivative of equation (7.5) evaluated at the steady state reads $1 - \delta + b(N_i + N_j)$. This is less than 1 if Condition (7.17) holds. Hence the positive steady state is asymptotically stable. This proves the first point.

Inserting equation (7.15) into equation (7.16) we can reduce the condition for the convergence of resources to a strictly positive long-run level to a condition for the initial population (see above). This proves the second point.

Finally, when $\omega = 0$, $s_t = \pi_t^\omega$. At steady state the two groups have the same population, and so $\bar{\pi}^\omega = 1/2$. Therefore we also have $\bar{s} = \bar{\pi}^\omega = 1/2$. ∎

With Assumption 7.1, the ecosystem can sustain a long-run equilibrium providing the initial population is not too high; in other circumstances an environmental trap occurs. The dynamics for more general cases, and the role of factors affecting the occurrence of an environmental collapse, are studied through numerical simulations in section 7.3.2. At this stage it is possible to see from equation (7.5) that a higher population uses more resources, and from equation (7.16) that the occurrence of an environmental trap depends on the long-run dynamics of the total population. Therefore, any change in parameters which has the effect of increasing equilibrium fertility rates also has the effect of increasing the likelihood of an environmental trap. This implies that two similar societies with different ζ's may end up in very different situations: the one where ζ is low may experience a moderate population growth and so achieve a long-run stable equilibrium, whereas the society where ζ is high may be doomed to collapse.

Table 7.1. *Benchmark parameterization of the population race model*

λ	α	χ	β	A	$N_{1,t}$	$N_{2,t}$	δ	b	K
0	1	0.8	1	10	90	100	0.08	$1.2 \cdot 10^{-4}$	12000

7.3 Numerical simulations and robustness analysis

In the previous section we derived some theoretical results for a specific configuration of the parameters. In this section we investigate whether these results still hold when the parameters take different values.

7.3.1 The Nash Equilibrium

Let us begin by setting some values for the parameters, which are summarized in Table 7.1. A few words on these values: setting $\chi = 0.8$ implies that, for instance, young adults with two siblings support their parents with 20 percent of their income, and the parent receives a total of 60 percent of the income of a young adult in this group. For the sake of simplicity the discount factor β is set to 1. The returns parameter α and the coefficient on child disutility λ are set to 1 and 0 respectively, as in Assumption 7.1. From section 7.2.3 we know that fertility rates are increased (decreased) by a lower α (a greater λ). We take initial population levels of 90 and 100 respectively, the fact that group 2 is bigger than group 1 implying that it is more likely to win if there is a conflict. The total factor productivity $A()$ depends on the stock of resources. For the sake of simplicity we assume $A(R_t) = AR_t$ and set $A = 10$.

When we consider the dynamics, then the environmental parameters δ, b, and K also play a role, as shown in the law of motion in equation (7.5). Assuming that one period lasts for twenty years, the intrinsic regeneration growth rate δ can be set at 0.08 (in accord with Dalton and Coats (2000) and Matsumoto (2002), that suggest a 4 percent growth rate per decade). Using the same assumptions as Matsumoto, the coefficient for the human impact on resources b turns out to have the order of magnitude of 10^{-4} on our scale. The carrying capacity K, which acts as a scaling parameter, is set at 12000.

Here we will focus on the parameters ζ and ω in two cases. In case I they take the same values as in section 7.2.2: $\{\omega = 0; \zeta = 1\}$, so that case I is a numerical example satisfying Assumption 7.1. Case II is characterized by a larger value for both parameters: $\{\omega = 0.1; \zeta = 1.3\}$. For both cases we consider the fertility

Table 7.2. *Outcome for generation born at t,*
cases I and II

Case	$n_{1,t}$	$n_{2,t}$	s_t	s_{t+1}
I	1.036	0.965	0.474	0.491
II	1.465	1.356	0.469	0.492

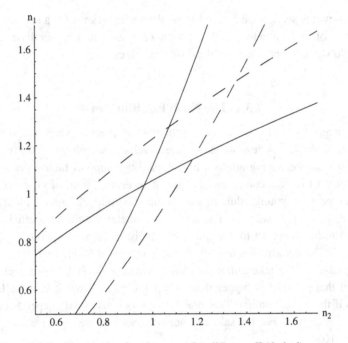

Figure 7.5 Fertility reaction functions: case I (solid); case II (dashed)

choice problem at given t.[11] The resulting equilibrium fertility choices and bargained share are shown in Table 7.2 and in Figure 7.5. In both cases optimal fertility is higher for group 1 than for group 2 because its size is initially lower. Moreover, in case II, there is a higher equilibrium level of fertility for both groups. This arises because the probability of success in war is more sensitive to the groups' relative sizes, giving a stronger incentive to have children. This is also reflected in the fact that, for given population size, group 1's share (s_t)

---

[11] Notice that in the fertility problem R_{t+1} is exogenous. Moreover, given that $\lambda = 0$, the resource stock is just a multiplicative term that does not affect the fertility choice.

is smaller in case II than in case I. Finally, we verified that the slopes of the reaction functions, which were shown to be positive in the neighborhood of the equilibrium under Assumption 7.1 (see Proposition 7.2), are still positive when the values of ζ and ω are somewhat different.

7.3.2 Resources and population dynamics

In section 7.2.4 we studied the dynamics of the particular configuration which allows analytical solutions. Here we will use numerical simulations to extend the analysis to the general model, so as to see which factors make the occurrence of a collapse more likely. The aim is to discover under which configuration of parameters the dynamics converge to a steady state.

Non-convergence can reflect two different situations. The first – which we label "population collapse" – arises when the population converges asymptotically to zero while resources achieve their carrying capacity K. This represents a world where fertility is below replacement level in the long run. The second situation – labeled "environmental collapse" – arises when resources are exhausted following a population boom. This also causes the extinction of the population, as no crops are produced. Contrary to the "population collapse" case, the "environmental collapse" leads to the extinction of population in finite time.

For the benchmark parameterization we focus on the role of the parameters ω and ζ, which have not been considered so far in the literature. The parameters for the benchmark specification are as shown in Table 7.1, but for λ which is set to 1. If $\lambda = 0$ fertility does not depend on resources and on actual clans' populations but just on their ratio: if this is the case, then fertility remains generally different from 1 (except in the case described in Proposition 7.3), leading either to population collapse or to environmental collapse. Instead, with a strictly positive λ, fertility is related to the actual stock of resources and populations and there exists a range of parameters ζ and ω such that collapse can be avoided. The setting $\lambda = 1$ is chosen for the sake of simplicity. The values for $N_{1,t}$ and $N_{2,t}$ are used as initial values, and the value for K is taken as the initial value for R_t. Figure 7.6 shows the three regions in the $\{\zeta; \omega\}$ space separated by bold curves.

The top-left region represents the zone of population collapse, the central area is the no-collapse zone where a long-run stable equilibrium of population and resources can be reached, and the bottom right represents environmental collapse. We can see that the frontiers all have positive slopes: a collapse is avoided if neither of these two parameters is "too large" compared with the

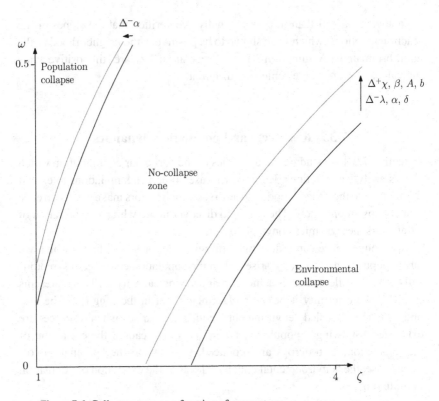

Figure 7.6 Collapse zones as a function of parameters

other. In particular, an environmental collapse becomes more likely if, for a given ω, ζ is high, or if for a given ζ, ω is low.

By performing a *ceteris paribus* perturbation of the parameters we can assess the effects of other model parameters on the collapse zones.[12] Figure 7.6 shows how the borderlines move as the parameters change. Both borderlines are affected by every parameter, but the effect on the left frontier is so small in some cases that we do not report it systematically. This shows that:

- a drop in the disutility of children λ reduces the stable population zone and increases the environmental collapse zone;
- higher old-age transfers χ enlarge the zone of environmental collapse and shrink the zone of no collapse;

---

[12] All the simulations are available from the authors upon request.

- less severe decreasing returns to labor ($\Delta^-\alpha$) reduce the scope for population collapse, enlarge the zone of environmental collapse, and move the zone of no collapse;
- lower discounting with time (higher β) enlarges the zone of environmental collapse and reduces the zone of no collapse;
- higher productivity A reduces the stability zone and enlarges the zone of environmental collapse;
- lower δ or higher b, both implying a more fragile ecosystem, reduces the zone of no-collapse and enlarges the zone of environmental collapse.

Basically, the parameters which have been proved in Corollaries 7.1 and 7.2 to have a positive impact on fertility enlarge the scope for environmental collapse by increasing the pressure on resources.

As Kirch (1997) remarks, the "diversification of the Oceanic societies and cultures resulted in part from the process of island settlement and inevitable isolation, in part from adaptation to contrastive island environments, *and in no small measure from internal social dynamics.*"[13] In this respect, the model adds new factors (e.g. ω, ζ) that play a role influencing human decisions to the elements already considered in the literature on fragile ecosystems (δ, b). Even if two societies are similar with respect to the second group of parameters, they may experience very different patterns if they differ substantially with respect to the first group. Though simple, the model highlights how these factors can affect fertility decisions when crop sharing is decided by bargaining.

7.3.3 Simulation of transition paths

As an example of dynamics we report in Figure 7.7 a simulation for the case of an environmental collapse (panel A) and one for the case of no collapse (panel B). In our model an "environmental collapse" occurs when the law of motion of resources (eq. (7.5)) given the current stocks of R, N_1, and N_2 would imply a negative stock of resources in the next period. Should this happen, in the simulation resources are set to zero since they cannot be negative, with the eventual extinction of population following from the lack of crop. In this sense we model the process that can lead to a collapse but not what happens thereafter. In the collapse scenario, the basic structure of our model no longer makes sense and one must turn to a different model.[14]

---

[13] P. 31, italic is ours.
[14] This seems in line with what happened on Easter Island, since it seems that cultural practices changed drastically once the resources were exhausted.

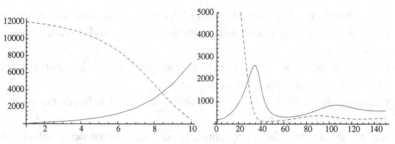

Young Population $N_{1,t} + N_{2,t}$ (solid); Resources (dashed). Panel A: $\{\omega = .4; \zeta = 1.22\}$;
Panel B: $\{\omega = .5; \zeta = 1.12\}$.
Other parameters as in Table 7.1 but for $\lambda = 1$, $\alpha = .5$.

Figure 7.7 Simulation for environmental collapse and no collapse

Panel A shows an economy with a relatively high ζ and low ω, high fertility
and high population growth. At some point (after ten periods in the example),
resources are depleted and we reach a state with $R = 0$. In panel B, a lower
ζ and higher ω allow the collapse to be avoided. The strategic motive toward
fertility is still at work and for high initial levels of resources, population initially
increases, but as resources are more and more depleted, the decrease in A_t
lowers fertility, offsetting the strategic incentive. The reduction in fertility turns
out to be enough in the setting of panel B to allow the resource stock to recover;
then, when resources are again high enough, population increases again, but
more slowly than before, and one can observe that the model is able to display
oscillatory behavior in the long run, as in Brander and Taylor (1998).

In Proposition 7.3 the long-run population turned out to be highly depen-
dent on initial values of N_1 and N_2. This result was obtained under the specific
parameterization of Assumption 7.1. Away from that setting the dynamics lose
such a serious dependence on initial values of population. By repeating simulation for different $N_{1,0}$ and $N_{2,0}$, we can observe whether a collapse occurs:
in the case of panel A a collapse occurs also for small initial levels of population, whereas in the case of panel B also for relatively high initial values,[15]
population exhibits an initial hump shape and then it oscillates with resources
in a similar fashion as in the benchmark case of panel B. What is affected is the
timing of the peak, that is achieved earlier for high initial values.

7.4 Extension to the sustainability of diverse societies

We have seen in Chapter 5 that the distribution of income and of political power
in a society affects the educational system, which in turn affects differential

---

[15] Clearly $N_{1,0}$ and $N_{2,0}$ cannot be "too high" otherwise a collapse follows almost immediately.

fertility between groups, and thus population dynamics. Population dynamics describe the growth or decline of a particular group, and are thus related to the dynamics of diversity in a society.

If we extend our notion of clans above to encompass ethnic or religious dimensions, the set-up provided here can be used to analyze the sustainability of a diverse society. First, one needs to define what a diverse society is. In economics, there is the notion of intragenerational heterogeneity, which describes a model economy where households differ not only by age but also by another dimension. This other dimension can be either "preferences" or "endowments." Preferences describe how people rank different outcomes, while endowments cover aspects such as abilities. Both can be related to the notions used in other social sciences, such as ideology, culture, or ethnicity. The two dimensions can sometimes be interweaved. For example, imagine a society with two types of people, "traditionals" and "liberals." The two groups will have different preferences, for example with respect to the type of public good that should be provided by the government, but could also have different abilities to work with other people: traditional having an advantage when working with other traditional people because of the high level of trust between them, while liberals being more able to work with any type of person, see e.g. Melindi Ghidi (2012).

Definition 7.2 Diverse society
A diverse society is one in which there are different types of households. Types reflect ideology, culture, or ethnicity.

We now provide a definition of sustainability that is adapted to the notion of diversity (from de la Croix (2011)). A weak notion of sustainability would require that no type disappears in the long run. In other words, the weight of each group in the society should remain positive for the society to remain diverse. There are two straightforward ways to measure the weight of a group: the demographic weight and the share in income or wealth.

Definition 7.3 Sustainability of a diverse society
Sustainability is achieved when the population shares and the income shares of all types do not converge to zero in the long run, i.e. when diversity is preserved.

Imposing that both the population share and the income share remain positive is a way to avoid "repugnant" situations where some type would still have some population but would be infinitely poor.

The above definitions put a general frame to any analysis of the sustainability of diverse societies. Here, we have only provided a new way of looking at fertility choices. The mechanism through which being larger yields an advantage provides a further motive for fertility choices, in addition to those generally highlighted (old-age support, family altruism, etc.). In our model this motive can be traced back to the absence of property rights over output, but the principle can easily be extended to any situation where the relative size of a group influences its expected pay-offs. Consider, for instance, tensions between two groups where one feels much weaker in war or weapon technology: enlarging its population can be seen as a means to increase its power and partly bridge the gap. Moreover, in many bargaining situations the bigger group can take advantage of its size by making its voice louder (for example, in subsidy seeking).

An interesting extension to the set-up developed here would be to introduce education as another way of gaining power. A key parameter would then be the relative importance of education versus number of people in gaining political power. A priori, if education is relatively important in getting power compared with population, the framework should lead to an "education race," which might be a better outcome than a "population race." The possibility of an education race will depend on the availability (funding) of education for all groups. A public funding scheme at the federal level seems an appropriate set-up to frame an education race between groups, as it would incite everyone to participate.

7.5 Conclusion

In this model, fertility is not determined through mechanistic Malthusian dynamics but is the outcome of a rational choice by decision makers, with a finite life-span, who are aware of some tradeoff in choosing how many children to raise. In particular one of the motives related to fertility choice has a strategic nature, since it is related to bargaining over crop sharing in the next period.

A new way to look at fertility is proposed, suggesting that strategic complementarities can characterize fertility behavior across groups. When the relative size provides advantages, as in this model in relation to military power, each group's fertility decision is affected by expectations about the other group's decision. We studied under what conditions this can result in over-population. Up to now the number of children has usually been studied as automatically determined by nutrition (in a Malthusian fashion), as a consumption good (assuming altruistic motives), or as an investment good (for old-age support). Our framework has elements of all these traditions, but differs substantially from them since the relative size also matters, thus determining fertility complementarity.

7.6 Additional material – concave utility

Let us here remove the assumption of a linear utility function. The function becomes CRRA (constant relative risk aversion): $(c_{i,t}^{1-\xi} + \beta d_{i,t+1}^{1-\xi})/(1 - \xi) - \lambda n_{i,t}$ where $\xi \geqslant 0$ is the parameter capturing the degree of relative risk aversion.[16] Notice that the solution to the bargaining problem still does not depend on second-period consumption (since it is unaffected by current bargaining) or on the disutility of child rearing (as fertility is chosen before the clans begin their bargaining). However, the solution to the bargaining problem is no longer given by equation (7.8) because risk aversion has been introduced. Clans still have foresight over s_{t+1}, internalizing the fact that it depends on their relative size, but the way in which s_{t+1} responds to current fertility is different from the response without risk aversion.

We can now study the effect of an increase in risk aversion ξ on s which results from bargaining in a neighborhood of the analytically treatable solution. This allows us to study the conditions under which increasing risk aversion implies a greater share for group 1 than in the linear case (i.e. when $\xi = 0$). Abstracting from constant terms, and omitting for simplicity the temporal subscript for π^ω and s, the maximization of the Nash product (7.7) yields the first-order condition:

$$\frac{1}{2((1 - \pi^\omega)(1 - \omega)(1 - s)^\xi - (1 - s)(1 - \omega)^\xi)}$$
$$= \frac{1}{2(\pi^\omega s^\xi (1 - \omega) - s(1 - \omega)^\xi)}.$$

By applying the implicit function theorem it is possible to derive an expression for $\frac{ds}{d\xi}$. Although such an expression is not easy to handle, we can study the situation in the neighborhood of $\xi = 0$ as our aim is to study the effect of introducing risk aversion into the expression. As in section 7.2.2 we focus on the neighborhood of $\omega = 0$, obtaining:

$$\frac{ds}{d\xi} = (1/2)(\pi^\omega \ln(\pi^\omega) - (1 - \pi^\omega)\ln(1 - \pi^\omega)).$$

---

[16] We assume that both clans are risk averse to the same extent. If the parties differ in their degree of risk aversion, the bargaining position of the less risk-averse party is improved (Binmore *et al.* (1986)). It would be possible to relax the assumption of the linear disutility of children as well, but the qualitative results would not change. What would occur is that, *ceteris paribus*, introducing decreasing returns in child disutility would increase fertility.

Table 7.3. *Risk aversion (ξ), fertility rates and bargained shares*

	$\xi = 0$	$\xi = 0.1$	$\xi = 0.2$	$\xi = 0.5$	$\xi \to 1$	$\xi = 2$
Case I						
$n_{1,t}$	1.036	1.065	1.096	1.253	1.036	0.340
$n_{2,t}$	0.965	0.993	1.020	1.163	0.965	0.326
s_t	0.474	0.473	0.472	0.471	0.474	0.487
s_{t+1}	0.491	0.491	0.492	0.491	0.491	0.492
Case II						
$n_{1,t}$	1.465	1.500	1.545	1.989	1.936	0.706
$n_{2,t}$	1.356	1.387	1.428	1.830	1.782	0.664
s_t	0.469	0.468	0.468	0.465	0.466	0.478
s_{t+1}	0.492	0.492	0.492	0.493	0.493	0.491

Rearranging this expression gives:

$$\frac{ds}{d\xi} \geqslant 0 \quad \Leftrightarrow \quad \frac{(1 - \pi^{\omega}) \ln(1 - \pi^{\omega})}{\pi^{\omega} \ln(\pi^{\omega})} \geqslant 1.$$

Since the left-hand side of this inequality turns out to be unambiguously increasing in π^{ω} as $\pi^{\omega} \in (0, 1)$, it is clear that the effect of introducing risk aversion is more likely to increase group 1's share if π^{ω} is high enough. The rationale behind these results is that when risk aversion is introduced, the clan with greater military power (π^{ω} and $1 - \pi^{\omega}$) benefits. This occurs because groups are more anxious to avoid the risky outcomes associated with a lack of agreement, and hence the most powerful group has an advantage. In particular, this means that the bargained share becomes more sensitive to relative population, since this affects the groups' military power. This means that the strategic motive is enhanced when risk aversion is introduced into the model.

Numerical simulations are needed to obtain results for the fertility choice as risk aversion increases further.[17] The results of such simulations on fertility rates and bargained share as risk aversion increases for cases I and II are shown in Table 7.3. We can see how, for a given risk aversion, fertility rates are always greater in case II, because the relative size is more decisive in this case. As expected, greater risk aversion initially brings about higher fertility rates. However, such an effect is not monotonic: when ξ is close to 1, fertility rates begin to decrease. This down-turn occurs because, if ξ is high enough, s is less affected by the groups' relative size (see s_t rows) and the strategic motive

---

[17] We cannot compute a closed-form solution s_t as a function of $n_{1,t}$ and $n_{2,t}$ and hence the second step (the choice of fertility) cannot be solved explicitly, even under Assumption 7.1.

becomes weaker and weaker. Notice, however, that, in both cases, for utility function approaching the logarithmic form (i.e. $\xi \to 1$) we do not observe less fertility than in the benchmark model with risk neutrality. Therefore the model seems to be robust to introduction of risk aversion.

Hence, introducing small risk aversion turns out to benefit the clan with higher military power, thus enhancing the strategic motive for fertility. For a higher degree of risk aversion, numerical analysis shows a non-monotonic effect on fertility, since at some point clans are both so averse to the uncertain outcome of war that a greater military power is no more effective as a threat. For moderate risk aversion (as in the log-utility case) the effects on fertility are close to those predicted by the model.

8

Production, reproduction, and pollution caps

In the previous chapter we have seen that, in the absence of coordination, the interactions between individual choices may lead to an unsustainable outcome. The objective of environmental policies is to make agents internalize the effect of their behavior on the environment. Under a Kyoto type of regime, the main motivation for capping greenhouse gas emissions arises from a concern for future generations. The aim is to make sure that the climatic conditions they will experience either will not be worse than ours or, at the very least, will not prevent them from leading a decent life.

In the literature on environmental policy, population is considered as exogenous – not necessarily constant, but exogenous, following, for example, some predetermined path provided by forecast agencies or demographers (see e.g. the projections of Lutz *et al.* (2001) predicting the end of population growth). It means that there is no feedback from policy to population. This might be a good approximation in the short run, but these studies often deal with horizons of one or two centuries, over which population obviously has time to change. In this chapter, we deal with environmental policies when population is endogenous. We will show that environmental policies that restrict pollution have an unintended consequence of population boost, which in turn lowers the effectiveness of the original policy. Hence, the endogeneity of fertility is important when we deal with environmental policy. In short, pollution quotas act as a tax on production of goods which generate pollution. This provides an incentive for households to allocate more time to leisure and rearing children – activities which do not generate pollution and therefore are not taxed.

Substitution of procreation for production is at the heart of this chapter. It occurs as soon as rearing children takes time (whether or not raising children costs goods). One may have doubts about both the very existence and the

A variant of this chapter is published in de la Croix and Gosseries (2012).

strength of this substitution effect. As to its existence, it is assumed to be realistic that rearing children entails an opportunity cost due to the time it takes. People's income (and level of production) is thus affected by the time spent on procreation. They experience a tradeoff between production and procreation. Facing a drop in the net return on production, they would invest more time in procreation and leisure. How robust is this substitution effect? We have argued in the introduction that the negative relationship between education and fertility holds both over time and across countries. In addition, many microeconometric studies show that fertility is negatively related to mothers' wages or education (for example, Fernández and Fogli (2006) for migrants in the US, Deb and Rosati (2004) for India, and Baudin (2009) for France). This tends to confirm that opportunity costs such as women's income are essential to determine fertility.

One challenge of the modeling approach here is to build a growth model in which population is constant along the balanced growth path. Indeed, it would make no sense to have a benchmark model where population either grows to infinity or reaches asymptotically zero. In the standard neo-classical growth model of Solow (1956), the growth rate of population is considered as exogenous and generically different from 0. This is because, at Solow's time, demography was considered as exogenous to the economy, and the growth rate of population was seen as exogenous to the economic growth. In order to obtain a long-run level of population, one needs to introduce Malthusian elements into the model. According to Malthus' theory, net fertility depends positively on consumption per capita, either because infant mortality depends on nutrition ("positive checks" in Malthus' words) or because households desire less children in bad times ("preventive checks"). Production takes place in farms where land is fixed and labor input is subject to decreasing returns. As a consequence, any increase in active population leads to a drop in farm real wages. Everything else being equal, the combination of these two elements, endogenous net fertility and decreasing returns, leads necessarily to a stable population in the long run.

To generate a constant population in the long run, we will assume that land is an input in the production function of children. When households have small dwellings, child production is more costly and people have fewer children (this has been known since Thompson (1938) and Goodsell (1937)). As a consequence, when population grows, land becomes scarcer, and it is more costly to produce children. Fertility drops and population stabilizes.[1]

---

[1] Alternatively, one might have supposed that there is a subsistence level of land services consumption, as in Peretto and Valente (2011). This would deliver the same stable long-run population through a different mechanism.

8.1 The model

Time is discrete and goes from zero to infinity. Each individual lives for only two periods: childhood and (active) adulthood. We consider a closed economy, possibly the whole Earth, endowed with a certain quantity of land L, having an initial level of assets per person k_0, an adult population size N_0, and an initial pollution level P_{-1}. We first describe how pollution is generated. Then we consider the household maximization problem and, finally, the implied aggregate dynamics.

8.1.1 Production and pollution

We assume that technology is exogenous. This does not need to imply that technology is fixed, but rather that technological progress does not depend on the policy that is conducted. In fact, what we really have in mind here is the exogenous nature of the energy efficiency of technologies. The impact of environmental policy on technological choice by firms has been studied by many people. We abstract from this dimension here in order to focus on two other adjustment variables: production per capita and population size. Admittedly, even if technology were fixed, one could still face a diversity of activities allowing at every moment in time to shift from energy-intensive activities to less energy-intensive ones. This is actually what happens when we substitute procreation for production. However, we assume here that within productive activities, only one type of technology is available.

At a given time, for a given technology, polluting emissions E_t are proportional to total output Y_t:

$$E_t = a_t Y_t.$$

Variable a_t represents the pollution coefficient, i.e. the degree to which production generates polluting emissions. Total output is itself the product of adult population size N_t and production per person y_t:

$$E_t = a_t N_t y_t.$$

The stock of pollution S_t accumulates according to:

$$S_t = (1 - g(S_{t-1}))S_{t-1} + E_t, \quad \forall t \in \mathbb{N}.$$

Function $g(S_{t-1})$ refers to the degradation rate, i.e., the share of past pollution S_{t-1} that has been absorbed by the environment. It depends on the absorptive capacity of the natural environment as well as on the extent of past pollution.

8.1.2 Households

At each date t, there is a new adult generation of size N_t deriving utility from consumption c_t, leisure ℓ_t, number of children n_t, and assets left to the future generation k_{t+1}. Leisure should be understood standardly as non-market and emission-free activities, such as chatting with friends, sleeping, sweeping the floor, etc. Households are homogeneous. We assume a logarithmic utility function:

$$u(c_t, \ell_t, n_t, k_{t+1}) = \ln c_t + \varphi \ln \ell_t + \gamma \ln(n_t k_{t+1}),$$

with $\varphi, \gamma \in \mathbb{R}_+$. Parameter φ is the taste for leisure. Parameter γ is the altruism factor. Notice that parents care about the total assets of their descendants, $n_t k_{t+1}$, i.e. the product of child quantity n_t with quality k_{t+1}. Notice also that parents do not care about their children utility, as would be the case with dynastic altruism. Our formulation of altruism is referred to in the literature as "joy-of-giving" (or warm glove), because parents have a taste for giving (see, e.g., Andreoni (1989)). As our aim here is not to assess how agents should behave, impure altruism seems an acceptable assumption as a means to obtain clearcut analytical results.

The choice of a logarithmic utility function is defended in Prescott (1986) on the grounds that leisure showed no secular trend despite growing wages. This can be accounted for only when the elasticity of substitution between leisure and consumption is close to 1.

Bequest b_t is given to the next generations and invested in a productive asset k_{t+1}. b_t can be interpreted as education, in which case k_{t+1} best describes human capital. The accumulation function is assumed Cobb Douglas:

$$k_{t+1} = \mu b_t^\eta k_t^\tau \tag{8.1}$$

with the following parametric restrictions: $\mu \in \mathbb{R}_+$, $\tau, \eta \in (0, 1)$. We assume moreover that $\eta + \tau < 1$, which will imply that assets and output per person will converge in the long run to a constant level.[2] Parameter μ is a measure of productivity. Parameter η is the elasticity of assets k_{t+1} to investment b_t. Parameter τ captures the strength of an externality from parents assets to children assets. In the case of human capital, this externality represents the usual parental influence on children outcome (see Chapter 2).

---

[2] The alternative case $\eta + \tau = 1$ would generate endogenous growth, which could be analyzed as well with the tools developed here.

Producing x children requires time T_t and space L/N_t (land per household), with the following technology:

$$x = m \left(\frac{L}{N_t} \right)^{\iota} T_t.$$

Parameter m measures total factor productivity of the procreation activity. Parameter $\iota \in (0, 1)$ captures the importance of space to produce children. The time needed to produce n_t children is given by:

$$\frac{1}{m} \left(\frac{N_t}{L} \right)^{\iota} n_t = \phi N_t^{\iota} n_t,$$

with

$$\phi = \frac{1}{m} \left(\frac{1}{L} \right)^{\iota}.$$

Compared with the models developed in Chapters 1–5, the introduction of land per person as an input in the child production technology implies that population will be stationary. Indeed, as population increases, it becomes more and more costly to have children, lowering progressively the fertility rate to its replacement level.

Households face a budget constraint stating that consumption plus bequests cannot exceed income y_t:

$$c_t + n_t b_t \leqslant y_t. \tag{8.2}$$

Households have a total time endowment equal to 1. They face a time constraint, expressing that time spent working h_t, rearing children, and having leisure should not exceed 1.

$$h_t + \phi N_t^{\iota} n_t + \ell_t \leqslant 1 \tag{8.3}$$

Households are self-employed and produce using assets k_t and hours of work h_t. The production function is linear. One hour of work produces k_t units of goods:

$$y_t \leqslant h_t k_t. \tag{8.4}$$

Replacing the saturated constraints (8.1), (8.2), (8.3), and (8.4) into the objective, the households maximization problem can be written as:

$$\max_{\ell_t, n_t, b_t} \ln((1 - \ell_t - \phi N_t^\iota n_t)k_t - n_t b_t) + \varphi \ln \ell_t + \gamma (\ln(n_t)$$

$$+ \tau \ln(k_t) + \eta \ln(b_t) + \ln(\mu))$$

The first-order conditions are:

$$\frac{-k_t}{(1 - \ell_t - \phi N_t^\iota n_t)k_t - n_t b_t} + \frac{\varphi}{\ell_t} = 0$$

$$\frac{-\phi k_t - b_t}{(1 - \ell_t - \phi N_t^\iota n_t)k_t - n_t b_t} + \frac{\gamma}{n_t} = 0$$

$$\frac{-n_t}{(1 - \ell_t - \phi N_t^\iota n_t)k_t - n_t b_t} + \frac{\gamma \eta}{b_t} = 0.$$

As the maximization problem is convex, the first-order conditions are necessary and sufficient for a maximum. Solving the set of first-order conditions and saturated constraints (8.2)–(8.3)–(8.4) for c_t, ℓ_t, n_t, b_t, and y_t yields closed-form solutions:

$$c_t = \frac{k_t}{1 + \varphi + \gamma}. \tag{8.5}$$

$$\ell_t = \frac{\varphi}{1 + \varphi + \gamma}. \tag{8.6}$$

$$n_t = \frac{\gamma(1 - \eta)}{(1 + \varphi + \gamma)\phi N_t^\iota}. \tag{8.7}$$

$$b_t = \frac{\eta \phi N_t^\iota k_t}{1 - \eta}. \tag{8.8}$$

$$y_t = \frac{\gamma \eta}{1 + \varphi + \gamma} k_t. \tag{8.9}$$

8.1.3 Aggregate dynamics

Adult population dynamics are given by:

$$N_{t+1} = N_t n_t. \tag{8.10}$$

Replacing the expressions for b_t (8.8) and n_t (8.7) into the equations describing the dynamics of assets (8.1) and population (8.10) leads to:

$$k_{t+1} = \mu \left(\frac{\eta \varphi}{1 - \eta} \right)^\eta N_t^{\eta \iota} k_t^{\tau + \eta}. \tag{8.11}$$

$$N_{t+1} = \frac{\gamma(1 - \eta)}{(1 + \varphi + \gamma)\phi} N_t^{1-\iota}. \tag{8.12}$$

This system is recursive as the second equation can be solved independently of the first one. The second equation shows that N_{t+1} is an increasing and concave function of N_t which does not depend on k_t. It has a unique non-trivial steady state:

$$\bar{N} = \left(\frac{\gamma(1 - \eta)}{(1 + \varphi + \gamma)\phi} \right)^{\frac{1}{\iota}} \tag{8.13}$$

which is globally stable. Dynamics of population are monotonic. For a given N_t, the first equation also describes an increasing and concave relation between k_{t+1} and k_t. When N_t is close enough to $\bar{N}$, the dynamics of k_t are also monotonic and converge to:

$$\bar{k} = \left(\frac{\mu^{1/\eta} \gamma \eta}{1 + \varphi + \gamma} \right)^{\frac{\eta}{1 - \tau - \eta}} \quad \text{for } \iota > 0.$$

Income per capita converges to:

$$\bar{y} = \mu^{\frac{1}{1 - \tau\eta}} \left(\frac{\gamma \eta}{1 + \varphi + \gamma} \right)^{\frac{1 - \tau\eta + \eta}{1 - \tau\eta}}.$$

A bigger country (higher L, lower ϕ) will have a bigger population. A more productive country (higher μ) will have higher income per capita.

If $\iota = 0$, space is not useful to produce children. Population growth unboundedly at rate $\gamma(1 - \eta)/((1 + \varphi + \gamma)\phi)$ and assets converge to:

$$\bar{k} = \left(\frac{\mu^{1/\eta} \eta \varphi}{1 - \eta} \right)^{\frac{\eta}{1 - \tau\eta}} \quad \text{for } \iota = 0.$$

8.2 Pollution cap and tradable rights

At each date, past pollution is given. A given pollution target $S_t^\star$ can be achieved by imposing an emission target $E_t^\star$ such that:

$$S_t^\star = (1 - g(S_{t-1}^\star))S_{t-1}^\star + E_t^\star, \quad \forall t \in \mathbb{N}.$$

Since in this chapter, we do not provide a utility-based justification for a given pollution target, the latter is taken to be exogenous. As a result, the path of emission targets $\{E_t^\star\}_{t=0..+\infty}$ is exogenous, too.

Remember that, for simplification purposes, we have assumed that the output is produced by self-employed households. To meet the sequence of emission targets, two policy schemes are available and interchangeable. First, a Pigovian tax on emissions, hence on production, the revenue of which is transferred back to households in a lump-sum way. Second, a tradable pollution rights system with a free initial allocation of rights to households. In a world where information is perfect about both the objective that is being pursued and the deep parameters of the model, tradable quotas schemes and price-oriented schemes are fully equivalent. This implies that, despite our focus on tradable rights schemes, the results will be of direct relevance for those willing to implement a Pigovian tax.

8.2.1 Households

Tradable pollution rights systems, such as the Kyoto system, impose on each household to buy pollution rights in proportion to the output that would exceed their initial endowment. Let us denote the price of the pollution right by p_t and the initial endowment of rights by q_t. The budget constraint of the household is now:

$$y_t \geqslant c_t + n_t b_t + p_t(a_t y_t - q_t). \tag{8.14}$$

The constraint can be rewritten:

$$(1 - a_t p_t)y_t + p_t q_t \geqslant c_t + n_t b_t$$

which shows clearly that the price of pollution permits p_t weighted by the pollution coefficient a_t acts like an income tax, and $p_t q_t$ as a lump-sum transfer.

Replacing the saturated constraints (8.1), (8.14), (8.3), and (8.4) into the objective, the households maximization problem can be written as:

$$\max_{\ell_t, n_t, b_t} \mathcal{L}_t = \ln((1 - a_t p_t)(1 - \ell_t - \phi N_t^t n_t)k_t - n_t b_t + p_t q_t)$$

$$+ \varphi \ln \ell_t + \gamma (\ln(n_t) + \tau \ln(k_t) + \eta \ln(b_t) + \ln(\mu)).$$

The first-order conditions can be written under the form "marginal cost = marginal benefit":

$$\frac{\partial \mathcal{L}_t}{\partial \ell_t} = 0 \Rightarrow \frac{(1 - a_t p_t)k_t}{c_t} = \frac{\varphi}{\ell_t}.$$

$$\frac{\partial \mathcal{L}_t}{\partial n_t} = 0 \Rightarrow \frac{(1 - a_t p_t)\phi k_t - b_t}{c_t} = \frac{\gamma}{n_t}.$$

$$\frac{\partial \mathcal{L}_t}{\partial b_t} = 0 \Rightarrow \frac{n_t}{c_t} = \frac{\gamma \eta}{b_t}.$$

The price p_t affects the first-order conditions for ℓ_t and n_t by lowering their marginal cost.

As the maximization problem is convex, the first-order conditions are necessary and sufficient for a maximum. Solving the system formed by the first-order conditions and the constraints leads to:

$$c_t = \frac{1}{1 + \varphi + \gamma} ((1 - a_t p_t)k_t + p_t q_t).$$

$$\ell_t = \frac{\varphi}{1 + \varphi + \gamma} \frac{(1 - a_t p_t)k_t + p_t q_t}{(1 - a_t p_t)k_t}.$$

$$n_t = \frac{\gamma (1 - \eta)}{(1 + \varphi + \gamma)\phi N_t^t} \frac{(1 - a_t p_t)k_t + p_t q_t}{(1 - a_t p_t)k_t}. \tag{8.15}$$

$$b_t = \frac{\eta \phi N_t^t k_t}{1 - \eta}(1 - a_t p_t). \tag{8.16}$$

$$y_t = \frac{(1 - a_t p_t)k_t(1 + \gamma \eta) - (\varphi + \gamma - \gamma \eta)p_t q_t}{(1 - a_t p_t)(1 + \varphi + \gamma)}.$$

From these expressions, we observe that the time spent on emission-free activities, i.e. leisure and procreation, increases with the price of pollution permits p_t. Indeed, p_t acts as a tax on time spent on production. Hence, increases in p_t lower the opportunity cost of leisure and procreation:

$$\frac{\partial \ell_t}{\partial p_t} > 0, \quad \frac{\partial n_t}{\partial p_t} > 0.$$

Leisure and procreation also increase with the endowment of pollution permits. This is because they are both normal goods:

$$\frac{\partial \ell_t}{\partial q_t} > 0, \quad \frac{\partial n_t}{\partial q_t} > 0.$$

Asset accumulation (education) is reduced by the price of pollution permits because of a substitution of quantity (n_t) for quality (k_{t+1}) of children:

$$\frac{\partial b_t}{\partial p_t} < 0.$$

Finally, net individual income and production are reduced by the price p_t:

$$\frac{\partial y_t}{\partial p_t} = -\frac{(\varphi + \gamma(1 - \eta))q_t}{(1 - p_t)^2(1 + \varphi + \gamma)} < 0.$$

8.2.2 Equilibrium

The equilibrium on the market for tradable pollution rights implies that total pollution $N_t a_t y_t$ equals the total number of quotas $N_t q_t$, unless the price p_t is nil:

$$p_t(N_t a_t y_t - N_t q_t) = 0.$$

Two cases may arise depending on whether the cap is binding or not. A cap is binding if it is set lower than the otherwise total amount of pollution. This occurs when:

$$q_t < a_t y_t$$

where y_t is computed in the business-as-usual scenario. Replacing y_t by its value from equation (8.9) leads to:

$$q_t < a_t \frac{1 + \gamma \eta}{1 + \varphi + \gamma} k_t.$$

Proposition 8.1 Equilibrium with binding and non-binding cap

At time t, the equilibrium satisfies:

$$\text{If } q_t \leqslant a_t \frac{1 + \gamma \eta}{1 + \varphi + \gamma} k_t$$

$$\text{then } p_t = \frac{k_t(1 + \gamma \eta) - q_t(1 + \varphi + \gamma)}{(k_t - q_t)(1 + \gamma \eta)}. \tag{8.17}$$

$$y_t = \frac{q_t}{a_t}$$

$$\text{If } q_t > a_t \frac{1+\gamma\eta}{1+\varphi+\gamma}k_t$$

$$\text{then } p_t = 0$$

$$y_t = \frac{\gamma\eta}{1+\varphi+\gamma}\frac{k_t}{q_t}.$$

If the pollution endowment is sufficiently restrictive, there will be a positive price of pollution permits and production will match the target. If the pollution quota is large, the policy is non-binding. The price of permits then falls to zero, and the output corresponds with the one of the business-as-usual scenario.

8.2.3 Dynamics

Let us consider a constant pollution cap $E^\star$. As a consequence, the pollution endowment per household will be:

$$q_t = \frac{E^\star}{N_t}.$$

We now analyze how different levels of the pollution cap $E^\star$ affect the dynamics of population N_t. To simplify, we keep technical progress constant $a_t = 1$ and we assume full degradation of pollution within one period ($g() = 1$).

The dynamics of assets k_t and population N_t are obtained by replacing b_t, n_t, and p_t from (8.16), (8.15), and (8.17) into (8.1) and (8.10):

$$k_{t+1} = \mu k_t^\tau \left(\frac{\eta\phi N_t^\iota k_t}{1-\eta} \left(1 - \frac{k_t(1+\gamma\eta)-q_t(1+\varphi+\gamma)}{(k_t-q_t)(1+\gamma\eta)} \right) \right)^\eta.$$

$$N_{t+1} = N_t \left(\frac{\gamma(1-\eta)}{(1+\varphi+\gamma)\phi N_t^\iota} \left(1 + \frac{\frac{k_t(1+\gamma\eta)-q_t(1+\varphi+\gamma)}{(k_t-q_t)(1+\gamma\eta)}}{1-\frac{k_t(1+\gamma\eta)-q_t(1+\varphi+\gamma)}{(k_t-q_t)(1+\gamma\eta)}} \frac{q_t}{k_t} \right) \right).$$

Using $q_t = E^\star/N_t$ and simplifying leads to:

$$k_{t+1} = \mu k_t^{\tau+\eta} \left(\frac{\eta\phi N_t^\iota E^\star(\varphi+\gamma-\gamma\eta)}{(N_t k_t - E^\star)(1-\eta)(1+\gamma\eta)} \right)^\eta.$$

$$N_{t+1} = \frac{\gamma(1-\eta)(N_t k_t - E^\star)}{\phi N_t^\iota k_t(\varphi+\gamma-\gamma\eta)}.$$

To analyze these dynamics let us first look for steady states $\bar{k}$, $\bar{N}$. Solving the last equation for k at steady state leads to:

$$\bar{k} = \frac{\gamma(1 - \eta)E^{\star}/N}{\gamma(1 - \eta) - \phi N^{\iota}(\varphi + \gamma - \gamma\eta)}.$$

Replacing k_{t+1} and k_t by this value in the first dynamic equation, we find:

$$\mu\left(\frac{\bar{N}}{E^{\star}}\right)^{1-\tau-\eta}\left(\frac{\gamma\eta}{1 + \gamma\eta}\right)^{\eta} = \left(\frac{\gamma(1 - \eta)}{\gamma(1 - \eta) - \phi\bar{N}^{\iota}(\gamma + \varphi - \gamma\eta)}\right)^{1-\tau}. \tag{8.18}$$

This equation cannot be solved explicitly for $\bar{N}$. Let us rewrite this equality as

$$\Psi_1(E^{\star}, \bar{N}) = \Psi_2(\bar{N}).$$

Figure 8.1 represents these two functions. The left-hand side Ψ_1 is an increasing and concave function of $\bar{N}$, starting from 0 when $\bar{N} = 0$ and going to infinity

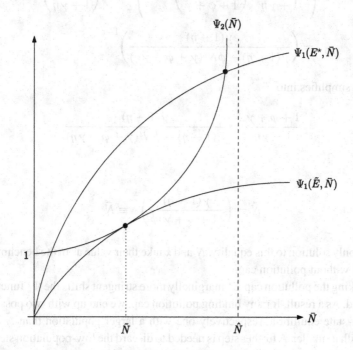

Figure 8.1 Steady state population with pollution cap

as $\bar{N} \to \infty$. The right-hand side Ψ_2 is an increasing and convex function of $\bar{N}$, starting from 1 when $\bar{N} = 0$ and going to infinity as $\bar{N} \to \hat{N}$ (vertical asymptote), with:

$$\hat{N} = \left(\frac{\gamma(1 - \eta)}{\phi(\gamma + \varphi - \gamma\eta)} \right)^{1/\iota}.$$

Hence, given the characteristics of the two functions, there are two, one or no steady state, depending on the stringency of the cap $E^\star$.

We can show that, when the cap $E^\star$ is set at its most stringent and yet non-binding level $\tilde{E}$, i.e. such that $p = 0$ and $y = q$, the steady state is unique. Indeed, in that case:

$$\tilde{E} = Nk \frac{1 + \gamma\eta}{1 + \varphi + \gamma}.$$

Equation (8.18) would be, in that case:

$$\mu \left(\frac{1 + \varphi + \gamma}{1 + \gamma\eta} \left(\frac{\mu^{1/\eta} \, \gamma\eta}{1 + \varphi + \gamma} \right)^{\frac{-\eta}{1-\tau-\eta}} \right)^{1-\tau-\eta} \left(\frac{\gamma\eta}{1 + \gamma\eta} \right)^{\eta}$$

$$= \left(\frac{\gamma(1 - \eta)}{\gamma(1 - \eta) - \phi\bar{N}^\iota(\gamma + \varphi - \gamma\eta)} \right)^{1-\tau}$$

which simplifies into

$$\frac{1 + \varphi + \gamma}{1 + \gamma\eta} = \frac{\gamma(1 - \eta)}{\gamma(1 - \eta) - \phi\bar{N}^\iota(\gamma + \varphi - \gamma\eta)}$$

and

$$\bar{N} = \left(\frac{\gamma(1 - \eta)}{(1 + \varphi + \gamma)\phi} \right)^{\frac{1}{\iota}} \equiv \tilde{N}$$

is the only solution to this equality. $\bar{N}$ and $\bar{k}$ take their value as in the benchmark model without pollution cap.

Making the pollution cap $E^\star$ marginally more stringent shifts the Ψ_1 function upward. As a result, for any binding pollution cap, we end up with two possible steady-state equilibria, respectively one with a larger population than $\tilde{N}$ and one with a smaller. A further step is needed to discard the low-population steady state and demonstrate the pro-natalist effect of lowering $E^\star$.

If $E^\star$ is restrictive enough, the low-population steady state has a population close to zero, and the high-population steady state has a population close to the value of the vertical asymptote $\hat{N}$. The first one is increasing in $E^\star$, the second one is decreasing in $E^\star$. We can show that the steady state where population is large and increasing with the restrictiveness of the pollution cap is the stable one.

Proposition 8.2 Population and the pollution cap
For a sufficiently stringent pollution cap $E^\star$, there is a stable-steady state population, decreasing in $E^\star$.

Proof: Linearizing the dynamic system around the steady state leads to the following Jacobian matrix:

$$
\begin{bmatrix}
\eta + \tau - \dfrac{\gamma\eta(1-\eta)}{(\varphi+\gamma-\eta\gamma)\phi\bar{N}^\iota} & -\dfrac{E^\star\gamma\eta(1-\eta)\left(\gamma(1-\eta)-\iota(\varphi+\gamma-\eta\gamma)\phi\bar{N}^\iota\right)}{\bar{N}^2(\varphi+\gamma-\eta\gamma)\phi\bar{N}^\iota\left((\varphi+\gamma-\eta\gamma)\phi\bar{N}^\iota+\gamma(1-\eta)\right)} \\[2ex]
\dfrac{\bar{N}^2\left(\gamma(1-\eta)-(\varphi+\gamma-\eta\gamma)\phi\bar{N}^\iota\right)^2}{E^\star\gamma(\varphi+\gamma-\eta\gamma)(1-\eta)\phi\bar{N}^\iota} & \dfrac{\gamma(1-\eta)}{(\varphi+\gamma-\eta\gamma)\phi\bar{N}^\iota}-\iota
\end{bmatrix}
$$

The determinant of this matrix is:

$$
\frac{\gamma(1-\eta)\tau}{(\varphi+\gamma-\eta\gamma)\phi\bar{N}^\iota}-\iota\tau.
$$

It is decreasing in $\bar{N}$. Its trace is:

$$
\frac{\gamma(1-\eta)^2}{(\varphi+\gamma-\eta\gamma)\phi\bar{N}^\iota}-\iota+\eta+\tau
$$

also decreasing in $\bar{N}$.

For the steady state close to $\hat{N}$, the determinant has a value close to $\tau(1-\iota)$ and a trace close to $1-\iota+\tau$. It is therefore stable. ∎

As long-run population $\bar{N}$ is higher if the pollution cap is set at a more stringent level, income per capita will unambiguously be lower, as $y = E^\star/N$.

From the dynamic point of view, the pro-population tilt of pollution caps is worrying. For a given $E^\star$, emission endowments per person inevitably become more and more stringent as generations pass. Because of this pro-natalist effect, capping emissions impoverishes the successive generations more than in a conventional set-up with exogenous fertility.

It is worth spelling out why capping emissions tends to reduce production rather than procreation. This is the case because production generates emissions from the moment it takes place onwards, whereas procreation rather generates delayed emissions. This rests on two assumptions. First only physical good production generates pollution. Second, children do not consume

Table 8.1. *Calibration: a summary*

Parameter		Value
Taste for children	γ	0.471
Weight of leisure in utility	φ	2.279
Return to education	η	0.531
Intergenerational transmission of human capital	τ	0.072
Importance of space in the cost of rearing children	ι	0.598
Productivity of education	μ	24.042
Time–cost parameter	ϕ	0.016

physical goods. This implies that the emissions of a person take place at adulthood. In a more general set-up, it would be sufficient to assume that pro-creation and leisure are less emission-intensive activities than production. This is why capping emissions at period t puts less pressure on procreation than on production. In a way, if procreation generates emissions only through future production (i.e. when children will themselves become producers), the capping scheme generates a specific form of externality. Current adults willing to procreate at a rate higher than the replacement rate do not internalize the fact that tomorrow's pollution cap will have to be divided into smaller pollution endowments.[3]

8.3 Numerical experiment

In order to provide a meaningful example of the mechanisms studied analyti-cally above, we calibrate the parameters of the model and we simulate the effect of introducing pollution caps on the dynamics of income and population.

8.3.1 Calibration

Assume that each period lasts twenty-five years. Table 8.1 summarizes the calibration results. We first identify the five parameters γ, φ, η, τ, and ι with the following five restrictions:

1. The share of consumption in GDP is 80 percent (corresponds to public and private consumptions of the national accounts). Using equations (8.5)

---

[3] If the degradation rate were lower one, there would be an additional externality related to the accumulation of pollution stock.

and (8.9), we find that:

$$\frac{c_t}{y_t} = \frac{1}{1+\gamma\eta} = 0.8.$$

2. The time spent on leisure (ℓ_t) and procreation ($\phi\bar{N}^\iota$) amounts to two-thirds of total available time. (This has become a standard value in the literature since Ghez and Becker (1975) found that households allocate approximately one-third of their time to market activities.) Using (8.13):

$$\phi\bar{N}^\iota = \frac{\gamma(1-\eta)}{1+\varphi+\gamma}.$$

From (8.6):

$$\ell_t + \phi\bar{N}^\iota = \frac{\varphi}{1+\varphi+\gamma} + \frac{\gamma(1-\eta)}{1+\varphi+\gamma} = \frac{\varphi+\gamma(1-\eta)}{1+\varphi+\gamma} = \frac{2}{3}.$$

3. At steady state, the time spent rearing children is equal to 15 percent (see Chapter 2) of the time remaining after leisure has been accounted for:

$$\frac{\phi N^\iota}{1-\ell_t} = 0.15.$$

This implies:

$$\frac{\gamma(1-\eta)}{1+\gamma} = 0.15.$$

4. Following the literature on conditional convergence (see Abreu *et al.* (2005) for a survey), the convergence speed of income per capita is 2 percent per year. For the dynamic equation (8.11) we get:

$$\frac{k_{t+1}}{k_t} = \left(\frac{k_t}{k_{t-1}}\right)^{\tau+\eta} \left(\frac{N_t}{N_{t-1}}\right)^{\iota\eta}.$$

The required convergence speed is obtained with $\tau + \eta = 0.98^{25}$.

5. The dynamics of population are calibrated to match the forecasted evolution of world population between 2008 ($t-1$), 2033 (t), and 2058 ($t+1$). From

Table 8.2. *Benchmark simulation – world economy 1983–2208*

t	k_t	N_t	c_t	n_t	ℓ_t	b_t	y_t	Y_t
1983	16.027	4.680	4.274	1.425	0.608	0.750	5.342	25.002
2008	29.307	6.670	7.815	1.153	0.608	1.694	9.769	65.164
2033	47.210	7.692	12.589	1.059	0.608	2.972	15.737	121.052
2058	65.863	8.146	17.564	1.023	0.608	4.291	21.954	178.847
2083	82.001	8.336	21.867	1.009	0.608	5.416	27.334	227.862
2108	94.283	8.414	25.142	1.004	0.608	6.262	31.428	264.432
2133	102.871	8.445	27.432	1.002	0.608	6.848	34.290	289.596
2158	108.556	8.458	28.948	1.001	0.608	7.233	36.185	306.058
2183	112.191	8.463	29.918	1.000	0.608	7.478	37.397	316.498
2208	114.465	8.465	30.524	1.000	0.608	7.630	38.155	322.992

the dynamic equation (8.12) we get:

$$\frac{N_{t+1}}{N_t} = \left(\frac{N_t}{N_{t-1}}\right)^{1-\iota}$$

and we have $N_{t-1} = 6.67$, $N_t = 8.18$, and $N_{t+1} = 8.88$ from the 2007 IIASA World Population Projection.

Solving this system gives $\gamma = 0.470588$, $\varphi = 2.27941$, $\eta = 0.53125$, $\tau = 0.0722147$, and $\iota = 0.5976$. Notice that η is in line with estimates of the return from education (see the discussion in section 2.3.1). Moreover, this η is almost enough to obtain the required speed of convergence of income per capita, as the additional parameter τ is small. Notice finally that the parameter ι implies an annual convergence speed for population of 3.56 percent per year.

The two productivity levels, μ and ϕ, are parameters that determine the size of population and income per capita. Imposing initial conditions so as to start in 1983 requires $N_0 = 4.68$ (measured in billions inhabitants) and $y_0 = 4.541$ (measured in thousands dollars per person and per year). Inverting (8.9) gives us $k_0 = 16.0271$. In order to obtain the right levels $N_1 = 6.67$ and $y_1 = 7.614$ in 2008, we need to have $\phi = 0.0164$ and $\mu = 24.0417$.

8.3.2 Simulation

Table 8.2 provides the simulation from 1983 (initial conditions) to 2208 when no pollution cap is imposed. It illustrates the properties of the benchmark model: monotonic convergence of population, which tends to 8.47 billion, and income

Table 8.3. *Simulation with a constant pollution cap – 1983–2208*

t	q_t	k_t	N_t	p_t	n_t	ℓ_t	b_t	y_t	Y_t
1983	21.368	16.027	4.680	0.000	1.425	0.608	0.750	5.342	25.002
2008	14.991	29.307	6.670	0.000	1.153	0.608	1.694	9.769	65.164
2033	13.000	47.210	7.692	0.240	1.151	0.661	2.259	13.000	100.000
2058	11.294	56.928	8.855	0.505	1.171	0.731	1.929	11.294	100.000
2083	9.647	53.070	10.366	0.556	1.087	0.746	1.774	9.647	100.000
2108	8.871	50.501	11.272	0.574	1.042	0.752	1.703	8.871	100.000
2133	8.513	49.231	11.746	0.582	1.020	0.754	1.669	8.513	100.000
2158	8.346	48.624	11.982	0.586	1.010	0.755	1.653	8.346	100.000
2183	8.266	48.335	12.097	0.587	1.005	0.756	1.646	8.266	100.000
2208	8.229	48.197	12.153	0.588	1.002	0.756	1.642	8.229	100.000

per capita (38155 dollars per capita in 2208). Fertility declines rapidly to its replacement level. Leisure is constant.

Let us now impose a constant pollution cap:

$$E^\star = 100,$$

starting to bind in 2033 (one should read the twenty-five-year period surrounding 2033). Table 8.3 provides the results. There are now two new columns: the endowment of rights per households q_t and price of the pollution right p_t. The price in 2033 is 0.24, corresponding to an implicit tax of 24 percent on production. Following the tax, total output Y_t is indeed limited to 100. As a consequence of this tax, the households retreat from market activities to devote more time to leisure (66.1 percent instead of 60.8 percent in the benchmark) and to procreation (1.151 child per person instead of 1.059 in the benchmark, to be multiplied by 2 to compare to fertility rates per woman). The rise in procreation does not look big, but it is large enough to have immense consequences for the future, through its cumulative effect over time. Population in 2058 is now 8.85 billion instead of 8.15 billion in the benchmark and converges in the long run to more than 12 billion instead of 8.5 billion in the benchmark.

Figure 8.2 compares the benchmark and the constant pollution cap paths together with an iso-pollution curve. The benchmark follows a convex path in this plane, and crosses the iso-pollution line $E^\star = 100$ early on. The constant cap path, on the contrary, moves south-east as soon as the cap is binding. It will converge to a situation with a large population and an income per capita only slightly above the 1983 level.

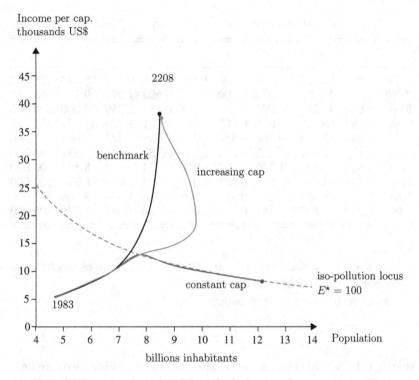

Figure 8.2 Income and population dynamics in the examples

Suppose now that the pollution cap is changing over time exogenously. We assume that there is some technical progress making production more and more clean over time. Precisely, we assume that

$$a_t = (1.01)^{-25(t-2)},$$

which reflects a technical progress of 1 percent per year. t is equal to 2 in 2033, this formulation is the same as previously for the year 2033, but the cap is becoming less and less stringent as time passes. Table 8.4 provides the results and Figure 8.2 compares the path with increasing cap with the two previous ones. This new path is an intermediate case. In the short run (which means here a few generations), it follows the constant cap path, with lower income per person and higher population. In the long run though, the cap is not binding any more thanks to technical progress, and the path converges to the benchmark steady state. As population has risen fast in the beginning, it actually

Table 8.4. *Simulation with an increasing pollution cap – 1983–2208*

t	q_t	k_t	N_t	p_t	n_t	ℓ_t	b_t	y_t	Y_t
1983	12.992	16.027	4.680	0.000	1.425	0.608	0.750	5.342	25.002
2008	11.690	29.307	6.670	0.000	1.153	0.608	1.694	9.769	65.164
2033	13.000	47.210	7.692	0.240	1.151	0.661	2.259	13.000	100.000
2058	14.483	56.928	8.855	0.318	1.089	0.680	2.660	14.483	128.243
2083	17.058	62.944	9.641	0.256	1.012	0.665	3.372	17.058	164.463
2108	21.622	71.912	9.755	0.140	0.964	0.638	4.487	21.622	210.913
2133	28.768	84.502	9.402	0.000	0.939	0.608	5.998	28.167	264.830
2158	39.279	99.747	8.831	0.000	0.975	0.608	6.819	33.249	293.627
2183	51.657	108.076	8.611	0.000	0.990	0.608	7.278	36.025	310.229
2208	66.922	112.532	8.525	0.000	0.996	0.608	7.533	37.511	319.761

overshoots its long-run level, and converges from above to its steady state. The cost of this policy in terms of income is still very large. For example, income per person would be $17058 per year in 2083 with the cap, and $27334 in the benchmark.

In future research, it would be interesting to consider a policy under which we cap population rather than emissions, for example along the lines proposed in Chapter 9. One question could be the following: is there a population cap $N^\star$ such that the desired emission level $E^\star$ could be met? If yes, does $N^\star$ allow for higher income per capita than under the model capping emissions directly? If the answer to these two questions is positive, the next question will become: under which conditions does it follow that we should cap population rather than emissions?

8.4 Conclusion

Pollution control, and especially greenhouse gas emission reduction, are matters of great importance. However, we have shown that such policies unexpectedly impact on the population dynamics through a production–procreation substitution effect. Capping pollution may therefore delay the demographic transition in developing countries and the drop in global fertility. Such an increase in population, compared with a business-as-usual scenario, may in turn be damaging either in environmental terms if the pollution scheme is ineffective, or in terms of average standard of living – both independently and through the operation of the pollution cap at the next period.

Our approach highlights the same tradeoff between being "warmer and richer" and "cooler but poorer" as the one popularized by Ridley (2010). The cost of curbing carbon emissions can be huge for developing countries. Our set-up makes clear one of the mechanisms through which this happens: by delaying the demographic transition.

9
Population policy

In many countries, a gap obtains between the actual fertility rate and what is perceived as the optimal fertility rate. In some cases, fertility is deemed too high, typically out of concern for the ability of our natural environment to cope with such an anthropic pressure (climate change being a possible example) or for the capacity of the land to feed and provide enough space to so many people (a motive present, among others, in China's one-child policy, see Greenhalgh (2003)). In other cases, the actual fertility is perceived as too low. It can be due to the need to be numerous enough to support an endangered cultural identity, for example. In some cases, it is the relative size of the various cohorts coexisting in a country that is at stake, a low fertility rate being one of the factors threatening the financial viability of pension schemes and health care systems. Other concerns about relative size of different groups within a population arise as well with respect to ethnic composition or educational level, fertility and mortality rates differing along such characteristics.

In the presence of under-population, various measures have been proposed and adopted. For example, at least in some contexts such as post-World War Two, one justification for the introduction of family benefits was a pro-natalist one. Other measures include extensive parental (paid or unpaid) leave schemes, parent-friendly workplaces or the public provision of day-care. More recently, it has been argued that linking pension benefits to fertility would be a way to restore optimality (see Schoonbroodt and Tertilt (2011)). In contrast, whenever over-population obtains, there is a variety of measures available to control population, ranging from information campaigns on contraception means, the liberalization of abortion or the leveling up of women's educational level, to China's one-child policy.

This chapter relies on material published in de la Croix and Gosseries (2009).

Population policy is searching for tools able to deal with both over- and under-population, the latter being a more recent concern in developed countries. In this chapter, we show that tradable entitlements provide an interesting tool to deal with population-control problems. We generalize the framework with both tradable procreation allowances and tradable procreation exemptions, in order to tackle the two sides of the problem. We next address two central concerns regarding such a scheme, namely distributive and educational concerns. The former refers to the fact that such a scheme, especially through its tradability component, would be detrimental to the poor. The latter refers to the inter-dependency of fertility and education choices stressed in Chapters 2 and 5. Third, we also investigate the implications of a global version of procreation entitlements, in line with comparable attempts to fight global warming (Kyoto agreement).

One contribution of this chapter is to show how population policy is inter-connected to redistribution and inequality dimensions. Starting with Malthus' policy advises, population control has often been a way to limit the fertility of the poor. The relationship between Malthusian views and the eugenic approach of the late nineteenth and early twentieth centuries is well explained in Pearce (2010). Is this a reason to abandon the idea of population-control policy? By taking into account education decisions, this chapter shows a different angle to the problem: population control might well reduce the number of children from poor parents, but it will increase their education and their chance of becoming skilled. The quality–quantity tradeoff is of particular relevance when population policy is discussed: taxing birth has the same effects as subsidizing education, and helps to reduce poverty among the living.

It remains an open question whether each of these grounds is legitimate, especially for those giving a significant importance to people's freedom (not) to procreate. Philosophers have actually shown that the very idea of an opti-mal population raises an even more fundamental challenge: as soon as we ask "optimal for whom?" it becomes clear that the answer may end up remaining unstable since the very existence of the agent with regard to whom we need to assess the benefit is itself a choice variable. The question of the (Pareto-) optimality criterion with endogenous fertility rate is present in the literature, for two recent contributions see Golosov *et al.* (2007) and Michel and Wigniolle (2006). In the present chapter, we shall leave aside such questions, assuming that in a given territory at a given point in time it can be meaningful to aim at a fertility rate different from the one expected in the absence of any state intervention. Hence, assuming that a fertility target may be defined in a mean-ingful manner, we shall be concerned here with the means to reach such a target.

9.1 Procreation entitlements

One measure that could serve both pro-natalist and anti-natalist purposes has never been put in place so far: tradable procreation entitlements. Tradable quotas schemes have been promoted as a policy tool for several decades. They have typically been proposed and widely implemented to combat air pollution,[1] overproduction (e.g. tradable milk quotas in the EU), and over-exploitation of natural resources (e.g. individual transferable fish quotas). It has also been proposed in other areas such as inflation control (Lerner and Colander (1980)), asylum policy (Schuck (1997) and Hathaway and Neve (1997)), immigration policy (Crettez (2011)), or deficit control (Casella (1999)), and, more recently, airport noise reduction (Bréchet and Picard (2010)) while never being implemented. The idea is always to agree on a cap to reduce the extent of a given problem (over-production, over-inflation, pollution, excessive unemployment, etc.), to allocate the corresponding rights to the various actors involved (states, firms and/or individuals), and to allow for tradability of such rights between the actors, in order to take into account differences in marginal reduction costs. One of the oldest of such proposals is Boulding's (1964) idea of tradable procreation licenses to combat over-population:

> I have only one positive suggestion to make, a proposal
> which now seems so far-fetched that I find it creates only amusement
> when I propose it. I think in all seriousness, however, that a system of
> marketable licenses to have children is the only one which will combine
> the minimum of social control necessary to the solution to this problem
> with a maximum of individual liberty and ethical choice. Each girl on
> approaching maturity would be presented with a certificate which will
> entitle its owner to have, say, 2.2 children, or whatever number would
> ensure a reproductive rate of one. The unit of these certificates might
> be the "deci-child," and accumulation of ten of these units by purchase,
> inheritance, or gift would permit a woman in maturity to have one legal
> child. We would then set up a market in these units in which the rich
> and the philoprogenitive would purchase them from the poor, the nuns,
> the maiden aunts, and so on. The men perhaps could be left out of these
> arrangements, as it is only the fertility of women which is strictly relevant
> to population control. However, it may be found socially desirable to
> have them in the plan, in which case all children both male and female
> would receive, say, eleven or twelve deci-child certificates at birth or at
> maturity, and a woman could then accumulate these through marriage.

---

[1] The US 1990 Clean Air Act Amendments initiated the first large-scale use of the tradable permit approach to pollution control. The empirical analysis of Joskow *et al.* (1998) shows that the emission rights market created in 1990 had become reasonably efficient within four years.

On top of a separate and short discussion by Tobin (1970) with no reference to Boulding, Heer (1975) and Daly (1991, 1993) discuss Boulding's proposal. They both propose amendments or complements to the scheme's design. Such proposals essentially revolve around four issues: the need for continuous adjustments of the birth rate target, the issue of shifting up the reproduction age through the system, the problem of early mortality, and the definition of the license beneficiaries.

9.2 Implementing tradable procreation rights

The salient features of the benchmark economy described in Chapter 1 and in which we shall introduce procreation entitlements consists in fertility and education choice by households belonging to different income groups. Households are heterogeneous in terms of human capital, and low-skilled households choose to have more children than skilled ones. Differential fertility will turn out to be a key element in the analysis of procreation entitlements. Remember we can interpret agents either as households in a country or as countries at the global level.

The government (or an international organization) has a fertility objective of v children per person. We do not question this objective, but only impose the reasonable condition that it should be biologically feasible, i.e.:

$$0 < v < \frac{1}{\phi}. \tag{C1}$$

Considering the problem of a given country, the implementation sequence of procreation entitlements is detailed in Table 9.1. Let us first consider the sequence for allowances, which are designed to prevent fertility from being above the target. At her majority, each parent receives for free[2] v procreation allowances from the Procreation Agency. We assume that each procreation allowance corresponds with the right to give birth to one child. Each time she gives birth to a child, a parent has to cede one procreation allowance back to the Procreation Agency. Procreation rights can be sold and purchased at any moment in time at a price g_t.

We now consider the sequence for exemptions, which are designed to prevent fertility from being below the target. Each time a parent gives birth to a child, and as soon as observed parent's fertility n_t becomes larger than v, she will receive free of charge from the Procreation Agency one exemption right. At the

---

[2] An alternative mode of initial allocation consists in an auction. The distributive impact of such an alternative will depend to a large extent on the way in which the regulator will spend the hence collected resources.

Table 9.1. *Implementation sequence of procreation entitlements for a country*

	Allowances (price $g_t \geqslant 0$)	Exemptions (price $q_t \geqslant 0$)
At majority	receives v rights	
At each birth	cedes back 1 right	if number births $> v$ receives 1 right
At menopause		if $n_t < v < 0$ gives back $v - n_t$ rights
Over complete life	Procreation and exemption rights can be sold and purchased	

standard menopausal age, each parent having fewer biological children than v has to give the Procreation Agency $v - n$ exemptions, which she will have purchased on the procreation exemptions market at a price $q_t \geqslant 0$. Parents with more children than v can sell on the market the unused exemptions.

We assume that fines are such that everyone will be deterred from violating such rules at equilibrium.[3] Table 9.1 makes visible three specific properties of a tradable entitlement scheme aimed at addressing a problem of under-provision. First, the exemptions are allocated ex post facto rather than initially. Second, in comparison with taxation, our proposal exhibits two properties. Not only is it quantity focused as opposed to price focused, but the joint operation of allowances and exemptions guarantees that the target will strictly be met; in case of tradable exemptions, we see from the table that their amount is not limited ex ante otherwise than through the biological constraint ($n_t \leqslant 1/\phi$); in the absence of an upper limit, reaching strictly the target cannot be guaranteed unless the system is coupled with a tradable allowances scheme, which is the case here. Third, contrary to a subsidy, the value of the exemption will fluctuate as a function of market conditions.

In our model there is no child mortality or infertility risk. In a more general set-up, these issues could be addressed by assuming a perfect insurance market which would cover those risks.

After inclusion of the procreation entitlements, the budget constraint for an adult becomes:

$$c_t^i = \left[w_t^i(1 - \phi n_t^i) - n_t^i e_t^i \right] + g_t(v - n_t^i) + q_t(n_t^i - v). \qquad (9.1)$$

---

[3] Fines would have to be targeted in such a way as not to affect the children themselves. Otherwise children would be sanctioned as a matter of fact for what they are not responsible for – see Dworkin (2000).

The variable g_t is the price of one procreation allowance, while q_t is the price of one procreation exemption. Since the two types of entitlements are put in operation simultaneously, only the difference $g_t - q_t$ matters. We call this difference "procreation price" and accordingly define:

$$p_t = g_t - q_t.$$

In equilibrium, p_t can be positive or negative. Equilibria with positive procreation price p_t reflect situations where fertility is discouraged, while equilibria with negative p_t obtain in cases in which fertility is promoted. Definition 9.1 stresses that there is one additional market compared with Definition 1.1.

Definition 9.1 Inter-temporal equilibrium with procreation rights

Given initial population sizes P_0^A and P_0^B, an equilibrium is a sequence of individual quantities $(c_t^i, e_t^i, n_t^i)_{i=A,B.t\geqslant 0}$, group sizes $(P_t^i)_{i=A,B.t\geqslant 0}$, and prices $(p_t)_{t\geqslant 0}$, such that:

- *consumption, education, and fertility maximize households' utility (1.1) subject to the budget constraint (9.1);*
- *group sizes evolve according to (1.3);*
- *labor market clears, i.e. equation (1.4) holds, and wages are equal to marginal productivity, υ^A for unskilled and υ^B for skilled;*
- *asset market clears, i.e.:*

$$\sum_i (n_t^i - v)P_t^i = 0. \tag{9.2}$$

Fertility and education choices

In this section we drop the time index to save notation. A condition for the problem to be well defined requires the endowment of the household to be positive: $w + pv > 0$. This condition will hold for all households if it holds for the unskilled:

$$\upsilon^A + pv > 0. \tag{C2}$$

This condition is always satisfied when fertility is discouraged ($p > 0$). When fertility is promoted, condition (C2) imposes a lower bound on the price of procreation (i.e. an upper bound on the price of exemptions). The condition implies that a poor household wanting to have no children should be able to afford it.

As in the benchmark model, the solution to the household decision problem can either be interior or at a corner. There is an additional difficulty compared with the problem without procreation entitlements. If fertility is strongly encouraged by a negative procreation price p, the biological constraint $n \leqslant 1/\phi$ might be binding, i.e. some households may want to have more children than is biologically feasible. In the benchmark model, the optimal n is always below the biological maximum $1/\phi$. Were this not the case, households would have no income at all. As soon as another source of income is assumed, that constraint should be taken into account (another example of the role played by this constraint can be found in de la Croix and Vander Donckt (2010)).

To find the solution to the household maximization problem, we study the following Kuhn–Tucker problem:

$$\max_{c,e,n} \{\ln[c] + \gamma \ln[n] + \gamma \eta \ln[\theta + e];$$

$$w(1 - \phi n) - ne + p(v - n) \geqslant c \geqslant 0, 1/\phi \geqslant n, e \geqslant 0\}.$$

It is obvious from the properties of the utility function (non-satiety and $u'(0) = +\infty$) that optimal consumption is positive and that the budget constraint holds with equality. We can thus substitute c from the budget constraint into the utility function. The problem becomes:

$$\max_{e,n} \{\ln[w(1 - \phi n) - ne + p(v - n)] + \gamma \ln[n]$$

$$+ \gamma \eta \ln[\theta + e]; 1/\phi \geqslant n, e \geqslant 0\}.$$

The Kuhn–Tucker conditions are:

$$a + \frac{\gamma \eta}{e + \theta} - \frac{n}{-(en) + w(1 - n\phi) + p(-n + v)} = 0$$

$$-b + \frac{\gamma}{n} + \frac{-e - p - w\phi}{-(en) + w(1 - n\phi) + p(-n + v)} = 0$$

$$ae = 0$$

$$b\left(-n + \frac{1}{\phi}\right) = 0$$

$$a \geqslant 0$$

$$b \geqslant 0$$

$$n \leqslant \frac{1}{\phi}$$

$$e \geqslant 0.$$

The first four equations define a system that we can solve for (a, b, n, e). There are four solutions:

$$b = \frac{\phi\left((1+\gamma)\theta - w\left(1+\gamma\eta\right)\phi - p\left(1+\gamma - \gamma\left(1-\eta\right)v\phi\right)\right)}{\theta - p\left(1 - v\phi\right)}, \quad a = 0,$$

$$e = \frac{-\theta - p\gamma\eta\left(1 - v\phi\right)}{1 + \gamma\eta}, \quad n = \frac{1}{\phi}. \tag{9.3}$$

$$b = \frac{\phi\left(w\phi + p\left(1 + \gamma(1 - v\phi)\right)\right)}{p(1 - v\phi)}, \quad a = -\frac{\gamma\eta}{\theta} - \frac{1}{p(1 - v\phi)}, \quad e = 0, \quad n = \frac{1}{\phi}. \tag{9.4}$$

$$b = 0, \quad a = \gamma\left(\frac{1}{p + w\phi} - \frac{\eta}{\theta}\right), \quad e = 0, \quad n = \frac{\gamma\left(w + pv\right)}{(1 + \gamma)\left(p + w\phi\right)}. \tag{9.5}$$

$$b = 0, \quad a = 0, \quad e = \frac{\eta\left(p + w\phi\right) - \theta}{1 - \eta}, \quad n = \frac{\gamma\left(1 - \eta\right)\left(w + pv\right)}{(1 + \gamma)\left(p - \theta + w\phi\right)}. \tag{9.6}$$

From these equations we can fully characterize the solution to the individual problem.

Proposition 9.1 Solution to the individual problem
Define the following threshold values for the procreation price:

$$\hat{p}(w) \equiv \frac{\theta - \eta\phi w}{\eta}. \tag{9.7}$$

$$\tilde{p}(w) \equiv \frac{\theta(1 + \gamma) - (1 + \eta\gamma)\phi w}{\gamma(1 - (1 - \eta)\phi v) + 1}. \tag{9.8}$$

$$\bar{p}(w) \equiv \frac{-\phi w}{\gamma(1 - \phi v) + 1} < 0. \tag{9.9}$$

$$\check{p} \equiv \frac{-\theta}{\gamma\eta(1 - \phi v)} < 0. \tag{9.10}$$

Assume that (C1) and (C2) hold.

R1 If $p < \check{p}$ and $p < \tilde{p}(w)$, $n = 1/\phi$, and

$$e = \frac{-\gamma\eta(1 + \phi v)p - \theta}{1 + \gamma\eta} > 0. \tag{9.11}$$

R2 If $p > \check{p}$ and $p < \bar{p}(w)$, $e = 0$ and $n = 1/\phi$.

R3 If $p < \hat{p}(w)$ and $p > \tilde{p}(w)$, $e = 0$ and

$$n = \frac{\gamma(w + vp)}{(\phi w + p)(1 + \gamma)} < \frac{1}{\phi} \qquad (9.12)$$

R4 If $p > \hat{p}(w)$ and $p > \tilde{p}(w)$,

$$e = \frac{\eta \phi w - \theta + \eta p}{1 - \eta} > 0, \qquad and: \qquad (9.13)$$

$$n = \frac{(1 - \eta)\gamma(w + vp)}{(\phi w - \theta + p)(1 + \gamma)} < \frac{1}{\phi}. \qquad (9.14)$$

Proof: The function $\hat{p}(w)$ is obtained by solving for p the condition $e = 0$ in equation (9.6) or the condition $a = 0$ in equation (9.5). The function $\tilde{p}(w)$ is obtained by solving for p the condition $n = 1/\phi$ in equation (9.6) or the condition $b = 0$ in equation (9.3). The function $\bar{p}(w)$ is obtained by solving for p the condition $b = 0$ in equation (9.4) or the condition $n = 1/\phi$ in equation (9.5). The threshold $\check{p}$ is obtained by solving for p the condition $a = 0$ in equation (9.4) or the condition $e = 0$ in equation (9.3). ∎

There are therefore four different regimes depending on the procreation price and the income:

- *R1* Procreation price p is very negative and wage w is low. The household does not work and specializes entirely in the production of children. This reproductive activity is so well paid that they can afford to provide some education to their children.
- *R2* p is negative and w is low. The household specializes entirely in the production of children, but is too poor to provide any education.
- *R3* p is positive or moderately negative and w is low. The household has some children, works, and does not provide education. This corresponds to the corner regime with no education that we already found in the model without procreation rights.
- *R4* p is positive or moderately negative but w is high. It corresponds to the interior solution. It is obtained when the price of the procreation rights is not too low. If it was, either households would like to offer no education at all to their children (the constraint $e \geqslant 0$ binds), or their economically optimal

fertility would be above the biological maximum (the constraint $n \leqslant 1/\phi$ binds).

Obviously, regimes R1 and R2 are anecdotic because the procreation prices for which they obtain are unrealistically negative (for such prices to occur at equilibrium, we would need a radical pro-natalist target) but still need to be considered when studying the general equilibrium with procreation rights.

The threshold procreation prices defined in Proposition 9.1 display two interesting properties. First, we can unambiguously rank them when the wage is equal to zero:

$$\hat{p}(0) > \tilde{p}(0) > \bar{p}(0) = 0 > \check{p}.$$

Second, they all intersect at the same point:

$$\text{at } w^{\star} = \frac{\theta(1 + \gamma(1 - \phi v))}{\gamma \eta \phi(1 - \phi v)}, \qquad \hat{p}(w^{\star}) = \tilde{p}(w^{\star}) = \bar{p}(w^{\star}) = \check{p}.$$

We represent these four lines and the corresponding regimes R1 to R4 in Figure 9.1.

Let us now consider a household with wage w. Starting from a very high price p, the solution will be in regime R4. Letting the price drop, and abstracting from the constraint (C2), two situations can arise. If $w < w^{\star}$, the succession of regimes will follow R4 $\rightarrow$ R3 $\rightarrow$ R2 $\rightarrow$ R1 as prices drop; if $w \geqslant w^{\star}$, we will pass from R4 to R1 directly. When we take into account the constraint (C2), regime R1 will never be a possible outcome for households with a very high wage.

We can now establish the properties of fertility and education as a function of income and procreation prices. Let us start with the effect of income.

Proposition 9.2 Fertility, education and income *For low income and low procreation price (regimes R1 and R2), small changes in income neither affect educational investment nor influence fertility.*

For low income and high procreation price (R3), small changes in income influence fertility negatively while leaving educational investment unaffected.

For a high level of income (R4), small changes in income affect spending on education positively. They also adversely influence fertility if and only if the price of procreation is low enough:

$$\frac{\partial n}{\partial w} < 0 \Leftrightarrow p < \frac{\theta}{1 - \phi v}.$$

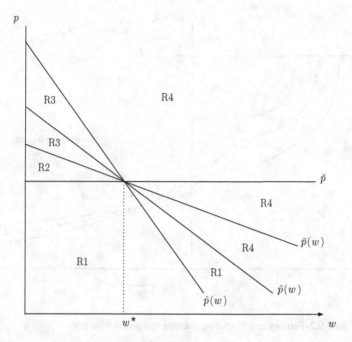

Figure 9.1 Solution to the individuals problem: regimes R1 to R4

Proof: All claims are a direct consequence of the results of Proposition 9.1. From equation (9.14), $\partial n/\partial w = -\gamma(1-\eta)(\theta - p(1-\phi v))/[(1+\gamma)(p-\theta+\phi w)^2]$. ∎

This stresses that if p is below a threshold given by $\theta/(1-\phi v)$, the usual result that high-income parents have fewer children applies. If procreation is made sufficiently expensive through a positive price of procreation, then the usual pattern is reversed, and high-income parents have more children than poor parents. For the same procreation price, the cost of children relative to total income is higher for the poor than for the rich. This feature will have important implications when it comes to assessing the distributive impact of the scheme.

Having assessed the impact of income on fertility for a given procreation price, we now move to investigating the effect of price changes on fertility rates. Proposition 9.3 summarizes the result.

Proposition 9.3 Fertility and procreation price
The individual fertility rate n is a decreasing function of procreation prices $p \in (-1/v, +\infty[$.

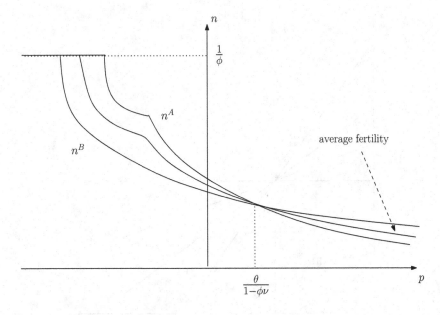

Figure 9.2 Fertility as a function of income and procreation price

Proof: From the expression for n given in Proposition 9.1 we find that:

$$\text{R1 \& R2: } \frac{\partial n}{\partial p} = 0, \qquad \text{R3 \& R4: } \frac{\partial n}{\partial p} < 0.$$

∎

Proposition 9.3 reflects that the demand for the quantity of children decreases with the price of children, i.e. children quantity is a non-Giffen good. Figure 9.2 represents an example of fertility for the two groups A and B as a function of the procreation price. Starting from the left-hand side at a very negative price, the fertility rate of group A first remains constant as p increases because we remain in the zone in which procreation price is such that parents want more children than their biological constraint allows (regimes R1 and R2). At a certain point the price becomes such that fertility starts to decrease (regime R3). We then observe a point at which the fertility function is non-differentiable, which corresponds to the shift from a regime with no education investment (R3) to the one in which parents invest also in quality (R4). The fertility function of group B is different as it shifts straight from the regime with maximum fertility (R1) to the interior regime (R4).

As discussed above, as long as p remains below the threshold $\theta/(1 - \phi v)$ defined in Proposition 9.2, the fertility rate of group A is equal to or greater than the fertility rate of group B. In case p is large, however, the differential fertility is reversed.

Equilibrium

Having analyzed the effect of procreation entitlements on individual behavior, it now remains to be shown that there is a procreation price such that actual average fertility will meet the demographic target set by the government.

The property outlined above states that households' fertility rates are decreasing and continuous functions of the procreation price. This implies that average fertility is also a decreasing and continuous function of p: average fertility decreases from $1/\phi$ for very low p to 0 for large positive p. The continuity of the fertility function is then sufficient to establish the existence of an equilibrium procreation price, which implies that the target fertility rate v is reached. The uniqueness of the equilibrium follows from the monotonicity of the fertility function.

Proposition 9.4 Existence and uniqueness of equilibrium
If $\tilde{p}(v^B) > -1/v$ the equilibrium procreation price exists and is unique.

Proof: $\tilde{p}(\omega)$ is defined in (9.8). If $\tilde{p}(v^B) > -1/v$, both fertility levels tend to $1/\phi$ when p approaches $-1/v$. Hence, for p going from $-1/v$ to $+\infty$, total fertility $(P^A n^A + P^B n^B)/(P^A + P^B)$ goes monotonically from $1/\phi$ to zero. At each date, there exist therefore a price p_t for which:

$$(P_t^A n_t^A + P_t^B n_t^B)/(P_t^A + P_t^B) = v \in]0, 1/\phi[,$$

which is the equilibrium price satisfying equation (9.2). This price is unique because fertility is a monotonous function of p. ∎

Besides the technical constraint $\tilde{p}(v^B) > -1/v$, it follows that the structure of the economy as such will not impose constraints as to the possible level of the demographic target v. This does not preclude the possibility of constraints due to other reasons, such as political feasibility or ethical reasons.

At equilibrium, our measure of income inequality Δ^T (T for tradable) is given by (from (1.10)):

$$\Delta^T = v^B(1 - \phi n^B) + p(v - n^B) - \left[v^A(1 - \phi n^A) + p(v - n^A) \right]$$
$$= v^B(1 - \phi n^B) - v^A(1 - \phi n^A) + p(n^A - n^B). \qquad (9.15)$$

Hence, on top of the difference in wages, one should take into account the transfer which is generated by procreation rights $p(n^A - n^B)$.

Corollary 9.1 states the known result that quantity-oriented policy is equivalent to price-oriented measures when the government has full information.[4]

Corollary 9.1 *Assume that $p > 0$ in equilibrium. Then, the same allocation can be reached without tradable entitlements by levying a tax p per child and giving a lump sum transfer pv per person.*

Assume that $p < 0$ in equilibrium. Then, the same allocation can be reached without tradable entitlements by providing a family allowance $|p|$ per child and levying a poll tax $|p|v$ per person.

In a case of under-population, for example, setting family allowances whose amount has been computed by the government to match the equilibrium procreation price level would lead to the same equilibrium as introducing a tradable exemptions scheme.

9.3 Effects on inequality

Examining the impact of tradable quotas schemes would be incomplete without providing a comparison of such effects with either those of a business-as-usual[5] situation or those of alternative measures aimed at reaching the same demographic target. There are two families of such alternative policies.

The first family includes a variety of price-oriented measures, such as family allowances, free education (in case of under-population), or taxation (in case of over-population). In the case of price-oriented methods, potential parents remain totally free to choose the number of children they wish to have, subject to incentives or disincentives as set up by regulatory authorities. In a world where information is perfect about both the objective that is being pursued and the elasticity of the supply function (fertility), tradable quotas

---

[4] For an example of price-oriented measures, see Fan and Stark (2008).
[5] Benchmark model and business-as-usual are used indifferently.

schemes and price-oriented schemes are fully equivalent (Corollary 9.1). Differences between taxes/subsidies and permits/exemptions arise when information is imperfect.

The second alternative to tradable quotas is quantity-oriented as well, but would consist in fixed rather than tradable quotas. Hereinafter, we compare tradable quotas with fixed ones. Quotas, including fixed ones, as illustrated by the Chinese case, are admittedly an exception.[6] And yet such a scheme will be our starting point here, because our goal is primarily to understand the properties of the model rather than to compare it with fiscal alternatives, which should be the focus of future research. Let us stress as well the fact that when comparing fixed and tradable quotas, we should assume the same type of initial allocation (here: equality per head).[7]

Two effects of fixed quotas on income inequality

Formally, fixed quotas imposes an additional constraint $n \leqslant v$ to the maximization problem studied in Chapter 1. If this constraint is tight for the skilled parents, i.e. if they would otherwise have more children, it will also be tight *a fortiori* for the unskilled. Hence, the constraint $n \leqslant v$ is tight for both groups if and only if:

$$v \leqslant \frac{(1 - \eta)\gamma v^B}{(\phi v^B - \theta)(1 + \gamma)} = \hat{n}^B.$$

The reverse situation, where the government imposes a minimum fertility level, can also be analyzed. In that case, the constraint is written $n \geqslant v$. It will be tight for the poor and even more so for the rich if and only if:

$$v \geqslant \frac{(1 - \eta)\gamma v^A}{(\phi v^A - \theta)(1 + \gamma)} = \hat{n}^A.$$

Hereinafter we envisage only the former case, dealing with over-population, unless specified otherwise. The results we obtain apply *mutatis mutandis* to the policy dealing with under-population.

Assuming tight constraints, the solution to the maximization problem is as follows.

---

[6] A careful macroeconomic analysis of the one-child policy can be found in Liao (2009).

[7] Notice that, in the Chinese one-child policy, the fixed quotas are not uniformly distributed: two children are allowed for in the countryside, only one in cities. This illustrates that the uniform allocation is not the only possible option, and that allocations of quotas on the basis of other factors, such as existing fertility levels, are also possible. This point is further developed in section 9.5.

If $w > \theta/(\gamma\eta(1/v - \phi))$ [interior regime]:

$$e = \frac{\gamma\eta w(1/v - \phi) - \theta}{1 + \gamma\eta}.$$

Otherwise:

$$e = 0.$$

In the interior regime, we have $\partial e/\partial v < 0$. This confirms that as parents react to the quantitative constraint by having fewer children, they will be able to afford to spend more on each of their children.

As to income inequality, the difference between high-skilled and low-skilled income, Δ^F (F for fixed), is given by:

$$\Delta^F = v^B(1 - \phi v) - v^A(1 - \phi v). \tag{9.16}$$

Comparing with equation (9.15) of the tradable rights case, transfers do not obtain in this case as a result of population policy.

We compute the change in income difference resulting from the introduction of fixed quotas:

$$\frac{\Delta^F - \Delta^B}{\phi} = \underbrace{(\hat{n} - v)(v^B - v^A)}_{\text{differential productivity effect} > 0} + \underbrace{v^B(\hat{n}^B - \hat{n}) - v^A(\hat{n}^A - \hat{n})}_{\text{differential fertility effect} < 0}$$

where $\hat{n} = (\hat{n}^A \hat{P}^A + \hat{n}^B \hat{P}^B)/(\hat{P}^A + \hat{P}^B)$ is average fertility in the benchmark case. The first effect, labeled "differential productivity effect," can be understood as follows. Let us envisage a hypothetical business-as-usual situation in which high-income and low-income people have the same fertility level $\hat{n}$. Assume that this level is higher than the one required by our demographic target v. With the introduction of non-tradable quotas, the extent to which the rich will procreate less than the poor is identical. Both the skilled and the unskilled will increase their income as a result of the time made available by such lower fertility. However, since the hourly wage (and underlying it, the productivity) of the high-income is higher than the one of the low-income people, the income of the rich will increase relatively more than that of the poor. In short, the introduction of fixed quotas to fight over-population in a world in which the fertility rate does not vary with the level of income will make the poor-income relatively poorer than the high-income.

The second effect, labeled "differential fertility effect," relaxes the assumption regarding the absence of initial fertility differential (and it is equal to zero if $\hat{n}^B = \hat{n}^A$). In the benchmark situation low-income people tend to have more children than high-income people. Here, a second type of effect can be singled out, of a redistributive rather than of an anti-distributive nature. It can be explained as follows. If the fixed quotas scheme requires the same fertility level from the poor and the rich, the poor will have to reduce their fertility level much more than the rich. As a result, they will also increase their working time more than the rich. This effect will reduce income inequality between the rich and the poor, when compared with the income differential in the business-as-usual situation.

The sign of the total effect of introducing fixed quotas on income difference depends on which of the two effects dominates. One parameter affecting the relative weight of the two effects is the elasticity of educational outcomes over investment in education, represented by η. Remember from (1.9) that the maximum differential fertility is:

$$\frac{1}{1-\eta}.$$

If this elasticity η is large, the fertility differential will tend to be large as well, to such an extent that the "differential fertility effect" may actually dominate the differential productivity effect. The reason underlying this connection between outcome-investment elasticity and fertility differential is the following. The poor are equally concerned about education as the rich. However, for the poor, the cost of investing in education as well as the opportunity cost of having children is lower than for the rich. A higher outcome investment elasticity will not affect the poor much, but will definitely push the rich to replace quantity with quality even more. Hence, the differential fertility is larger when η is large.

We now replace fixed quotas with tradable quotas. In order to identify the difference it makes, we compute the change in income gap between the benchmark and the model with tradable rights:

$$\frac{\Delta^T - \Delta^B}{\phi} = \underbrace{(\hat{n} - v)(v^B - v^A)}_{\text{differential productivity effect} > 0} +$$

$$\underbrace{\left[v^B(\hat{n}^B - \hat{n}) - v^A(\hat{n}^A - \hat{n}) \right] - \left[v^B(n^B - v) - v^A(n^A - v) \right]}_{\text{differential fertility effect}}$$

$$+ \underbrace{\frac{p}{\phi}(n^A - n^B)}_{\text{tradability effect}}. \quad (9.17)$$

Here, a third type of effect obtains, referred to as the tradability effect and represented through the expression $p(n^A - n^B)/\phi$. Contrary to the two other effects, its sign is indeterminate. Depending on the price of the procreation entitlements, tradability will either be redistributive (when $p(n^A - n^B)/\phi > 0$) or anti-distributive (when $p(n^A - n^B)/\phi < 0$). Proposition 9.5 specifies the conditions under which each case occurs.

Proposition 9.5 Redistributive nature of tradability
(i) If $\theta > 0$, tradability is redistributive if and only if:

$$p < 0 \ or \ p > \min\left\{\frac{\theta}{1 - \phi v}, \hat{p}(v^A), \tilde{p}(v^A)\right\}.$$

(ii) If $\theta = 0$ tradability is always redistributive.

Proof: The tradability effect is given by:

$$M = \frac{p}{\phi}(n^A - n^B).$$

(i) To analyze the sign of M, we should consider the different possible regimes. From Figure 9.1, if the poor is in R1, the rich can be in either R1 or in R4. If the poor is in R2, the rich can be in R2, R3, or R4. If the poor is in R3, the rich can be in R3 or R4. If the poor is in the interior regime R4, the rich is in R4, too. We thus have eight situations to consider.

Cases where both types of households are either in R1 or in R2 are excluded by assumption (C1). Indeed, in that case, aggregate fertility per person would be $1/\phi$ and the equilibrium condition (9.2) would be violated. This leaves us with six different cases.

When the poor is in R2, the procreation price is necessarily negative, and $n^A = 1/\phi > n^B$. When both individuals are in R3, the procreation price can be either positive or negative, but we always have $n^A > n^B$ because fertility decreases in income in regime R3. Hence, $p < 0 \rightarrow M < 0$ in this regime. When the poor is in R3 and the rich in R4, we also always have $n^A > n^B$ (compare (9.12) to (9.14)), which implies in this regime $p < 0 \leftrightarrow M < 0$. Finally, if both individuals are in the interior regime R4, we can use Proposition 9.2 to infer that if $p < 0$ ($n^A > n^B$) or if $p > \frac{\theta}{1 - \phi v}$ ($n^B > n^A$), then $M < 0$. The min term in the condition of the proposition gathers the requirement of being in regime R4 with the condition of Proposition 9.2.

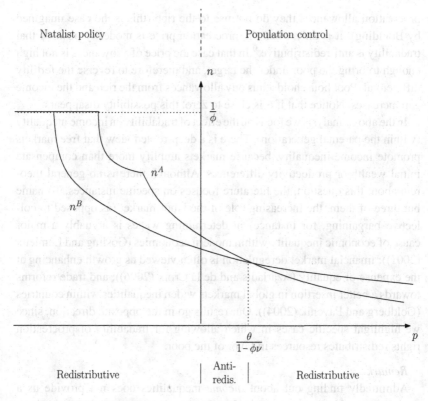

Figure 9.3 Redistributive nature of tradability

(ii) If $\theta = 0$ the expression

$$\min\left\{\frac{\theta}{1-\phi v}, \hat{p}(v^A), \tilde{p}(v^A)\right\}$$

is negative and the condition in (i) is always true. ∎

Figure 9.3 helps capture the intuition underlying Proposition 9.5. When p is negative, fertility is encouraged. Poor households have more children than the fertility target while the rich have fewer. Poor people sell the exemptions they receive to the rich, which reduces the income gap between the rich and the poor. When p is positive and large, having children is so expensive that rich people have more children than poor ones. This time, the poor end up below the target and the rich above.[8] Yet this is also redistributive because poor people sell the

---

[8] At equilibrium the target is always equal to average fertility.

procreation allowances they do not use to the rich (this is the case imagined by Boulding). It is only when the procreation price is modestly positive that tradability is anti-redistributive.[9] In that case the price of allowances is not high enough to bring the poor under the target, and therefore to reverse the fertility differential. Poor households thus buy allowances from the rich and the income gap increases. Notice that if θ is close to zero, this possibility disappears.

In the above analysis we focus on the effect of tradability on income inequality (within the parental generation). There is a deep-rooted view that free markets promote income inequality, because markets amplify more than compensate initial wealth or productivity differences. Although there is no general theorem about this question, the literature focuses on specific instances. To name but three of them, the increasing role of the labor market (as opposed to collective bargaining, for instance) in determining wages is arguably a major cause of economic inequality within modern economies (Gosling and Lemieux (2001)); financial market deregulation is often viewed as growth enhancing at the expense of equality (Azariadis and de la Croix (2006)); and trade reforms towards a better insertion in global markets widen inequalities within countries (Goldberg and Pavcnik (2004)). Our results go in the opposite direction, since we highlight specific cases in which allowing for tradability of procreation rights redistributes resources in favor of the poor.

Remark

Admittedly finding out about *income* inequalities does not provide us a straightforward indication as to the impact on *welfare* inequalities (within both the current and the next generation).[10] In order to draw conclusions on the latter, we need to consider the effect of tradable rights on indirect utility. Indirect utility is obtained by replacing demand functions derived above into the utility function (1.1). In the interior regime, which will prevail for high enough procreation price p, we obtain the following expression for the indirect utility function of household of type i:

$$(1 + \gamma) \ln(\upsilon^i + p\nu) - \gamma(1 - \eta) \ln(\phi \upsilon^i - \theta + p) + \text{constant terms}.$$

The first term of the sum reflects that utility is increasing in endowment $\upsilon^i + p\nu$. The second term involves the real price of children $\phi \upsilon^i - \theta + p$ (i.e. the

---

[9] This invites us to consider with a critical eye the widely shared view, also implied e.g. in Tobin (1970), that tradability promotes by nature inequality.

[10] Extending this assessment to the welfare of future generations would necessitate taking a stand on a difficult philosophical question: can we compare at all (and if yes, how) in terms of welfare two states of the world that do not contain the same set of individuals? Can we meaningfully say that it's better for a person to be conceived and brought into existence than not? (Arrhenius (2000))

price of children compared with the price of the physical good), including the opportunity cost ϕv^i, the free education provided by nature θ, and the procreation price p.

Exercise: Compute the indirect utility in the other three regimes and assess the effect of tradable quotas in these cases.

The question is now whether an increase in the relative price of children p, or equivalently a decrease in the target fertility rate v, will generate an increase in welfare inequality. Considering first the effect on the endowment $v^i + pv$, everything will depend on whether equilibrium prices will rise by less or more than the decrease in target v. If pv increases when policy becomes more anti-natalist, everyone's endowment increases, but the poor benefit more than the rich because pv weights more for them in their total endowment. In that case, utility inequality would be reduced by the rise in p via the endowment effect. Inequality would be increased in the opposite situation where pv decreases when policy becomes more anti-natalist. In general, the effect of stronger anti-natalist policies on utility inequality via the change in endowment is indeterminate.

On the contrary, the effect on the price of children $\phi v^i - \theta + p$ is not ambiguous. The rise in p will reduce utility of both types of households since children become more expensive, but it will reduce more the utility of the unskilled; indeed

$$\frac{\partial \gamma (1 - \eta) \ln(\phi v^i - \theta + p)}{\partial p} = \frac{\gamma (1 - \eta)}{\phi v^i - \theta + p}$$

is stronger if v^i is small. We can therefore conjecture that, at given endowment inequality, an increase in the price of children will hurt the unskilled more. The reason is that their opportunity cost of having children is lower.

To sum up, an increase in the relative price of children, or equivalently a decrease in the target fertility rate, will in some cases generate an increase in welfare inequality. This implies that the possible income inequality-reducing effect of strong anti-natalist policies may be mitigated by this relative price effect on welfare inequalities. Opponents to anti-natalist quotas may thus be right in fearing an increase in welfare inequality despite being wrong in predicting an increase in income inequalities. Poor people may end up relatively richer while becoming relatively less happy, being more affected by the high price of children.

9.4 Effects on education

Let us now turn our attention to the effect of procreation entitlements on education. This is an important question because both social mobility and long-run income are positively affected by education spending. Proposition 9.6 shows how education depends on procreation price.

Proposition 9.6 Education and procreation price
Assume that the threshold $\dot{p} = \min\{\breve{p}, \tilde{p}(w)\} < -1/v$. Investment in education e is increasing in procreation price p.

Proof: From the expression for e given in Proposition 9.1.   ∎

An increase in the procreation price reduces fertility (Proposition 9.3) and increases education, which is the usual quantity–quality tradeoff facing a rise in the cost of children. In this case, natalist policy would be bad for education, social mobility, and long-run income, while population control would be good.[11]

To illustrate the effect on education of pro-natalist policy, let us take a numerical example. Suppose that the parameters are as follows: $\gamma = 0.0167, \theta = 0.1$, $\eta = 0.6$, $\phi = 0.075$, $v^A = 0.5$, $v^B = 2$, $\mu^A = 0.8$, $\mu^B = 1.8$. The initial condition is $z_1 = P_0^A/P_0^B = 6$. The parameters are such that, in the absence of policy, the growth rate of population converges to 0 in the long run. With those values, we obtain $n^A = 1.04$, $n^B = 0.82$. Social mobility is as follows. The probability to become skilled is equal to 68.5 percent for a child from skilled parents, and 10 percent for a child from unskilled parents. With this social mobility, the share of skilled persons increase in the economy, and the ratio z_t goes from 6 to 4.2 in the long run.

Let us now consider the effect of policy on fertility, social mobility, and dynamics. We first plot fertility as a function of the procreation price. Figure 9.4 redraws Figure 9.2 for the numerical example.

We now compare this benchmark outcome with what would prevail if some population policy is implemented. We considered three cases: $v = 0.8$, $v = 1$, and $v = 1.2$. When $v = 0.8$, the policy is anti-natalist compared with the benchmark. $v = 1$ is a neutral policy as the benchmark already delivers an average fertility of 1 (in the long run). When $v = 1.2$, the policy is pro-natalist.

---

[11] A special but practically marginal case arises when p is extremely low and $\dot{p} > -1/v$. In such a case, individual investment in education e is decreasing in p for $p < \dot{p}$ and increasing in p for $p > \dot{p}$. Poor households are in regime R1; they are entirely specialized into the production of children ($n = 1/\phi$). A small rise in p has no effect on fertility, but has a negative income effect, which entails that education spending is reduced.

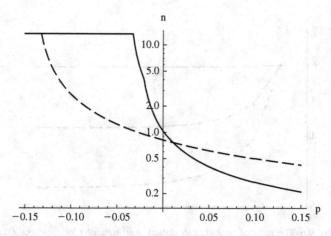

Figure 9.4 Fertility as a function of income and procreation price in the example.
Unskilled (solid line) and skilled (dashed)

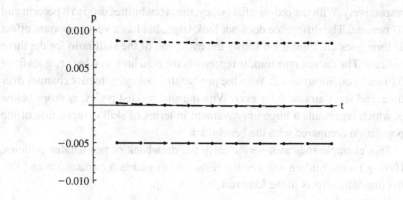

Figure 9.5 The procreation price in the example. Anti-natalist (dots), neutral (short
dashes), pro-natalist (long dashes)

Figure 9.5 shows the procreation price in the three cases. Notice the asymmetry:
to obtain a decrease in average fertility of 0.2, one needs a larger incentive
($p \approx 0.009$) than to obtain a decrease in fertility of 0.2 ($p \approx -0.005$). This is
because fertility is a convex function of p, as shown in Figure 9.4.

Now, the point of the exercise is to illustrate the effect of these policies on
education and social mobility. Let us first look at the probability of becoming
skilled in the three cases. With the anti-natalist policy, these probabilities are

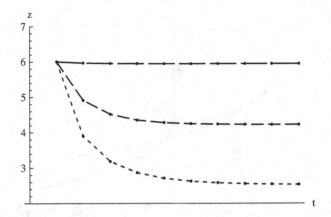

Figure 9.6 The ratio of unskilled to skilled. Anti-natalist (dots), neutral (short dashes), pro-natalist (long dashes)

equal to 12 percent and 71 percent for children from unskilled and skilled parents respectively. With the pro-natalist policy, the probabilities drop to 8 percent and 67 percent. The difference does not look large, but has a very important effect as time goes on. Figure 9.6 shows the evolution of the skill ratio for the three policies. The curve in the middle represents the benchmark, where z_t goes from 6 (initial condition) to 4.2. With the pro-natalist policy, z_t hardly changes over time, and stays around 6 for ever. With the anti-natalist policy, z_t drops below 3, which represents a huge improvement in terms of skill composition of the population compared with the benchmark.

This example indicates very clearly the drawback of pro-natalist policies. Having more children reduces the resources available for education and this has dramatic effects in the long run.

9.5 Moving from national to global level
Procreation entitlements at the global level

So far, we have assumed that tradable procreation permits were allocated at the domestic level. However, there may be good reasons to look at the way in which the scheme could be applied to countries rather than to individuals. One such reason is that those concerned with the scheme at the domestic level because of moral objections to its enforcement may still be ready to accept less coercive measures at the domestic level combined with a scheme of tradable procreation permits among countries. Such domestic measures may include raising incentives to invest in people (to trigger the quality–quantity tradeoff), reducing gender discrimination on the labor market (making women think twice before having an extra child), and developing pension systems (to reduce the need for procreation as a way of securing future old-age support). Moreover, those willing on the contrary to promote the instrument domestically will generally be positively inclined towards simultaneously implementing it at the global level. Another reason to look more closely at a global version of the scheme is that one often cited mode of initial allocation, i.e. grandfathering (see next section), could possibly make sense at the global level while being far less plausible at the individual level.

Applied at the global level, the system would work along the same lines as a domestic one, involving two key moments. First, a global demographic target should be set for a given period. Second, we would need to decide about an initial allocation rule to distribute the quotas to each of the countries. Let us first consider a situation with a uniform distribution of entitlements, which is the case analyzed so far. Understanding agents in our model as countries or sets of countries, all the results developed above can be applied at the global level. In particular, the market for procreation entitlements will clear at the equilibrium price, country-specific fertility and education reacting as described by Propositions 9.3 and 9.6. The effect of tradability on income (gross national income here) will depend on the condition set in Proposition 9.5.

Procreation rights with grandfathering

In the previous section, we asked ourselves whether a tradable procreation entitlement would necessarily have an anti-redistributive impact. The underlying intuition was that because of tradability, the wealthiest countries would be able to further increase the gap separating them from poorer countries. Our model demonstrates, however, that there is only one area in Figure 9.3 in which such anti-redistributive effects arise. Outside this zone, the scheme would rather have a redistributive impact. The key practical question was then to identify where practical schemes envisaged in specific real-life circumstances would be located. The simulations of the previous section have shown that for a moderate population-control policy, we may end in this anti-redistributive zone, while for stronger policies, it is more unlikely to be the case. In this section, we have a closer look at still another theoretical option that could have different distributive properties. Rather than implementing an equal per capita initial allocation of procreation quotas, we would do so on a grandfathering basis.

The idea of grandfathering usually refers nowadays to the exemption from new regulation granted on a temporary basis to actors already involved in a given activity.[12] More interestingly for us, it is used in the tradable emission permits context (such as the Kyoto context, see Bohringer and Lange (2005) and Gosseries (2007)) to refer to one mode of initial permits allocation, i.e. one that grants relatively larger shares of emission rights to those who already emit relatively more. This means that when facing a global emission-reduction target, larger polluters will have to reduce their emissions in the same proportion as lesser polluters. This means that the larger polluters are partly exempted from the application of the new rule (relative exemption).

In the pollution-reduction case, grandfathering can *prima facie* be expected to lead to anti-redistributive consequences when compared with an equal per capita allocation, for larger per capita polluters are also generally richer countries. In the procreation case, the relationship between fertility rate and wealth is not so straightforward and might actually be the reverse. This suggests that grandfathering in the case of tradable procreation entitlements could well have a distributive impact that differs both from the one exhibited in the case of grandfathering for tradable emission quotas and from the one unveiled in the previous section for tradable procreation entitlements allocated on a per capita basis. We now provide the analysis needed for the latter comparison.

We assume that countries receive an initial endowment of rights proportional to their fertility rate in the absence of procreation rights (benchmark):[13]

$$v^i = m \, n^i \mid_{p=0}.$$

Parameter m, when larger than 1, indicates a pronatalist policy. Conversely, if m is lower than 1, population policy is restrictive. The previously defined average fertility target v relates to the v^i through:

$$P^A v^A + P^B v^B = (P^A + P^B)v.$$

---

[12] Grandfathering is a concept that originates from the late nineteenth century in the southern US states (see Rose (1906)). It consists in an attempt at further delaying the electoral enfranchisement of black people. As the franchise was formally broadened, extending to both white and black men, the introduction of poll tax and/or literacy requirements was supposed to slow down the access of most black people to the suffrage. It was also excluding some white men however, which aroused concern in the white community. This led to the introduction of the so-called "grandfather clause" in the electoral regime of some of the southern US states, stating that those whose grandfather or father was already enfranchised would be exempted from poll tax and/or literacy requirements. In practice, this meant that all white males would have the right to vote while still preserving the exclusion of most black males through poll tax and/or literacy requirements, from which they could not be exempted since none had had a grandfather entitled to vote.

[13] This is standard practice for pollution rights. By referring to a base year preceding the conception of the scheme, we avoid the moral hazard problem consisting in trying to manipulate one's relative share before the entry into force of the system.

Since initial endowments are now different across countries, the income gap between countries becomes:

$$\Delta^G = \upsilon^B - \upsilon^A + p(\upsilon^B - \tilde{n}^B) - p(\upsilon^A - \tilde{n}^A)$$

where fertility levels with a tilde denote fertility in the grandfathering case. Computing the difference in income gap between the benchmark case and the grandfathering one, we obtain:

$$\frac{\Delta^G - \Delta^B}{\phi} = \underbrace{(\hat{n} - \upsilon)(\upsilon^B - \upsilon^A)}_{\text{differential productivity effect} > 0}$$

$$+ \underbrace{\left[\upsilon^B(\hat{n}^B - \hat{n}) - \upsilon^A(\hat{n}^A - \hat{n})\right] - \left[\upsilon^B(\tilde{n}^B - \upsilon) - \upsilon^A(\tilde{n}^A - \upsilon)\right]}_{\text{differential fertility effect}}$$

$$+ \underbrace{\frac{p}{\phi}(\tilde{n}^A - \tilde{n}^B)}_{\text{tradability effect}}$$

$$\underbrace{-\frac{pm}{\phi}(\hat{n}^A - \hat{n}^B)}_{\text{grandfathering effect}} \quad (9.18)$$

We can compare this expression with the one in equation (9.17). The differential productivity effect is unchanged. The differential fertility effect and the tradability effect have the same form as before, but n^A and n^B in (9.17) are now replaced by $\tilde{n}^A$ and $\tilde{n}^B$ in (9.18). The two latter effects would play the same role as before provided that fertility behavior is only marginally altered by grandfathering. A fourth effect is the grandfathering effect. Since the poor country initially received more procreation rights per head than the rich one, an income transfer from the rich to the poor obtains in exchange for extra entitlements in case of positive procreation price. The direction of transfer is reversed in case of negative procreation price.

Numerical simulations show that the essential difference between (9.18) and (9.17) is the last effect, which is a pure transfer. Grandfathering has a redistributive effect in the case of population control, simply by implementing a redistributive initial allocation of rights.

9.6 Conclusion

While being inspired by earlier proposals by authors such as Boulding or Tobin, this chapter should certainly not be read as an exercise in the history of economic ideas. This study should pave the way for a yet to come systematic exploration of the respective merits of alternative population policies.

In this chapter, we explored the idea of tradable procreation entitlements, within a general equilibrium model with endogenous fertility. Both tradable allowances and tradable exemptions were envisaged, aimed at addressing problems of respectively over- and under-population. An equilibrium with such assets exists. It can thus implement any desired growth rate of population. Having shown this, we focus on worries over the possible anti-redistributive nature of such a scheme, as well as possible adverse impacts in terms of educational investments.

Three effects are identified and contrasted. While two of them also obtain in the case of fixed quotas schemes, a third one, the tradability effect, is specific to the present scheme. Insofar as income distribution is concerned, with procreation exemptions (whatever their price) or allowances if they are expensive enough, tradability redistributes resources from the rich to the poor. In contrast, cheap procreation allowances redistribute resources towards the rich.

As far as human capital is concerned, natalist policy would tend to reduce the average educational level of the next generation, while population control would increase it. In the case of pro-natalist policies, sustaining education through additional measures may turn out to be helpful for future generations.

We finally indicated to what extent an alternative allocation rule of procreation entitlements, granting rights in proportion to existing fertility levels (grandfathering) rather than on a per capita basis, can make population control even more redistributive.

10
Conclusion: endogenous fertility matters

This book provides a set of general equilibrium models where heterogeneous households rationally choose their number of children. We show that if indeed fertility is not only determined by exogenous cultural factors but responds to economic incentives, it has important consequences for inequality, education, and sustainability.

First, as soon as one assumes that the most important cost of having children is a time cost, economic theory says that fertility negatively depends on the mother's labor income. This has strong implications for the relationship between income inequality and growth. A rise in inequality makes the rich richer, and leads them to have fewer highly educated children. The poor are poorer, and still have many uneducated children. Average human capital in the future is kept low by the mass of grown-up children from poor families. Hence, inequality is particularly damaging for growth when one takes into account fertility incentives.

Second, one key message of the theory is that fertility and education are joint decisions. Hence, the cost of education is an important factor determining fertility. A policy aimed at providing free public education to all would tend to equalize fertility across income group, which is good for inequality, but will also incentivize households to have more children than under private education, which might hamper growth. A mixed system combining private and public education might not be at the expense of the poor, as long as the quality of public schools is chosen in a democratic way.

Third, fertility can be seen as a strategic variable in the fight for power between different (cultural, ethnic, religious) groups. Neglecting such a role would be acceptable in the short run; however, effects on population growth are cumulative, and long-run outcomes may depend crucially on the fertility incentives of the different groups. The survival of ethnically diverse societies depends on these incentives.

Finally, fertility might be affected by policies targeted at other objectives. For example, taxing output to control pollution may delay the demographic transition. Hence, any evaluation of a policy should consider carefully its possible effects on fertility and population dynamics.

Bibliography

Abreu, Maria, Henri de Groot, and Raymond Florax. 2005. "A Meta-Analysis of β-Convergence: the Legendary 2%." *Journal of Economic Surveys* 19 (3): 389–420.

Acemoglu, Daron, and Joshua Angrist. 2000. "How Large are Human Capital Externalities? Evidence from Compulsory Schooling Laws." *NBER Macroeconomics Annual 2000*, pp. 9–59.

Alderman, Harold, Peter Orazem, and Elizabeth Paterno. 2001. "School Quality, School Cost, and the Public/Private School Choices of Low-income Households in Pakistan." *Journal of Human Resources* 36 (2): 304–326.

Althaus, Paul. 1980. "Differential Fertility and Economic Growth." *Zeitschrift für die gesamte Staatswissenschaft* 136 (2): 309–326.

Alvarez, Fernando. 1999. "Social Mobility: The Barro–Becker Children meet the Laitner–Loury Dynasties." *Review of Economic Dynamics* 2 (1): 65–103.

Andreoni, James. 1989. "Giving with impure altruism: applications to charity and Ricardian equivalence." *Journal of Political Economy* 97 (6): 1447–1459.

Angrist, Joshua, and Alan Krueger. 1991. "Does Compulsory School Attendance Affect Schooling and Earnings?" *The Quarterly Journal of Economics* 106 (4): 979–1014.

Arcalean, Calin, and Ioana Schiopu. 2010. "Inequality and Education Funding: Theory and Evidence from the US School Districts." ESADE Business School.

Arrhenius, Gustaf. 2000. "An Impossibility Theorem for Welfarist Axiologies." *Economics and Philosophy* 16: 247–266.

Ashenfelter, Orley, and Alan Krueger. 1994. "Estimates of the Economic Return to Schooling from a New Sample of Twins." *American Economic Review* 84 (5): 1157–1173.

Azariadis, Costas, and David de la Croix. 2006. "Financial Institutional Reform, Growth, and Equality." In *Institutions, Development, and Economic Growth*, edited by Teo Eicher and Cecilia Garcia Peñalosa, CESifo Seminar Series, 35–64. MIT Press.

Bar, Michael, and Oksana Leukhina. 2010a. "The Role of Mortality in the Transmission of Knowledge." *Journal of Economic Growth* 15 (4): 291–321.

2010b. "Demographic Transition and Industrial Revolution: A Macroeconomic Investigation." *Review of Economic Dynamics* 13 (2): 424–451.

Bardet, Jean-Pierre. 1983. *Rouen au XVIIe et XVIIIe siècles*. Edited by SEDES. Paris.

Barro, Robert. 2000. "Inequality and Growth in a Panel of Countries." *Journal of Economic Growth* 5 (1): 5–32.

Barro, Robert, and Gary Becker. 1989. "Fertility Choice in a Model of Economic Growth." *Econometrica* 57 (2): 481–501.

Baudin, Thomas. 2009. "Religion and Fertility: The French Connection." CORE mimeo.

2011. "Family Policies: What Does the Standard Endogenous Fertility Model Tell Us?" *Journal of Public Economic Theory* 4 (13): 555–593.

Baudin, Thomas, David de la Croix, and Paula Gobbi. 2011. "DINKS, DEWKS and co. Marriage, Fertility and Childlessness in the US." IRES, Université catholique de Louvain.

Bearse, Peter, Gerhard Glomm, and Debra Patterson. 2005. "Endogenous Public Expenditures on Education." *Journal of Public Economic Theory* 7 (4): 561–577.

Becker, Gary. 1960. "An Economic Analysis of Fertility." *Demographic and Economic Change in Developed Countries*. Princeton University Press.

Becker, Gary, and Gregg Lewis. 1973. "On the Interaction between the Quantity and Quality of Children." *Journal of Political Economy* 81 (2): S279–S288.

Becker, Gary, Kevin Murphy, and Robert Tamura. 1990. "Human Capital, Fertility, and Economic Growth." *Journal of Political Economy* 98 (2): 12–37.

Bedi, Arjun, and Ashish Garg. 2000. "The Effectiveness of Private versus Public Schools: The Case of Indonesia." *Journal of Development Economics* 61 (2): 463–494.

Beltrami, Daniele. 1951. "Lineamenti di storia della popolazione di Venezia nei secoli XVI, XVII e XVIII." *Atti dell'Istituto Veneto di Scienze, Lettere ed Arti*, vol. 109.

Bénabou, Roland. 1996. "Inequality and Growth." *NBER Macroeconomics Annual*, pp. 11–74.

2000. "Unequal Societies: Income Distribution and the Social Contract." *American Economic Review* 90 (1): 96–129.

Ben-Porath, Yoram. 1967. "The production of human capital and the life-cycle of earnings." *Journal of Political Economy* 75 (4): 352–365.

Binmore, Ken, Ariel Rubinstein, and Asher Wolinsky. 1986. "The Nash bargaining solution in economic modelling." *Rand Journal of Economics* 17 (2): 176–188.

Bohringer, Christoph, and Andreas Lange. 2005. "On the design of optimal grandfathering schemes for emission allowances." *European Economic Review* 49 (8): 2041–2055.

Boucekkine, Raouf, David de la Croix, and Omar Licandro. 2002. "Vintage Human Capital, Demographic Trends, and Endogenous Growth." *Journal of Economic Theory* 104 (2): 340–375.

2003. "Early Mortality Declines at the Dawn of Modern Growth." *Scandinavian Journal of Economics* 105 (3): 401–418.

Boucekkine, Raouf, David de la Croix, and Dominique Peeters. 2007. "Early Literacy Achievements, Population Density and the Transition to Modern Growth." *Journal of the European Economic Association* 5: 183–226.

2008. "Disentangling the Demographic Determinants of the English Take-off: 1530–1860." Edited by Alexia Prskawetz, David Bloom, and Wolfgang Lutz, *Population and Development Review Supplement*, pp. 126–148.

Boucekkine, Raouf, Rodolphe Desbordes, and Hélène Latzer. 2009. "How Do Epidemics Induce Behavioral Changes?" *Journal of Economic Growth* 14 (3): 233–264.

Boulding, Kenneth. 1964. *The Meaning of the Twentieth Century*. London: George Allen and Unwin Ltd.

Brander, James, and M. Scott Taylor. 1998. "The Simple Economics of Easter Island: A Ricardo–Malthus Model of Renewable Resource Use." *American Economic Review* 88 (1): 119–138.

Bréchet, Thierry, and Pierre Picard. 2010. "The Price of Silence: Tradable Noise Permits and Airports." Mimeo, CORE, Louvain-la-Neuve.

Card, David, and Alan Krueger. 1996. "School Resources and Student Outcomes: An Overview of the Literature and New Evidence from North and South Carolina." *Journal of Economic Perspectives* 10 (4): 31–50.

Casella, Alexandra. 1999. "Tradable Deficit Permits. Efficient Implementation of the Stability Pact." *Economic Policy* 29: 323–347.

Cervellati, Matteo, and Uwe Sunde. 2009. "Longevity and Lifetime Labor Supply: Evidence and Implications Revisited." IZA mimeo.

Chen, Hung-Ju. 2008. "Life Expectancy, Fertility, and Educational Investment." *Journal of Population Economics* 23 (1): 37–56.

Chesnais, Jean Claude. 1992. *The Demographic Transition*. Oxford University Press.

Clark, Gregory. 2007. *A Farewell to Alms: A Brief Economic History of the World*. Princeton University Press.

Cohen, Joel. 1995. *How Many People Can the Earth Support?* New York and London: W. W. Norton and Company.

Cohen-Zada, Danny, and Moshe Justman. 2003. "The Political Economy of School Choice: Linking Theory and Evidence." *Journal of Urban Economics* 54 (2): 277–308.

Coughlin, Peter, and Shmuel Nitzan. 1981. "Electoral Outcomes with Probabilistic Voting and Nash Social Welfare Maxima." *Journal of Public Economics* 15 (1): 113–121.

Crettez, Bertrand. 2011. "Is Selling Immigration Rights Politically Sustainable?" *Louvain Economic Review* 77 (4): 33–55.

Dahan, Momi, and Daniel Tsiddon. 1998. "Demographic Transition, Income Distribution, and Economic Growth." *Journal of Economic Growth* 3 (1): 29–52.

Dalton, Thomas, and R. Morris Coats. 2000. "Could institutional reform have saved Easter Island?" *Journal of Evolutionary Economics* 10 (5): 489–505.

Daly, Herman. 1991. *Steady-State Economics*. Second Edition. Washington DC: Island Press.

    1993. "The Steady-State Economy: Toward a Political Economy of Biophysical Equilibrium and Moral Growth." In *Valuing the Earth. Economics, Ecology, Ethics*, edited by Herman E. Daly and Kenneth N. Townsend, pp. 325–363. Cambridge/London: The MIT Press.

Deb, Partha, and Furio Rosati. 2004. "Estimating the effect of fertility decisions on child labor and schooling." Unpublished manuscript.

Deininger, Klaus, and Lyn Squire. 1996. "Measuring Income Inequality: A New Database." Development Discussion Paper No. 537, Harvard Institute for International Development.

de la Croix, David. 2011. "Education Funding and the Sustainability of Diverse Societies." In *The Political Function of Education in Deeply Divided Countries*, edited by Theodor Hanf, pp. 321–332. Baden-Baden Nomos.

de la Croix, David, and Matthias Doepke. 2003. "Inequality and Growth: Why Differential Fertility Matters." *American Economic Review* 93 (4): 1091–1113.
2004. "Public Versus Private Education When Differential Fertility Matters." *Journal of Development Economics* 73 (2): 607–629.
2009. "To Segregate or to Integrate: Education Politics and Democracy." *Review of Economic Studies* 76: 597–628.
de la Croix, David, and Davide Dottori. 2008. "Easter Island Collapse: a Tale of a Population Race." *Journal of Economic Growth* 13 (1): 27–55.
de la Croix, David, and Axel Gosseries. 2009. "Population Policy through Tradable Procreation Entitlements." *International Economic Review* 50 (2): 507–542.
2012. "The Natalist Bias of Pollution Control." *Journal of Environmental Economics and Management* 63 (2): 271–287.
de la Croix, David, and Omar Licandro. 1999. "Life Expectancy and Endogenous Growth." *Economics Letters* 65 (2): 255–263.
de la Croix, David, and Philippe Michel. 2002. *A Theory of Economic Growth: Dynamics and Policy in Overlapping Generations*. Cambridge University Press.
de la Croix, David, and Philippe Monfort. 2000. "Education Funding and Regional Convergence." *Journal of Population Economics* 13 (3): 403–424.
de la Croix, David, and Alessandro Sommacal. 2009. "A Theory of Medical Effectiveness, Differential Mortality, Income Inequality and Growth for Pre-Industrial England." *Mathematical Population Studies* 16: 2–35.
de la Croix, David, and Marie Vander Donckt. 2010. "Would Empowering Women Initiate the Demographic Transition in Least-Developed Countries?" *Journal of Human Capital* 4 (2): 87–129.
Diamond, Jared. 2005. *Collapse. How Societies Choose to Fail or Survive*. New York: Viking Books.
Doepke, Matthias. 2004. "Accounting for Fertility Decline during the Transition to Growth." *Journal of Economic Growth* 9 (3): 347–383.
2005. "Child Mortality and Fertility Decline: Does the Barro–Becker Model Fit the Facts?" *Journal of Population Economics* 18 (2): 337–366.
Doepke, Matthias, and Fabrizio Zilibotti. 2005. "The Macroeconomics of Child Labor Regulation." *American Economic Review* 95 (5): 1492–1524.
Dottori, Davide, and I-Ling Shen. 2008. "Low-skilled Immigration and the Expansion of Private Schools." Bank of Italy Working Paper No. 726.
Dworkin, Ronald. 2000. *Sovereign Virtue. The Theory and Practise of Equality*. Cambridge, MA: Harvard University Press.
Ehrlich, Isaac, and Francis Lui. 1991. "Intergenerational Trade, Longevity, and Economic Growth." *Journal of Political Economy* 99 (5): 1029–1059.
Epple, Dennis, David Figlio, and Richard Romano. 2004. "Competition Between Private and Public Schools: Testing Stratification and Pricing Predictions." *Journal of Public Economics* 88 (7): 1215–1245.
Epple, Dennis, and Richard Romano. 1996. "Public Provision of Private Goods." *Journal of Political Economy* 104 (1): 57–84.
Erickson, Jon, and John Gowdy. 2000. "Resource Use, Institutions, and Sustainability: a Tale of Two Pacific Island Cultures." *Land Economics* 76 (3): 345–354.

Fan, Simon, and Oded Stark. 2008. "Looking at the Population Problem through the Prism of Heterogeneity: Welfare and Policy Analyses." *International Economic Review* 49 (3): 799–835.

Fernández, Raquel, and Alessandra Fogli. 2006. "Fertility: The Role of Culture and Family Experience." *Journal of the European Economic Association* 4 (2–3): 552–561.

Fernández, Raquel, and Richard Rogerson. 2001. "Sorting and Long-Run Inequality." *Quarterly Journal of Economics* 116 (4): 1305–1341.

Fioroni, Tamara. 2009. "Child Mortality and Fertility: Public vs Private Education." *Journal of Population Economics* 23 (1): 73–97.

Firth, Raymond. 1936. *We, the Tikopia: A Sociological Study of Kinship in Primitive Polynesia*. London: George Allen and Unwin.

1967. *The Work of the Gods in Tikopia*. Second Edition. New York: Humanities Press.

Flenley, John, and Paul Bahn. 2003. *The Enigmas of Easter Island*. Oxford University Press.

Flenley, John, A. Sarah King, Joan Jackson, C. Chew, J. Teller, and M. Prentice. 1991. "The Late Quaternary Vegetational and Climatic History of Easter Island." *Journal of Quaternary Science* 6 (2): 85–115.

Fletcher, Jesse, Jacob Apkarian, Robert Hanneman, Hiroko Inoue, Kirk Lawrence, and Christopher Chase-Dunn. 2011. "Demographic Regulators in Small-Scale World-Systems." *Structure and Dynamics* 5 (1): 1–31.

Galor, Oded. 2005. "From Stagnation to Growth: Unified Growth Theory." Chapter 4 of *Handbook of Economic Growth*, edited by Philippe Aghion and Steven Durlauf, Volume 1 of *Handbook of Economic Growth*, pp. 171–293. Amsterdam: Elsevier.

2011. *Unified Growth Theory*. Princeton University Press.

Galor, Oded, and David Weil. 2000. "Population, Technology, and Growth: From Malthusian Stagnation to the Demographic Transition and Beyond." *American Economic Review* 90 (4): 806–828.

Galor, Oded, and Hyoungsoo Zang. 1997. "Fertility, Income Distribution, and Economic Growth: Theory and Cross-Country Evidence." *Japan and the World Economy* 9 (2): 197–229.

Galor, Oded and Zeira, Joseph. 1993. "Income Distribution and Macroeconomics." *Review of Economics Studies* 60 (1): 35–52.

Ganzeboom, Harry, Paul De Graaf, and Donald Treiman. 1992. "A Standard International Socio-Economic Index of Occupational Status." *Social Science Research* 21 (1): 1–56.

Ghez, Gilbert, and Gary Becker. 1975. *The Allocation of Time and Goods over the Life Cycle*. Cambridge, MA: NBER Books. National Bureau of Economic Research, Inc.

Glomm, Gerhard, and B. Ravikumar. 1992. "Public Versus Private Investment in Human Capital: Endogenous Growth and Income Inequality." *Journal of Political Economy* 100 (4): 818–834.

1998. "Opting Out of Publicly Provided Services: A Majority Voting Result." *Social Choice and Welfare* 15 (2): 197–199.

Gobbi, Paula. 2011. "A Model of Voluntary Childlessness." IRES, Université catholique de Louvain.

Gokhale, Jagadeesh, Lawrence Kotlikoff, James Sefton, and Martin Weale. 2001. "Simulating the Transmission of Wealth Inequality via Bequests." *Journal of Public Economics* 79 (1): 93–128.

Goldberg, Pinelopi, and Nina Pavcnik. 2004. "Trade, Inequality, and Poverty: What Do We Know? Evidence from Recent Trade Liberalization Episodes in Developing Countries." Working Paper No. 10593, National Bureau of Economic Research.

Goldhaber, Dan. 1996. "Public and Private High Schools: Is School Choice the Answer to the Productivity Problem?" *Economics of Education Review* 15 (2): 93–109.

Golosov, Mikhail, Larry Jones, and Michele Tertilt. 2007. "Efficiency with Endogenous Population Growth." *Econometrica* 75 (4): 1039–1071.

Good, David, and Rafael Reuveny. 2007. "On the Collapse of Historical Societies." Paper presented at the Conference of the European Association of Environmental and Resource Economists.

Goodsell, Willystine. 1937. "Housing and Birth Rate in Sweden." *American Sociological Review* 2 (6): 850–859.

Gosling, Amanda, and Thomas Lemieux. 2001. "Labour Market Reforms and Changes in Wage Inequality in the United Kingdom and the United States." NBER Working Paper No. 8413, National Bureau of Economic Research, Inc.

Gosseries, Axel. 2007. "Cosmopolitan Luck Egalitarianism and the Greenhouse Effect." *Canadian Journal of Philosophy* 31: 279–309.

Greenhalgh, Susan. 2003. "Science, Modernity, and the Making of China's One-child Policy." *Population and Development Review* 29 (2): 163–196.

Haines, Michael. 1989. "Social Class Differentials during Fertility Decline: England and Wales Revisited." *Population Studies* 43: 305–323.

Hansen, Gary, and Edward Prescott. 2002. "Malthus to Solow." *American Economic Review* 92 (4): 1205–1217.

Hanushek, Eric. 1992. "The Trade-off between Child Quantity and Quality." *Journal of Political Economy* 100 (1): 84–117.

Hassler, John, Jose Rodriguez Mora, Kjetil Storesletten, and Fabrizio Zilibotti. 2003. "The Survival of the Welfare State." *American Economic Review* 93 (1): 87–112.

Hathaway, James, and Alexander Neve. 1997. "Making International Refugee Law Relevant Again: A Proposal for a Collectivized and Solution-Oriented Protection." *Harvard Human Rights Journal* 10: 115–211.

Haveman, Robert, and Barbara Wolfe. 1995. "The Determinants of Children's Attainments: A Review of Methods and Findings." *Journal of Economic Literature* 33 (4): 1829–1878.

Hazan, Moshe. 2009. "Longevity and Lifetime Labor Input: Evidence and Implications." *Econometrica* 77 (6): 1829–1863.

Hazan, Moshe, and Hosny Zoabi. 2006. "Does Longevity Cause Growth? A Theoretical Critique." *Journal of Economic Growth* 11: 363–376.

2011. "Do Highly Educated Women Choose Smaller Families?" Paper presented at the Second Workshop on "Towards Sustained Economic Growth", Barcelona.

Heer, David. 1975. "Marketable Licences for Babies: Boulding's Proposal Revisited." *Social Biology* 22 (1): 1–16.

Hollingsworth, T. 1964. "The Demography of the British Peerage." *Population Studies* 18 (2): 1–108.

Hotz, Joseph, and Robert Miller. 1988. "An Empirical Analysis of Life Cycle Fertility and Female Labor Supply." *Econometrica* 56 (1): 91–118.

James, Estelle. 1993. "Why Do Different Countries Choose a Different Public–Private Mix of Educational Services?" *Journal of Human Resources* 28 (3): 571–592.

Jones, Larry, and Alice Schoonbroodt. 2007. "Baby Busts and Baby Booms: The Fertility Response to Shocks in Dynastic Models." Unpublished Manuscript, University of Minnesota.

Jones, Larry, and Michele Tertilt. 2008. "An Economic History of Fertility in the U.S.: 1826–1960." In *Frontiers of Family Economics*, edited by Peter Rupert. Amsterdam: Elsevier.

Joskow, Paul, Richard Schmalensee, and Elizabeth Bailey. 1998. "The Market for Sulfur Dioxide Emissions." *American Economic Review* 88 (4): 669–685.

Kalemli-Ozcan, Sebnem. 2002. "Does the Mortality Decline Promote Economic Growth?" *Journal of Economic Growth* 7 (4): 411–439.

———. 2003. "A Stochastic Model of Mortality, Fertility, and Human Capital Investment." *Journal of Development Economics* 70 (1): 103–118.

Keegan, John. 1993. *A History of Warfare*. New York: Knopf.

Kelley, Allen, and Robert Schmidt. 1999. "Economic and Demographic Change: A Synthesis of Models, Findings, and Perspectives." Duke University Department of Economics Working Paper No. 99/01.

Kingdon, Geeta Gandhi. 1996. "The Quality and Efficiency of Private and Public Education: A Case-study of Urban India." *Oxford Bulletin of Economics and Statistics* 58 (1): 55–80.

———. 2005. "Private and Public Schooling: The Indian Experience." University of Oxford.

Kirch, Patrick. 1986. "Exchange Systems and Inter-island Contact in the Transformation of an Island Society." In *Island Societies: Archaeological Approaches to Evolution and Transformation*. Cambridge University Press.

———. 1997. "Microcosmic Histories: Island Perspective on 'Global Change'." *American Anthropologist* 99 (1): 30–42.

Kirch, Patrick, and D. Yen. 1982. "Tikopia: The Prehistory and Ecology of a Polynesia Outlier." *Bishop Museum Bulletin*. Honolulu.

Knowles, John. 1999a. "Can Parental Decisions Explain U.S. Income Inequality?" Working Paper, University of Pennsylvania.

———. 1999b. "Social Policy, Equilibrium, Poverty and Investment in Children." Working Paper, University of Pennsylvania.

Kremer, Michael. 1997. "How Much Does Sorting Increase Inequality?" *Quarterly Journal of Economics* 112 (1): 115–139.

Kremer, Michael, and Daniel Chen. 2002. "Income Distribution Dynamics with Endogenous Fertility." *Journal of Economic Growth* 7 (3): 227–258.

Krishna, K. L. 2004. "Patterns and Determinants of Economic Growth in Indian States." Indian council for Research on International Economic Relations, New Delhi, Working Papers No. 144.

Krueger, Alan, and Mikael Lindahl. 2001. "Education and Growth: Why and for Whom?" *Journal of Economic Literature* 39 (4): 1101–1136.

Lagerlöf, Nils-Petter. 2006. "The Galor–Weil Model Revisited: A Quantitative Exercise." *Review of Economic Dynamics* 9 (1): 116–142.

Bibliography

Leibowitz, Arleen. 1974. "Home Investments in Children." *Journal of Political Economy* 82 (2): S111–S131.

Lerner, Abba, and David Colander. 1980. *MAP. A Market Anti-Inflation Plan*. New York: Harcourt Brace Jovanovich.

Liao, Pei-Ju. 2009. "The One-child Policy: A Macroeconomic Analysis." Taiwan: Academia Sinica.

Lutz, Wolfgang, Warren Sanderson, and Sergei Scherbov. 2001. "The End of World Population Growth." *Nature* 412: 543–545.

Maddison, Angus. 2001. *The World Economy: A Millennial Perspective*. Development Centre Studies. Paris: OECD.

    2003. *The World Economy: Historical Statistics*. Development Centre Studies. Paris: OECD.

Mare, Robert. 1997. "Differential Fertility, Intergenerational Educational Mobility, and Racial Inequality." *Social Science Research* 26: 263–291.

Matsumoto, Akio. 2002. "Economic Dynamic Model for Small Islands." *Discrete Dynamics in Nature and Society* 7 (2): 121–132.

Maxwell, John, and Rafael Reuveny. 2005. "Continuing Conflict." *Journal of Economic Behavior and Organization* 58: 30–52.

Melindi Ghidi, Paolo. 2012. "A Model of Ideological Transmission with Endogenous Parental Preferences." *International Journal of Economic Theory* forthcoming.

Merrigan, Philip, and Yvan Saint-Pierre. 1998. "An Econometric and Neoclassical Analysis of the Timing and Spacing of Births in Canada from 1950 to 1990." *Journal of Population Economics* 11: 29–51.

Michel, Philippe, and Bertrand Wigniolle. 2006. "On Efficient Child Making." *Economic Theory* 27: 1–20.

Moav, Omer. 2005. "Cheap Children and the Persistence of Poverty." *Economic Journal* 115 (500): 88–110.

Morand, Olivier. 1999. "Endogenous Fertility, Income Distribution, and Growth." *Journal of Economic Growth* 4 (3): 331–349.

Neal, Derek. 1997. "The Effects of Catholic Secondary Schooling on Educational Achievement." *Journal of Labor Economics* 15 (1): 98–123.

Nechyba, Thomas. 2006. "Income and Peer Quality Sorting in Public and Private Schools." Chapter 22 of *Handbook of the Economics of Education, Vol. 2*, edited by Eric A. Hanushek and Finis Welch. Amsterdam: North-Holland.

Owsley, Douglas, G.W. Will, and Stephen Ousley. 1994. "Biological Effects of European Contacts on Easter Island." In *Easter Island in Pacific Context: South Seas Symposium: Proceedings of the Fourth International Conference on Easter Island and East Polynesia*, Edited by Christopher Moore Stevenson, Georgia Lee, and F.J. Morin, pp. 129–134, Easter Island Foundation.

Pal, Parthapratim, and Jayati Ghosh. 2007. "Inequality in India: A Survey of Recent Trends." Working Paper No. 45, United Nations, Department of Economics and Social Affairs.

Pearce, Fred. 2010. *The Coming Population Crash and our Planet's Surprising Future*. Boston, MA: Beacon Press.

Peller, Sigismund. 1965. "Births and Deaths among Europe's Ruling Families since 1500." In *Population in History*, edited by D. Glass and D. Eversley. London: Edward Arnold.

Peretto, Pietro, and Simone Valente. 2011. "Growth on a Finite Planet: Resources, Technology and Population in the Long Run." Paper presented at the Second Workshop on "Towards Sustained Economic growth", Barcelona.

Perotti, Roberto. 1996. "Growth, Income Distribution, and Democracy: What the Data Say." *Journal of Economic Growth* 1 (2): 149–187.

Perrenoud, Alfred. 1975. "L'inégalité sociale devant la mort à Genève au XVIIe siècle." *Population* 30: 221–243.

1978. "La mortalité à Genève de 1625 à 1825." *Annales de démographie historique*, pp. 209–233.

Persson, Torsten, and Guido Tabellini. 2000. *Political Economics: Explaining Economic Policy*. Cambridge, MA: MIT Press.

Ponting, Clive. 1991. *A Green History of the World: The Environment and the Collapse of Great Civilizations*. New York: Penguin.

Prescott, Edward. 1986. "Theory ahead of business-cycle measurement." *Carnegie-Rochester Conference Series on Public Policy* 25 (1): 11–44.

Preston, Samuel, and Cameron Campbell. 1993. "Differential Fertility and the Distribution of Traits: The Case of IQ." *American Journal of Sociology* 98 (5): 997–1019.

Pritchett, Lant. 1994. "Desired Fertility and the Impact of Population Policies." *Population and Development Review* 20 (1): 1–55.

Psacharopoulos, George. 1994. "Returns to Investment in Education: A Global Update." *World Development* 22 (9): 1325–1343.

Ramsey, Frank. 1927. "A Contribution to the Theory of Taxation." *Economic Journal* 37 (145): 47–61.

Rangazas, Peter. 2000. "Schooling and Economic Growth: A King–Rebelo Experiment with Human Capital." *Journal of Monetary Economics* 46 (2): 397–416.

Reuveny, Rafael, and John Maxwell. 2001. "Conflict and Renewable Resources." *The Journal of Conflict Resolution* 45 (6): 719–742.

Ridley, Matt. 2010. *The Rational Optimist. How Prosperity Evolves*. London: Harper-Collins.

Rose, John. 1906. "Negro Suffrage: The Constitutional Point of View." *American Political Science Review* 1 (1): 17–643.

Rosenzweig, Mark, and Kenneth Wolpin. 1994. "Are There Increasing Returns to the Intergenerational Production of Human Capital? Maternal Schooling and Child Intellectual Achievement." *Journal of Human Resources* 29 (2): 670–693.

Ruggles, Steven, Matthew Sobek, Trent Alexander, Catherine A. Fitch, Ronald Goeken, Patricia Kelly Hall, Miriam King, and Chad Ronnander. 2004. "Integrated Public Use Microdata Series: Version 3.0." [Machine-readable database]. Minneapolis, MN: Minnesota Population Center.

Sahlins, Marshall. 1955. "Esoteric Efflorescence in Easter Island." *American Anthropologist* 57 (5): 1045–1052.

Saint-Paul, Gilles, and Thierry Verdier. 1997. "Power, Distributive Conflicts and Multiple Growth Paths." *Journal of Economic Growth* 2 (2): 155–168.

Schoonbroodt, Alice, and Michèle Tertilt. 2011. "Property Rights and Efficiency in OLG Models with Endogenous Fertility." Mimeo.

Schuck, Peter. 1997. "Refugee Burden-Sharing: A Modest Proposal." *Yale Journal of International Law* 22 (2): 243–297.

Shell, Karl. 2008. "Sunspot Equilibrium." *The New Palgrave Dictionary of Economics*, Second Edition. Edited by Steven N. Durlauf and Lawrence E. Blume. New York: Palgrave Macmillan.

Skaperdas, Stergios. 1996. "Contest Success Functions." *Economic Theory* 7 (2): 283–290.

Skirbekk, Vegard. 2008. "Fertility Trends by Social Status." *Demographic Research* 18: 145–180.

Solow, Robert. 1956. "A Contribution to the Theory of Economic Growth." *Quarterly Journal of Economics* 70 (1): 65–94.

Stevenson, Thomas. 1920. "The Fertility of Various Social Classes in England and Wales from the Middle of the Nineteenth Century to 1911." *Journal of the Royal Statistical Society* 83: 401–444.

Stiglitz, Joseph. 1974. "The Demand for Education in Public and Private School Systems." *Journal of Public Economics* 3 (4): 349–385.

Tamura, Robert. 1991. "Income Convergence in an Endogenous Growth Model." *Journal of Political Economy* 99 (3): 522–540.

1994. "Fertility, Human Capital, and the Wealth of Families." *Economic Theory* 4 (4): 593–603.

2001. "Teachers, Growth and Convergence." *Journal of Political Economy* 109 (5): 1021–1059.

Thompson, Warren S. 1938. "The Effect of Housing upon Population Growth." *The Milbank Memorial Fund Quarterly* 16 (4): 359–368.

Tobin, James. 1970. "On Limiting the Domain of Inequality." *Journal of Law and Economics* 13 (2): 263–277.

Van Tilburg, Jo Anne, and John Mach. 1995. *Easter Island: Archeology, Ecology and Culture*. Washington, DC: Smithsonian Institution Scholarly Press.

Weiland, Heribert. 2011. "Education and Political Change in Namibia. Equality in Inequality." In *The Political Function of Education in Deeply Divided Countries*, edited by Theodor Hanf. Baden-Baden Nomos.

Wiggins, Stephen. 1990. *Introduction to Applied Nonlinear Dynamical Systems and Chaos*. New York: Springer-Verlag.

Williamson, Jeffrey. 1985. *Did British Capitalism Breed Inequality?* Boston, MA: Allen and Unwin.

Wilson, Chris, and Robert Woods. 1991. "Fertility in England: A Long-term Perspective." *Population Studies* 45: 399–415.

Wrigley, Edward Anthony, and Roger Schofield. 1981. *The Population History of England 1541–1871*. Cambridge, MA: Harvard University Press.

Author index

Acemoglu, Daron 38
Alderman, Harold 106
Althaus, Paul 4
Alvarez, Fernando 26
Andreoni, James 10, 187
Angrist, Joshua 37, 38
Apkarian, Jacob 154
Arcalean, Calin 97
Arrhenius, Gustaf 225
Ashenfelter, Orley 37
Azariadis, Costas 225

Bahn, Paul 155
Bailey, Elizabeth 207
Bar, Michael 58, 63
Bardet, Jean-Pierre 49
Barro, Robert 10, 40, 41
Baudin, Thomas 2, 10, 17, 20, 185
Bearse, Peter 92
Becker, Gary 3, 10, 12, 48, 199
Bedi, Arjun 106
Beltrami, Daniele 62
Ben-Porath, Yoram 62
Bénabou, Roland 21, 69, 81, 111, 133
Binmore, Ken 161, 181
Bohringer, Christoph 231
Boucekkine, Raouf 45, 56, 62
Boulding, Kenneth 207
Brander, James 154, 155, 178
Bréchet, Thierry 207

Campbell, Cameron 73
Card, David 37
Casella, Alexandra 207
Cervellati, Matteo 63

Chase-Dunn, Christopher 154
Chen, Daniel 2, 4, 20
Chen, Hung-Ju 22
Chesnais, Jean Claude 41
Chew, C. 156
Clark, Gregory 2, 154
Coats, R. Morris 156, 173
Cohen, Joel 155
Cohen-Zada, Danny 135
Colander, David 207
Coughlin, Peter 99
Crettez, Bertrand 207

Dahan, Momi 21
Dalton, Thomas 156, 173
De Graaf, Paul 141
de la Croix, David 20, 30, 45, 49, 62, 69, 72,
    81, 91, 130, 153, 179, 184, 199, 203, 205,
    212, 225
Deb, Partha 17, 185
Deininger, Klaus 140
Desbordes, Rodolphe 56
Diamond, Jared 153, 161
Doepke, Matthias 20, 30, 45, 69, 91, 111, 130,
    199
Dottori, Davide 128, 153
Dworkin, Ronald 209

Ehrlich, Isaac 3, 159
Epple, Dennis 92, 135
Erickson, Jon 161

Fan, Simon 219
Fernández, Raquel 185
Figlio, David 135

Fioroni, Tamara 56
Firth, Raymond 157, 158
Flenley, John 155, 156
Fletcher, Jesse 154
Fogli, Alessandra 185

Galor, Oded 2, 4, 21, 43, 45, 46, 62
Ganzeboom, Harry 141
Garg, Ashish 106
Ghez, Gilbert 199
Ghosh, Jayati 69
Glomm, Gerhard 69, 71, 92
Gobbi, Paula 10, 20
Gokhale, Jagadeesh 73
Goldberg, Pinelopi 225
Goldhaber, Dan 106
Golosov, Mikhail 206
Good, David 155
Goodsell, Willystine 186
Gosling, Amanda 225
Gosseries, Axel 184, 203, 205, 231
Gowdy, John 161
Greenhalgh, Susan 205

Haines, Michael 63
Hanneman, Robert 154
Hansen, Gary 45, 46
Hassler, John 111
Hathaway, James 207
Haveman, Robert 36
Hazan, Moshe 20, 63
Heer, David 208
Hollingsworth, T. 63
Hotz, Joseph 2

Inoue, Hiroko 154

Jackson, Joan 156
James, Estelle 138
Jones, Larry 2, 10, 206
Joskow, Paul 207
Justman, Moshe 135

Keegan, John 155, 161
Kelley, Allen 4
King, A. Sarah 156
Kingdon, Geeta Gandhi 69, 106
Kirch, Patrick 157, 158, 177
Knowles, John 17, 36, 72
Kotlikoff, Lawrence 73

Kremer, Michael 2, 4, 20, 73
Krishna, K. L. 69
Krueger, Alan 37, 38

Lagerlöf, Nils-Petter 155
Lange, Andreas 231
Latzer, Hélène 56
Lawrence, Kirk 154
Leibowitz, Arleen 38
Lemieux, Thomas 225
Lerner, Abba 207
Leukhina, Oksana 58, 63
Lewis, Gregg 3
Liao, Pei-Ju 220
Licandro, Omar 45, 62
Lindahl, Mikael 37, 38
Lui, Francis 3, 159
Lutz, Wolfgang 184

Mach, John 156
Maddison, Angus 41, 45, 62
Mare, Robert 71
Matsumoto, Akio 160, 173
Maxwell, John 155, 162
Melindi Ghidi, Paolo 179
Merrigan, Philip 2
Michel, Philippe 72, 206
Miller, Robert 2
Moav, Omer 93
Monfort, Philippe 81
Morand, Olivier 21
Murphy, Kevin 48

Neal, Derek 106
Nechyba, Thomas 135
Neve, Alexander 207
Nitzan, Shmuel 99

Orazem, Peter 106
Ousley, Stephen 162
Owsley, Douglas 162

Pal, Parthapratim 69
Paterno, Elizabeth 106
Patterson, Debra 92
Pavcnik, Nina 225
Pearce, Fred 1, 206
Peller, Sigismund 63, 64
Peretto, Pietro 186

Perotti, Roberto 41
Perrenoud, Alfred 49, 61, 62
Persson, Torsten 99
Picard, Pierre 207
Ponting, Clive 155, 161
Prentice, M. 156
Prescott, Edward 45, 46, 187
Preston, Samuel 73
Pritchett, Lant 3
Psacharopoulos, George 37

Ramsey, Frank 113
Rangazas, Peter 24
Ravikumar, B. 69, 71, 92
Reuveny, Rafael 155, 162
Ridley, Matt 204
Rodriguez Mora, Jose 111
Rogerson, Richard 71, 73
Romano, Richard 92, 135
Rosati, Furio 17, 185
Rose, John 231
Rosenzweig, Mark 38
Rubinstein, Ariel 161, 181

Sahlins, Marshall 159
Saint-Paul, Gilles 111
Saint-Pierre, Yvan 2
Sanderson, Warren 184
Scherbov, Sergei 184
Schiopu, Ioana 97
Schmalensee, Richard 207
Schmidt, Robert 4
Schofield, Roger 63
Schoonbroodt, Alice 10, 205
Schuck, Peter 207
Sefton, James 73
Shell, Karl 110
Shen, I-Ling 128
Skaperdas, Stergios 162
Skirbekk, Vegard 2
Solow, Robert 185
Sommacal, Alessandro 49

Squire, Lyn 140
Stark, Oded 219
Stevenson, Thomas 63
Stiglitz, Joseph 92
Storesletten, Kjetil 111
Sunde, Uwe 63

Tabellini, Guido 99
Tamura, Robert 48, 72, 81
Taylor, M. Scott 154, 155, 178
Teller, J. 156
Tertilt, Michele 2, 206
Thompson, Warren S. 186
Tobin, James 208, 225
Treiman, Donald 141
Tsiddon, Daniel 21

Valente, Simone 186
Van Tilburg, Jo Anne 156
Vander Donckt, Marie 212
Verdier, Thierry 111

Weale, Martin 73
Weil, David 4, 43, 45, 46, 62
Weiland, Heribert 128
Wigniolle, Bertrand 206
Will, G.W. 162
Williamson, Jeffrey 41
Wilson, Chris 63
Wolfe, Barbara 36
Wolinsky, Asher 161, 181
Wolpin, Kenneth 38
Woods, Robert 63
Wrigley, Edward Anthony 63

Yen, D. 157, 158

Zang, Hyoungsoo 21
Zilibotti, Fabrizio 111
Zoabi, Hosny 20, 63

Printed in the United States
By Bookmasters